Billy the Kid

A
Short
and
Violent
Life

ROBERT M. UTLEY

University of Nebraska Press:
Lincoln
&
London

/13

The paper in this book meets the
minimum requirements
of American National Standard for
Information Sciences –
Permanence of Paper for Printed
Library Materials,
ANSI Z39.48-1984

Library of Congress Cataloging in
Publication Data
Utley, Robert Marshall, 1929-
Billy the Kid : a short and violent life /
Robert M. Utley.
p. cm.
Bibliography: p. Includes index.
Summary: Examines the career of
the young outlaw whose life and
death were an expression of the
violence prevalent on the American
frontier.
ISBN 0-8032-4553-X
1. Billy, the Kid.   2. Outlaws – Southwest, New – Biography.
3. Southwest, New – History – 1848-
4. Frontier and pioneer life –
Southwest, New. [1. Billy, the Kid.
2. Robbers and outlaws.
3. Frontier and pioneer life – West
(U.S.)]   I. Title.
F786.B54U87   1989
364.1'552'0924 – dc19   [B]
[92]
89-30022   CIP   AC

For Paul Andrew Hutton

Friend,

Neighbor, Valued Critic

Contents

ILLUSTRATIONS

Following page 110:

Following page 196:

MAPS

"Quien es? Quien es?"

With those words—"Who is it? Who is it?"—the youth threw away a critical moment of time. In the darkened bedroom, he could not make out the figure crouched at the head of Pete Maxwell's bed. He thought he was among friends, and his hesitation cost him his life.

The crouching form belonged to Pat Garrett, sheriff of Lincoln County, and those fateful words told Garrett exactly who faced him. He did not hesitate, but grabbed his six-shooter from its holster and fired two shots point-blank. One slammed into the boy's chest, the other rebounded from the adobe wall and splintered the headboard of Maxwell's bed. Billy the Kid crumpled to the floor, dead. He was but twenty-one years old.

All that was mortal died on the floor of Pete Maxwell's bedroom at old Fort Sumner, New Mexico, on that night of July 14, 1881; but almost at once an immortal Billy the Kid rose from the dead, ultimately to expand into a mighty legend of global impact. Few figures from the past have so profoundly stirred the human imagination. Among peoples everywhere, the name prompts instant recognition and evokes vivid images.

Stripping off the veneers of legendry accumulated over a century exposes neither hero nor villain, but a complex personality. Of the Kid as person and the Kid as outlaw, the reality both sustains and contradicts the legend.

By the time of his death, the public had already come to look on Billy the Kid as larger than life, a peerless outlaw in a land full of outlaws. Until near the end of his life, he could thank the newspapers for this standing. His actual exploits did not support the reputation. Then a sensational capture, trial, and escape gave validity to the newspaper portrait, and a violent death, publicized to the entire nation, fixed it indelibly in the public memory for all time.

Common outlaw, uncommon personality, inspiration for a giant in the pantheon of American heroes—such was Billy the Kid. So all-encompassing is the giant of legend that he has buried the man of reality.

Yet the reality is worth seeking. A legend cherished by all the world lends significance to a life that is otherwise of concern mainly to a handful of antiquarians. Because of the legend, the life invites scrutiny, to see if it can be compressed into its true human dimensions, and to discover what it tells about violence on the American frontier and, indeed, violence in American society.

ACKNOWLEDGMENTS

Either directly in the preparation of this book, or indirectly through my work on *High Noon in Lincoln: Violence on the Western Frontier* (Albuquerque: University of New Mexico Press, 1987), I have profited from the generous aid of many people, whose contributions I acknowledge with gratitude.

In Midland, Texas: J. Evetts Haley and his efficient and friendly staff of the Haley History Center—Beth Schneider, Robin McWilliams, and Cindy Burleson.

In Santa Fe, New Mexico: State Archivist Michael Miller and his able, always helpful associates at the New Mexico State Records Center and Archives; Orlando Romero, Arthur Olivas, and Richard Rudisill of the Museum of New Mexico History Library; Thomas Caperton, director of New Mexico State Monuments; Michael E. Pitel of the New Mexico Economic Development and Tourism Department; and Donald R. Lavash, formerly historian at the State Records Center and biographer of Sheriff William Brady.

In Lincoln, New Mexico: R. G. Miller, Robert L. Hart, and John Meigs of the Lincoln County Heritage Trust; Jack Rigney and his staff of the Lincoln State Monument; and Nora Henn of the Lincoln County Historical Society.

In Tucson, Arizona: Professor Harwood P. Hinton of the University of Arizona, whose wise counsel has been unfailingly helpful; Jerry Weddle, who generously shared his own new and important research findings; Bruce Dinges of the Arizona Historical Society;

and David Laird, university librarian, and Louis Hieb, head of Special Collections, University of Arizona Library.

Also John P. Wilson of Las Cruces, New Mexico, outstanding authority on Lincoln County; Doyce P. Nunis, Jr., of the University of Southern California; Allen Barker of Pine Grove, California; Jack DeMattos of North Attleboro, Massachusetts; Frederick W. Nolan and Joseph G. Rosa of London, England; Rose Diaz of the University of New Mexico Library in Albuquerque; Philip J. Rasch of Ojai, California; Don McAlavy of Clovis, New Mexico; Byron Price of the National Cowboy Hall of Fame in Oklahoma City; Claire Kuehn of the Panhandle-Plains Historical Museum in Canyon, Texas; Thomas A. Mason and Connie McBirney of the Indiana Historical Society in Indianapolis; Eileen Bolger of the Denver Federal Records Center; Professor Richard Maxwell Brown of the University of Oregon; and Kenneth Pate of Azle, Texas, who assembled the photographs of firearms and furnished the technical data.

Finally, my heartiest thanks are reserved for two people who commented constructively and often decisively on the entire manuscript: Professor Paul Andrew Hutton of the University of New Mexico, to whom this book is dedicated; and Melody Webb of the National Park Service, who also happens to be my wife.

The Kid

Until the final few months of his life, the youth destined for immortality as the West's most famous outlaw was known not as Billy the Kid but simply as "the Kid." He acquired the label as a teenager, when he first began to associate with men. To the day of his death, his boyish face and slim figure stamped him as a kid. So did his behavior, uniformly characteristic of youth, untouched by adult maturity. A kid he remained throughout his short and violent life, ended by a bullet at twenty-one. More than any other trait, youth shaped the personality and directed the life of Billy the Kid.

The Kid's origins are shrouded in mystery and buffeted by controversy. A corps of diligent researchers has tracked him in census records, city directories, baptismal and marriage registers, newspapers, and other sources. Discoveries have been tantalizingly suggestive but rarely conclusive.

That he was in Santa Fe, New Mexico, on March 1, 1873, is indisputable. On that day, as a lad of thirteen, Henry McCarty stood with his brother Joe as witness to his mother's marriage. The ceremony took place in the First Presbyterian Church, with the Reverend D. F. McFarland administering the vows as William Henry Harrison Antrim, age thirty, took in marriage the widow Catherine McCarty, age forty-three.[1]

The ceremony probably formalized a relationship of some years' duration. Bill Antrim and Catherine McCarty had known each other since 1865, when they met in Indianapolis, Indiana. A Civil

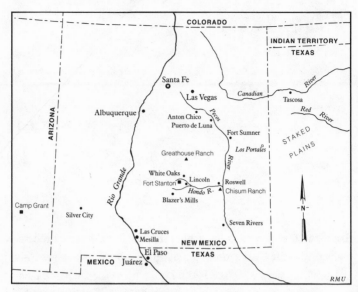

The West of Billy the Kid, 1873–81

War veteran, Bill drove a hack for an express company. How, when, where, and by whom Catherine had been widowed are disputed questions. Almost certainly she had moved with her two young sons from New York City, but why to Indianapolis is not known. She told the compilers of the Indianapolis city directory for 1868 that she was the widow of Michael McCarty.[2]

Without much doubt, Catherine and her husband (if she had one) were Irish immigrants, tiny specks in the multitude that rushed American shores as a result of Ireland's potato famine. Henry and Joe, therefore, probably lived their first years in the impoverished Irish ghettos of Manhattan (or maybe Brooklyn). If Catherine and a husband named Patrick resided at 210 Greene Street, then Henry was born on September 17, 1859, and Joe later. If Catherine lived at 70 Allen Street with an unnamed husband (or no husband), then Henry was born on November 20, 1859, and Joe five years earlier. Except as an irritatingly elusive question, it makes little difference which. Henry came out of New York's Irish slums, but he made his name and fame in New Mexico.[3]

In 1870 both Antrim and the McCartys turned up in Wichita,

Kansas. With Bill's help, Catherine had lifted her family from ghetto origins. Both grew sufficiently prosperous to acquire real estate in the infant frontier community, and Catherine ran a successful business in the heart of town. "The City Laundry is kept by Mrs. McCarty," heralded the local newspaper in the spring of 1871, "to whom we recommend those who wish to have their linen made clean." A decade later, after Henry had achieved renown as Billy the Kid, the Wichita editor observed that "many of the early settlers remember him as a street gamin in the days of longhorns."

Soon the "street gamin" became a suburbanite, for Catherine acquired a quarter-section homestead on the outskirts of Wichita. Antrim, surely with the aid of Henry and Joe, built a cabin, dug a well and storm cellar, and planted hedges and fruit trees. The McCartys and "Uncle Bill" Antrim gave every sign of putting down roots in their new Kansas home.[4]

Abruptly, however, in June 1871 the widow McCarty sold her property and two months later vanished from Wichita forever. Antrim left too, although his purchase of additional land that summer may have signified an intent to return some day. Almost certainly, a diagnosis of tuberculosis prompted Catherine to search for higher, drier, more healthful climes. The little group made its way to Denver, Colorado, and from there soon turned south to New Mexico.[5]

The Territory of New Mexico was a land of vast distances; of rugged mountains, parched deserts, and grassy plains; and of a cultural medley of Hispanic, Anglo, and Indian that did not always mix well. In the middle 1870s, before the Atchison, Topeka, and Santa Fe Railroad crept over Raton Pass bringing revolutionary change, New Mexico was also a land of rudimentary transportation, of isolation and parochialism, of poverty and privation relieved by only nominal prosperity, of centuries-old cultural institutions and infant political and economic institutions, of ineffective government, and of endemic violence.

Like all other western territories not yet pacified by the railroad, New Mexico knew violence as a condition of life. The raw frontier lured adventurers from all over the nation. They formed a population characterized by youth, daring, ambition, energy, recklessness, greed, contempt for restraints, and a casual view of suffering and death. They rocked New Mexico with violence and lawlessness.

In New Mexico as in other territories, four influences incited this class of men to violence. First was ambition—the scramble for quick money and the power that went with it. Second and third were liquor and guns. Nearly everyone went armed, and nearly everyone drank constantly and often heavily. The combination proved deadly.

Fourth, and possibly most compelling, was the "code of the West." Among the young bravos who flocked to the frontier, the code governed male relationships. "I'll die before I'll run," enjoined the tradition of violent self-defense and self-redress. The code had originated in Texas, flowing northward on the great cattle trails of the post–Civil War decades. Demanding personal courage and pride and reckless disregard of life, it commanded practitioners to avenge all insult and wrong, real or imagined; never to retreat before an aggressor; and to respond with any degree of violence, even death.[6]

Uncle Bill with Catherine and the two boys settled first in New Mexico's capital city. Santa Fe lay in a spacious and scenic valley rimmed by mountain ranges, with the peaks of the Sangre de Cristos looming in its rear. Setting the model for other Hispanic communities, it consisted of prosaic adobes rising fortresslike along narrow streets radiating from a central plaza. In this square the historic Santa Fe Trail, commercial link with "the states" since 1821 and now shrinking with the approach of the railroad, reached its destination. Travelers lodged at the Exchange Hotel, the *fonda* on the southeast corner of the plaza. The venerable "Palace of the Governors," moldering with almost three centuries of governmental use, fronted the plaza on the north.

Although predominantly a Hispanic community, Santa Fe gave business and political fealty to a small Anglo elite. The governor and other federal officials were party faithfuls with claims on the president's patronage—not large claims, however, for remote New Mexico was not looked on as a choice political reward, and appoin-

4

tees rarely transcended mediocrity. Together with a band of shrewd lawyers and businessmen, certain territorial officials made up a loose cabal of opportunists that political enemies labeled the "Santa Fe Ring." Members denied that it even existed, and except as an unorganized fraternity of common interest it may not have. But insiders enjoyed modest bonanzas by trafficking in old Spanish land grants, the public domain, and contracts for supporting the territory's huge federal establishment, especially Indian agencies and army forts.

From Santa Fe, shortly after the marriage of Bill and Catherine on March 1, 1873, the Antrims turned south. Slicing the territory down the center, the Rio Grande connected northern to southern New Mexico. Tracing the river, the Camino Real, New Mexico's colonial lifeline, still served as the thoroughfare south to Albuquerque and across the dreaded Jornada del Muerto to the lush Mesilla Valley.

A rich bottomland watered by the Rio Grande, the Mesilla Valley lay at the western foot of the jagged Organ Mountains. With a population of about three thousand, the valley was the agricultural, commercial, and social heartland of southern New Mexico. Mesilla, a Hispanic village on the banks of the Rio Grande, served as seat of Doña Ana County. Two miles distant, Las Cruces grew rapidly as Anglo businessmen competed for dominance over the economy. More than four hundred farms testified to the fertile soils of the valley.

Typical New Mexican towns of squat adobe structures and narrow streets, Mesilla and Las Cruces invited the scorn of eastern travelers. "They are the dirtiest and filthiest places I have yet visited," declared one; "the people seem to lack life and energy." Putting up at the Mesilla Hotel, this "tired and dusty stranger" discovered a drove of hogs rooting combatively beneath his window. "The noise day and night was intolerable, and the stench arising from them was excessively offensive."[7]

The Antrims veered west from the river to make their new home in Silver City, ninety miles northwest of the Mesilla Valley. Silver City nestled in the southern foothills of a tangled mass of mountains. For decades, Spaniard and American alike had mined the gulches of the area, but the strike that produced Silver City did not occur until 1870. By the middle 1870s, the settlement had evolved into a community that prided itself on "eastern" dwellings and a predominantly Anglo population. "Strangers who recently made their first visit to Silver City," noted a Las Cruces newspaper, "tell us they are astonished to find a real American town with fine two story brick buildings and a live energetic people so far on the southwestern frontier."[8]

In Silver City the Antrims established themselves in a log cabin at the head of the "Big Ditch," the stream bed that ran next to the town's main thoroughfare and carried runoff from mountain storms. Uncle Bill Antrim worked at odd jobs while indulging a lifelong compulsion to search for the elusive strike that would bring mineral riches. Catherine supplemented the meager income by taking in boarders. "Mrs. Bill Antrim was a jolly Irish lady, full of life and mischief," remembered a neighbor.[9]

Now known by his stepfather's name as well as McCarty, Henry ran with the other boys and did little to set himself apart from them. He was "a scrawny little fellow with delicate hands and an artistic nature," recalled his schoolteacher, "always willing to help with the chores around the school house. Billy (they called him Henry then) was no more of a problem in school than any other boy growing up in a mining camp."[10]

The New Mexico climate failed to head off Catherine's tuberculosis, and gradually she grew weaker. Bedridden for four months, she died on September 16, 1874, nineteen months after her marriage to Bill Antrim. The funeral took place the next day in the Antrim cabin, with burial following in the town cemetery.[11]

After Catherine's death, Bill Antrim and the two boys boarded at the home of Richard Knight. Uncle Bill exercised little parental oversight. In fact, he may have been absent for months at a time. With other restless denizens of Silver City, he was drawn by the new mineral strikes in Arizona that gave birth to the town of Globe.

Richard Knight ran a butcher shop in Silver City and a ranch at

6

the southern end of the Burro Mountains, southwest of the town. Mrs. Knight's younger brother, Tony Connor, became one of Henry's close friends. They worked together in Knight's butcher shop.

"Billy was one of the best boys in town," recalled Tony years later. "He was very slender. He was undersized and was really girlish looking." "I never remember Billy doing anything out of the way any more than the rest of us," he added. "We had our chores to do, like washing the dishes and other duties about the house."[12]

"He was quiet, I remember," related another friend, Chauncey Truesdell, "and never swore or tried to act bad like the other kids." For a time after their mother's death, Henry and Joe lived with the Truesdells.[13]

During these youthful months, Henry grew passionately fond of music. He and other boys formed a minstrel troupe that played to appreciative audiences at Morrill's Opera House. "Billy was Head Man in the show," commented a fellow thespian.[14] For the few years remaining to him, he would love to sing and dance.

Besides music, noted Tony Connor, "Billy got to be a reader. He would scarcely have his dishes washed until he would be sprawled out somewhere reading a book. It was the same down at the butcher shop." Soon, books gave way to lighter reading such as dime novels and the *Police Gazette*, which may have filled the young mind with fantasies of which his mother would not have approved.[15]

Whether incited by the *Police Gazette* or simply by the absence of parental restraint, Henry drifted toward petty thievery. "His first offense," recalled Sheriff Harvey Whitehill in later years, "was the theft of several pounds of butter from a ranchman by the name of Webb, living near Silver City, and which he disposed of to one of the local merchants. His guilt was easily established, but upon promise of good behavior, he was released."[16]

"He was a good kid," declared another friend, Louis Abraham, "but he got in the wrong company."[17] The wrong company was George Shaffer, locally known, because of his headgear, as "Sombrero Jack." According to the sheriff's son, another of Henry's friends, "Every Saturday night, George would get drunk. But he thought a lot of Billy and Billy used to follow him around. This fellow George liked to steal; he had a mania to steal and was always stealing."[18]

And so, thanks to Sombrero Jack, Henry Antrim took his first big step toward a life of crime. One night a year after his mother's death, Henry accompanied his inebriated friend on a foray against the local Chinese laundry. They made off with a bundle of clothing. Henry hid the loot at the home where the family now boarded. The proprietress, Mrs. Sarah Brown, discovered it and turned the boy in to Sheriff Whitehill. Hauled before the justice of the peace, Henry found himself in the toils of the law.[19]

"It did not amount to anything," observed Anthony Connor, "and Mr. Whitehill only wished to scare him."[20] The sheriff's son agreed: "He didn't want to put him in a cell. He was just a boy who had stole some clothes. . . . He didn't want to be mean."[21]

Henry did not regard the matter this lightly. With the combination of cunning and sincerity that marked his later escapades, he persuaded the sheriff to let him have the run of the corridor outside the cell. "And right there is where we fell down," conceded Whitehill. The sheriff left the boy unguarded for half an hour. "When we returned, and unlocked the heavy oaken doors of the jail, the 'Kid' was nowhere to be seen."[22] Not for the first time, the slim, wiry youth had climbed up a chimney to safety, as described satirically by the local editor in the first of the budding criminal's press notices:

Henry McCarty, who was arrested on Thursday and committed to jail to await the action of the grand jury, upon the charge of stealing clothes from Charley Sun and Sam Chung, celestials, sans cue, sans Joss sticks, escaped from prison yesterday through the chimney. It's believed that Henry was simply the tool of "Sombrero Jack," who done the stealing whilst Henry done the hiding. Jack has skinned out.[23]

The escape stamps fifteen-year-old Henry Antrim as clever, resourceful, and daring—traits that would carry him through many a scrape in the next few years. It also betrays the first stirrings of a reckless temper, together with a determination to do as he pleased.

8

The death of his mother, for whom he later voiced an abiding affection, had freed him from parental influence. He got along well enough with Bill Antrim, who treated Catherine's sons with kindness and consideration but did not attempt to impose authority. As Henry grew into adolescence, therefore, he also grew increasingly free willed and independent. The escape from Sheriff Whitehill's jail was the ultimate assertion of independence, cutting all family and social ties and, in his own mind at least, making him a fugitive from the law. Now on his own, with a mixture of anxiety and resolve that may be imagined, he fixed a westward course into the unknown.

The Adolescent

After squirming his way up the chimney of the Silver City jail in September 1875, Henry Antrim all but vanished from recorded history for nearly two years. Although reams of creative fantasy have filled the void, enough of his trail can be followed to suggest the outlines and even yield some of the contents.[1]

Henry's range for two years lay just beyond New Mexico's western border. Apache Indians claimed this tangle of mountain and desert, drained by the upper Gila River and its tributaries, but a scattering of white prospectors and cowmen had begun to challenge their dominion. Soldiers based at Camps Thomas, Grant, and Bowie scouted against Indian raiders and comprised a market that attracted still more whites.

Henry's activities centered on Camp Grant, a cavalry post picturesquely located at the southwestern base of Mount Graham. Not far from the parade ground, along the southern edge of the military reservation, civilian enterprises had begun to take root—the Hotel de Luna of Miles L. Wood, a general store run by Milton McDowell, the saloon of George Atkins, and the "hog ranches" that sprouted near every army post to cater to the soldiers' appetites. Rolling off to the south, the rich grasses of the Sulphur Springs Valley nourished the cattle herds of Henry C. Hooker, who supplied beef to the military posts as well as to the Apache Indian agency of San Carlos.

For a time Henry Antrim worked at the Hooker ranch.[2] In this setting the boy picked up the basic skills of punching cows, tending horses, handling wagon teams, riding and roping, and performing the myriad chores necessary to keep a ranch running. He also began to familiarize himself with rifle and pistol. His youth, however, unfitted him for a man's work, and the Hooker foreman, William Whelan, discharged him.[3]

Late in 1876 Henry turned up among the hangers-on who congregated at the edge of the Camp Grant reservation. At first he worked at Miles Wood's hotel but soon, as Wood recalled, "got to running with a gang of rustlers" based in the little community. With this bunch, he took his next step toward a life of crime.[4]

Henry's particular friend and cohort was John R. Mackie, a Scotsman who had served as a drummer boy in the Civil War and put in an enlistment in the Sixth Cavalry. Even before leaving the army, Mackie had collided with the law. In September 1875, in a dispute over cards, he had shot a civilian in the neck. The bullet was not fatal, and Mackie was released on a plea of self-defense. Discharged from the army in January 1876, he remained in the vicinity of Camp Grant and teamed up with Henry, who was ten years his junior.[5]

Henry and John specialized in petty thievery and occasional horse theft. According to Miles Wood, "Soldiers would come from Fort Grant to visit the saloons and dance homes here. Billy [he was still Henry] and his chum Macky would steal the saddles and saddle blankets from the horses and occasionally they would take the horses and hide them out until they got a chance to dispose of them." Wood recalled one occasion when two officers attempted to secure their mounts by running long picket ropes from the hitching rail outside to the bar inside. "Macky talked to the officers," said Wood, "while Billy cut the ropes from the horses leaving the officers holding the pieces of rope."[6]

On November 17, 1876, Henry, probably in tandem with John, stole one horse too many. Sergeant Lewis C. Hartman had tied his cavalry mount outside Milton McDowell's store, only to have it run off while he was inside. With four soldiers, Hartman took the trail and tracked the thieves northward to the vicinity of the new mining camp of Globe City. There the troopers recovered the horse and set Antrim afoot. Later, in February 1877, Hartman swore out a complaint against Antrim before Miles Wood, who served as justice of the peace and who duly issued an arrest warrant.[7]

The constable to whom the warrant was entrusted could not find the culprit, but on March 25 Wood himself looked out the window to see Antrim and Mackie entering the hotel dining room for breakfast. "I told the waiter that I would wait on them," Wood remembered. "I took a large server and tray and took it in and slipped it on the table in front of them and pulled a six gun from under it and told them to 'hands up.'" Wood marched his prisoners up to the fort and asked the commanding officer, Major Charles E. Compton, to hold them temporarily in the post guardhouse.[8]

As Sheriff Whitehill had discovered, Henry Antrim was hard to confine. Within an hour he had asked to be taken outside on some pretext. There he threw salt in the eyes of his guard and tried to run away. Other guards rushed to the scene and recaptured him. Summoned by the sergeant of the guard, Wood took Antrim to the blacksmith shop and had him shackled. That night Wood attended a social function at Major Compton's house. Called to the door, Compton returned to report that "the Kid was gone shackles and all."

Next Henry appeared in the Globe area, and Wood sent the arrest warrant to officials there. Twice a constable arrested him, and twice he slipped away.[9]

By mid-summer of 1877, Henry was back in the vicinity of Camp Grant. Gus Gildea, one of the Hooker hands, saw him arrive. "He came to town," recalled Gildea, "dressed like a 'country jake,' with 'store pants' on and shoes instead of boots. He wore a six gun stuffed in his trousers."[10]

Henry quickly ran into trouble with Francis P. Cahill, an ex-soldier working as a blacksmith at Camp Grant. "He was called 'Windy' because he was always blowin' about first one thing and another," said Gildea. "Shortly after the Kid came to Fort Grant, Windy started abusing him. He would throw Billy to the floor, ruffle his hair, slap his face and humiliate him before the men in the saloon."[11]

On the night of August 17, 1877, in George Atkins's saloon, Windy and Henry got into an altercation. Gildea declared that Windy slapped Henry around with the same sort of provocation that had occurred before. Cahill explained later that he had called Henry a pimp, Henry had called him a son-of-a-bitch, and the two had piled into each other. "I did not hit him, I think," said Cahill, who "saw him go for his pistol, and tried to get hold of it, but could not and he shot me in the belly." Whereupon, after giving this statement the next day, Windy Cahill died.

A coroner's jury convened at once. Considering the facts available to them, the jurors decided that the shooting "was criminal and unjustifiable, and that 'Henry Antrim alias Kid' is guilty thereof."[12]

The finding meant that Henry should be held for the action of a territorial grand jury, which would decide whether he would be indicted and stand trial for murder. But he would not be around for the grand jury's deliberations; he had fled immediately after the slaying. As Major Compton telegraphed the civil officials in Tucson, "Antrim, alias 'Kid,' was allowed to escape and I believe is still at large."[13]

He was indeed. In fact, Henry lost no time in placing himself beyond the jurisdiction of the Arizona authorities. By the first week in September, he had taken refuge at the Richard Knight ranch in the Burro Mountains southwest of Silver City. His friend Tony Connor, Mrs. Knight's brother, remembered Henry's arrival. "He told the folks what he had done," said Connor. "He remained there about two weeks, but fearing the officers from Arizona might show up almost any time, he left for Lincoln County and never returned."[14]

Henry had killed his first man of record. The coroner's jury declared it murder, but Henry never gave the courts a chance to decide. Almost certainly, he could have gone free on a plea of self-defense. The meager records do not indicate whether Windy Cahill had a gun. If so, it seems unlikely that a grand jury would have brought forth an indictment or that a petit jury would have convicted. Even if Cahill carried no weapons, his greater physical strength and (if Gildea and others may be credited) his record of bullying the boy would have solidly supported a self-defense plea.

At this juncture, Henry could have gone straight with little fear that his past would overtake him. Law-enforcement officers made serious efforts to apprehend only the most chronic and vexatious criminals, and even those managed to pursue their vocation with relative impunity. The Arizona authorities would have done nothing to search for a fugitive who had vanished, especially one who had not even been indicted and whose offense was fraught with extenuating circumstances. Nor would Sheriff Whitehill have bestirred himself to make an issue over the stolen laundry bag in Silver City. Moreover, Henry would have felt no public onus for his youthful indiscretions. Frontier citizens tended to excuse past transgressions so long as they did not recur with unacceptable frequency.

But Henry Antrim may not have realized how inconsequential he was to the authorities of both Arizona and New Mexico. He may truly have feared that deputies were on his trail and that the courts would treat him harshly. Or he may not have cared. He was only seventeen, not yet graduated from adolescence. To an avid reader of the *Police Gazette,* perhaps the adventurous life and potential rewards of the outlaw seemed attractive. Arizona had branded him an outlaw, and in fact he had been a rustler and horse thief for more than a year; why not continue in the profession?

★

At age fifteen, Henry Antrim had fled New Mexico a petty thief. In two years he acquired an adult range of skills and values typical of raw frontier society. He returned to New Mexico not only an accomplished stock thief but a personality shaped by his Arizona experiences and associates.

The Hooker cowboys and Henry's rustler comrades had introduced him to a culture that he had only glimpsed as a boy in Silver City. Their society emphasized horsemanship and gunmanship, which for Henry became time-consuming obsessions. He also absorbed the code of the West, in which the gun figured so prominently. Carousing, gambling, and whoring were part of this life.

14

Later testimony is conflicting, but the weight favors the conclusion that Henry rarely drank intoxicants and did not use tobacco. Even so, saloons offered plenty of attractions. There he enjoyed the camaraderie of friends, delighted in singing and dancing, and gambled almost compulsively. He grew particularly expert at monte, later achieving a modest reputation as a monte dealer. Whoring in its commercial form does not appear to have interested him, but young women did, especially Hispanic young women, for whom his charm proved unfailingly seductive.

Sometime during this period he may even have wandered into Mexico. When he resurfaced after the Arizona interlude, he spoke Spanish fluently. That proficiency could have been drawn from Hispanic friends in Arizona, but it would have come more swiftly and surely from a Mexican sojourn. Mastery of the language contributed to the instant rapport and popularity Henry enjoyed with people of Hispanic extraction for the rest of his life.

By the summer of 1877, Henry had reached late adolescence and taken on the physique and personality by which he would soon become well known.[15] Slim, muscular, wiry, and erect, weighing 135 pounds and standing about five feet seven inches tall, he was lithe and vigorous in his movements. Wavy brown hair topped an oval face betraying the down of incipient mustache and beard. Expressive blue eyes caught everyone's notice. So did two slightly protruding front teeth. They were especially visible when he smiled or laughed, which was nearly always, but people found them pleasing rather than disfiguring.

In attire, Henry kept himself neat. He affected none of the garish costumes in which sensationalist writers later dressed him, but wore simple, serviceable clothing, often the ubiquitous black frock coat, dark pants and vest, and boots. His only conspicuous garb was an unadorned Mexican sombrero—possibly drawn from the model of his friend Sombrero Jack—a utilitarian shield against the southwestern sun rather than an indulgent showpiece.

In personality, Henry combined good humor with a flaming, hair-trigger temper. Boldness verged on recklessness, and when provoked he could explode in deadly rage that carried no warning.

Yet his sunny, cheerful nature, his openness and generosity, and his laugh-studded smile made him well liked by almost everyone. He boasted a quick mind and superior intelligence, and he could read and write.

Because of his slight build and beardless countenance, his young years, and his appealing personality, Henry's friends called him "the Kid." The nickname became firmly attached during the Arizona years. "The Kid" meant Henry Antrim, or Henry McCarty, and sometimes he referred to himself as "Kid Antrim."

By accident or design, Kid Antrim was about to become the junior member of the most notorious outlaw gang in New Mexico.

The Outlaw

As Tony Connor stated, his friend Henry Antrim had left Silver City never to return. His destination: Lincoln County. Thus the boy headed for eastern New Mexico and the country that would provide the scene for his wanderings for the four years remaining to him.

Lincoln County sprawled across thirty thousand square miles of southeastern New Mexico, a vast jurisdiction the size of South Carolina claiming less than two thousand citizens. Geographically, economically, and socially, it fell into two distinct worlds: a mountain world and a plains world.

The mountain world consisted of the Capitan, Sacramento, and Guadalupe mountains and the Sierra Blanca. Little pockets of white settlement dotted the northern ranges, leaving the Guadalupes, to the south, as the undisputed domain of Apache Indians.

The county seat was Lincoln. It lay in the upland valley of the Rio Bonito, with the flat hump of the Capitan Mountains looming to the north and the Sierra Blanca peaks soaring to the southwest. With primitive tools, Hispanics tilled the fertile soils of the Bonito. Most of the Anglos, also farmers owning a few cattle as well, concentrated along the Ruidoso, the next stream south of the Bonito. The Ruidoso and the Bonito united to form the Hondo, which flowed out of the mountains to empty into the Pecos River.

An adobe village of four hundred people, largely Hispanic, Lincoln extended for a mile on both sides of a single tree-shaded street,

17

crowded on the north by the Bonito and on the south by a steep mountainside dappled with piñon and juniper. At the western edge of town stood the "big store" of L. G. Murphy & Co., the only two-story building in town. In the center of town rose the round tower, or *torreon*, a bastion of stone and adobe erected in 1862 for defense against Indians. Lincoln boasted no county courthouse, only a roomy adobe owned by "Squire" John B. Wilson that doubled as dance hall and, twice a year, courtroom for the itinerant district court based in Mesilla.[1]

Nine miles upstream from Lincoln, Fort Stanton perched on the banks of the Bonito. Like most frontier posts, it consisted of offi-cers' quarters, barracks, and storehouses fronting on a rectangular parade ground. The mission of the fort's garrison was to watch over the Mescalero Apache Indians, whose reservation and agency lay across the divide to the southwest at the forks of the Tularosa River. With the agency, the fort provided virtually the only market for the farmers and stockmen of the area.

Although sparsely populated and remote from the territory's main cities and travel routes, Lincoln and its environs excelled in habits of violence. The combination of whiskey and guns so preva-lent throughout the West seemed particularly volatile in Lincoln County. Adding to the mix were ethnic tensions of Anglos and His-panics, intensified by a racism that pitted Texans against "Mexi-cans," whites against the "nigger soldiers" at Fort Stanton, and everyone against the Indians of the Apache reservation. Casual law enforcement and ineffective courts imposed the weakest of formal restraints on the drunken killings and maimings that had grown routine.[2]

Few offenders paid for their crimes, whether murder, assault, or theft of stock. In fact, not until 1877 did Lincoln County even have a jail, and then only a hole in the ground topped by a log guardroom near the east end of town.

The little cluster of mountain dwellers on the Bonito and the Ruidoso depended on the Mesilla Valley for supply. The road to Mesilla, 140 miles to the southwest, climbed from Fort Stanton to the pass between the Sierra Blanca and the Sacramento Mountains, then descended the Tularosa River by way of the Mescalero Apache Indian agency and Blazer's Mills. Another little community had taken root here, where an Iowa dentist, Dr. Joseph H. Blazer, had established a sawmill and gristmill at the close of the Civil War. The road descended the Tularosa to the foot of the mountains, site of the Hispanic village of Tularosa. Just beyond, the river sank in the desert sand. Across a flat, barren desert strewn with black lava, along the edge of the glittering White Sands, and up through San Augustín Pass dividing the Organ and San Andres mountains, the traveler made his tortuous way in a journey that from Lincoln usually consumed three days.

East of Lincoln the dark mountain wall fell away to the shimmering Pecos Plains. This was cattle country, carpeted with grama grass as far as the eye could see—"knee high on every hill and mesa," marveled a traveler.[3]

Here John Simpson Chisum reigned as the "cattle king of New Mexico." Plain and unpretentious, with an angular, leathery face, Chisum was an affable extrovert and shrewd businessman who, at fifty-four, knew cows as few others did. He had arrived in 1867, trailing a herd of longhorns up the Goodnight-Loving Trail from Texas. By 1876 the Chisum herds had multiplied to eighty thousand head and ranged from old Fort Sumner down the Pecos 150 miles almost to the Texas line. The rich grasslands were public domain, free for the taking, but the swollen Chisum herds discouraged interlopers.

They came anyway. Along the southern edges of Chisum country, a handful of small cowmen crept up the Pecos from Texas to contest "Uncle John's" domination. They founded the community of Seven Rivers and began to build their own herds, mostly from Chisum "strays." Chisum fought back, and in the spring of 1877 the feud escalated into a shooting war.[4]

At the heart of the plains world stood Roswell and, nearby, Chisum's South Spring ranch. Roswell took root in 1869, the enterprise of Van C. Smith. A colorful, convivial character, Smith had sought refuge in this remote location in an effort to conquer his addiction to gambling. He erected two large adobe buildings and named the little community Roswell, for his father.

Roswell formed a pleasant green oasis amid the sweep of yellow plains, for no less than three streams united here to flow into the Pecos. Deep, crystal-clear, and swarming with all manner of fish, the North and South Spring rivers and the Hondo sent water coursing through a network of acequias to nourish cornfields, fruit orchards, and shady cottonwood trees. Chisum's South Spring ranch, another oasis, lay four miles to the southeast.

Van Smith failed to vanquish his compulsion and returned to Santa Fe to open a gambling house. He thus lost his chance to be remembered as the "Father of Roswell." That title went instead to Joseph C. Lea. A Confederate veteran full of shrewd ambition, "Captain" Lea bought the Smith property in 1877.

Lea's store clerk, and also Roswell's postmaster, was Marshall Ashmun Upson. "Intellectual handyman" for the surrounding area, Ash Upson was a restless journalist who loved words, people, and the bottle, in reverse order. He would meet Henry Antrim for the first time in October 1877 and ultimately decisively influence the world's image of the young outlaw.[5]

As Lincoln looked to Mesilla for its window on the outside world, Roswell and Seven Rivers looked northward, 160 miles up the Pecos River, to Las Vegas.

Las Vegas rested on a scenic fault, with the Great Plains rolling off to the east and the Sangre de Cristo Mountains rising in rugged splendor on the west. The remnant of the Santa Fe Trail linked Las Vegas with the advancing end of track of the Santa Fe Railroad in Colorado, and lumbering freight wagons pulled by oxen drew up in a plaza barren of vegetation and fronted on four sides by nondescript adobes. From the storehouses of the great mercantile firms such as the Ilfield Company, merchants from down the Pecos loaded their wagons with hardware, dry goods, firearms and ammunition, and groceries. Judging from appearances, an eastern reporter concluded, Las Vegas "certainly must date back to the birth of Christ."

The town boasted "the identical ass on which Jesus rode into Jerusalem," he added. "We saw it grazing just outside the city."[6]

Roughly midway between Las Vegas and Roswell, Fort Sumner stood on the east bank of the Pecos. Adobe barracks, residences, and storehouses arranged around a parade ground, the fort had been established during the Civil War to watch over the Navajo Indians colonized at the Bosque Redondo (Round Grove of Trees) after their conquest by the army. Government beef contracts for the Navajos and their guardian bluecoats had first drawn John Chisum and other Texas cowmen into New Mexico. After the Navajos went back to their homeland in 1868, Fort Sumner lost its mission and was abandoned.

Lucien Maxwell, who had recently sold the vast Maxwell Land Grant, bought Fort Sumner from the government in 1871. Some twenty-five or thirty Hispanic families accompanied him from his previous headquarters at Cimarron and settled in the buildings of the fort or built little adobes nearby. They farmed the irrigated fields abandoned by the Indians and ran sheep and cattle. Anglo cattlemen began to drift into the area in the middle 1870s, mingling their herds with the sheep pastured by Hispanics. Lucien died in 1875, but his son Pete—Pedro—carried on the Maxwell interest. Although a family enterprise, the fort served settlers and travelers as a town, complete with residences, stores, and saloons.[7]

Such was eastern New Mexico in 1877, when Kid Antrim first forded the Rio Grande to put his Arizona past behind him. In Lincoln County it was a volatile land, even then verging on explosion. To the north, in San Miguel County, it was a land of lively commerce verging on dramatic transformation as the railroad drew closer. Henry Antrim would come to know this land and its people intimately, and he would leave a lasting mark on both.

★

On October 1, 1877, a band of nine outlaws slipped into the Pass Coal Camp in the Burro Mountains, not far from Richard Knight's ranch, and made off with three horses. Included in the group were several of New Mexico's foremost desperadoes: Jesse Evans, Frank

Baker, Bob Martin, George "Buffalo Bill" Spawn, Nicholas Provencio, and one Ponciano. The next day, making their way through Cooke's Canyon on the road from Silver City to Mesilla, the thieves met a traveler named Carpenter. He recognized one of the horsemen and later named him: Henry Antrim.[8]

Thus the Kid had teamed up with the most notorious gang of outlaws in southern New Mexico. Evans and his men formed a loose coalition of bandits whose numbers varied between ten and thirty and whose depredations, aimed chiefly at horses and cattle, ranged from Silver City on the west to the Pecos River on the east. Sometimes they operated as one band, more often as several. They called themselves "The Boys." Albert J. Fountain, editor of the *Mesilla Valley Independent*, labeled them "The Banditti," and he waged a strident crusade against them that provoked first their ire and later their retribution.

The most prominent and professionally talented of The Boys was their leader, Jesse Evans—"Captain" Evans, as Editor Fountain scornfully branded him. Of medium stature and slight build, with gray eyes and light hair and complexion, Evans was about twenty-five in 1877. He pursued his calling with boldness, arrogance, rapacity, callousness toward his victims, and contempt for anyone who interfered or even protested, including the law. Yet he also projected an air of relaxed insolence and wry wit that some thought charming.

Evans had come to New Mexico from Texas in 1872 and gone to work for John Chisum on the Pecos. The cattle baron's horse remudas had suffered grievously from raids of the Mescalero Apache Indians, based on their reservation high in the mountains to the west. Determined to retaliate in kind, Chisum sent his cowboys on systematic plundering forays against the Indian herds. Evans participated.

Thus versed in the art of rustling, in 1875 Evans drifted westward to the Rio Grande and landed in the Mesilla Valley, where he found work on the ranch of John Kinney, three miles north of Mesilla. In Kinney, he found also a kindred soul, destined for a stature in the gallery of southwestern outlaws even greater than his own. A ruddy-faced New Englander, with brown hair and mustache, Kinney was about Evans's size, but five years older. During a stint in the U.S. cavalry, he had served at Fort Selden, fifteen miles north of Las Cruces, and on his discharge as a first sergeant in 1873 he had returned to go into the cattle business. For Kinney, the cattle business meant the same as it did for Evans, and by 1877 the Kinney ranch had acquired a reputation, as Fountain declared in the *Independent*, as "the headquarters and rendezvous for all the evil doers in the county."[9]

The offenses of both Evans and Kinney went beyond mere rustling. On New Year's Eve of 1876, Kinney, Evans, and several friends got into a brawl with some soldiers at a dance hall near Las Cruces, and Kinney was badly beaten. The vanquished withdrew, only to reappear at the doors and windows with blazing six-shooters. A soldier and an unlucky civilian who happened to be in the line of fire died instantly, and three soldiers were severely wounded, one mortally. No charges were brought against the murderers. As the victims' commanding officer reported, "It is much safer to kill a soldier in New Mexico than to be caught gambling, or defrauding the revenue."[10]

Within days of the New Year's Eve massacre, Evans got into another shooting affray. Accused, with two others, of putting six bullets into Quirino Fletcher on the main street of Las Cruces, he stood trial for murder. In that land of lax frontier justice, however, juries rarely convicted, and the defendants went free.[11]

By this time, Evans had his own gang. He undoubtedly continued his association with Kinney, who occasionally participated in the exploits of The Boys. They in turn used the Kinney ranch as a refuge, as Fountain charged. Evans's field of operations, however, extended all the way across southern New Mexico, whereas Kinney seems rarely to have strayed very far from his Mesilla Valley ranch.

Into this heady environment, in late September 1877, ventured Henry Antrim. Accused of murder in Arizona, he doubtless felt that he had found a suitable milieu and a congenial set of associates for the next stage of his life. Even if Arizona had taught him more about life than came to most teenagers, he must have been an impressionable adolescent, susceptible to the influences of the older men with whom he had cast his lot.

Typically, they and their kindred sported several aliases. Henry Antrim still went by his stepfather's name, and he brought with him from Arizona the nickname of "Kid." With his youth, his appearance, and his behavior, Kid Antrim fit the part. Increasingly, however, he adopted an alias of his own: William H. Bonney. Where that name came from remains a mystery, despite diligent efforts to find a Bonney family connection. At least one boyhood friend remembered his schoolmates using it in Silver City.[12] Within a matter of weeks, Henry Antrim became Billy Bonney, with Antrim regarded as an alias. People still called him the Kid, but not for another three years would anyone know him as Billy the Kid.

The escapades of the Evans gang in the two weeks following the theft of the horses at the Pass Coal Camp reveal the influences now playing on Billy Bonney and dramatize the values of his new world. Arizona had given him a taste of this world. In October 1877 he swallowed a heavy dose.[13]

After meeting Carpenter in Cooke's Canyon, Evans and his eight followers, including the Kid, continued on the road toward Mesilla. Seven miles east of old Fort Cummings, they stopped a westbound stagecoach. Assured by the driver that he carried no bullion, Evans replied, "Well, we'll let you pass this time," though he insisted that they have a drink together before the gang rode on. There were still nine men, according to the driver, each armed with two six-shooters and a Winchester rifle and draped with two belts full of cartridges.

At each of the three roadhouses along the way to Mesilla, The Boys partook of food and liquid refreshments, then told the proprietor to "chalk it up." "They desired to have it distinctly understood," reported the *Independent*, "that they were 'gentlemen,' and did not propose to be insulted by having beggarly tavern keepers thrust bills under their noses." At one of the stops, they found a copy of the *Independent*, containing one of Fountain's tirades against the "banditti." Irritated, Evans announced that he intended to present Fountain with "a free pass to hell."[14]

On October 5, at Mule Springs, three more of Evans's men

joined the group. They had stolen two horses at Santa Barbara, thirty-three miles up the valley from Mesilla, and had a six-man posse on their trail. When the possemen closed in, however, they found themselves outnumbered and outgunned. They carried only pistols, whereas the fugitives had rifles. The outlaws fired about forty shots, then attacked, drove the posse into a canyon, and rode off with "a shout of derision."[15]

Their number still further augmented, to seventeen, The Boys crossed the Rio Grande and took the road to the east, into Lincoln County. At Tularosa on October 9, they staged a big drunk, shot up the town and terrorized the residents, then proceeded up the road to the home of a man named Sylvester. He had once testified against one of The Boys, so they shot his dog and riddled the house with bullets. As Sylvester frantically shouted for his tormentors to spare his wife and children, they replied with more shots and shouts of drunken laughter, but apparently hurt no one.

Farther up the road, The Boys paused for provisions at the store of John Ryan near the Mescalero Apache Indian agency. Here, Evans gallantly entrusted to Ryan a horse previously stolen from Kate Godfroy, daughter of the Indian agent. He had heard that Kate was brokenhearted over the loss of her horse, Evans said, and he wanted Ryan to return it with an affectionate kiss. (It had been so badly used that it was no longer serviceable, commented the *Independent*.)

That night, near the mountain summit, The Boys continued their partying. For two travelers who chanced by in a buggy, the group turned out in mounted formation to parade along the road in mock honor. The two men were John H. Riley and James Longwell.

"A smart devil and a regular confidence man," according to one who knew him,[16] Riley was a partner in the mercantile firm of James J. Dolan & Co., formerly L. G. Murphy & Co. As both customer and client, he was an important personage for Evans and The Boys. Headquartered at Lincoln, across the mountains to the east, the Dolan firm dominated the economy of Lincoln County. Dolan and Riley supplied much of the contract beef used by the Apaches at the Indian agency and by the soldiers at Fort Stanton. Federal beef contracts had become so competitive, however, that no supplier could make a profit legitimately. One solution was to buy rustled stock at five dollars a head and turn it in on government contracts at fifteen. Evans and The Boys regularly furnished Dolan and Riley with stolen cattle while also occasionally performing other shady chores to which they preferred to have no visible link.

As friends and business associates of Evans's, therefore, Riley and Longwell, a company employee, probably stayed for the night's festivities. It is an easy guess that Riley penned the literate, satirical account that later appeared in the *Independent* under the pseudonym of "Fence Rail."[17]

The night's activities disclose much about The Boys and the examples they set for Billy Bonney. Evans mounted a stump to congratulate his men for their brilliant attainments and to suggest the need for "perfecting the organization." This took the form of electing Evans to the rank of colonel and Baker, Provencio, and Ponciano, "on account of their proficiency in horse lifting," to the rank of captain. All others, presumably including recruit Billy, received promotions to the grade of captain by brevet (an honorary military rank).

The revelers next adopted a series of resolutions. One thanked all who had aided or harbored them. Another thanked a friendly press (the *Mesilla News*) that had ridiculed the *Independent*'s claims of organized lawlessness in southern New Mexico. Still another castigated the *Independent*. And a final one proclaimed "that the public is our oyster, and that having the power, we claim the right to appropriate any property we may take a fancy to."

The ceremony ended around a huge bonfire. Nick Provencio produced a copy of the *Independent* and consigned it to the flames. While Frank Baker rendered the "Rogues March" on a comb, "Colonel" Evans led his band in a raucous procession around the "funeral pyre." The group then divided, one turning up the south fork of the Tularosa, the other taking the main road up the north fork, over the mountains to the Ruidoso, and on down to the Pecos.

Sometime in the middle of October, Evans and at least part of his gang reached the lower Pecos at Seven Rivers, where they put up at the ranch of crusty old Hugh Beckwith, patriarch of an extended family and the leader of the Chisum opposition.[18] For unknown reasons, Billy Bonney bunked with the neighboring Heiskell Jones family. The Joneses had eight sons ranging in age from one to twenty-two, and a twelve-year-old daughter besides. Barbara—"Ma'am Jones"—enjoyed a far-flung reputation for hospitality and hearty cooking.[19]

Whatever Billy's reasons for staying with the Joneses, they proved fortunate, for at the Beckwith ranch some of Jesse Evans's past sins caught up with him. On September 18 he and Frank Baker had stolen some horses and mules from the ranch of Richard Brewer, on the Ruidoso southeast of Lincoln. They belonged not only to Brewer but also to John H. Tunstall, a young Englishman who had come to New Mexico to make his fortune in stock raising. With some friends, Brewer gave chase, all the way to Mesilla, but had to return empty-handed. When district court convened in Lincoln early in October, Brewer served as foreman of the grand jury and made certain that indictments for larceny were returned against Evans and his friends. Brewer then enlisted a posse of fifteen men and persuaded Lincoln County Sheriff William Brady to lead it down to the Pecos, where Evans was known to be. On October 17 Brady's men closed in on the Beckwith ranch and, after a brief exchange of gunfire, arrested Evans, Baker, Tom Hill, and George Davis. Three days later, the four found themselves locked in the Lincoln jail.[20]

At the nearby Jones ranch, meantime, Billy Bonney made the acquaintance of the Casey family. Ex-soldier Robert Casey had come up from Texas in 1867 and established his growing family on the upper Hondo River east of Lincoln. For years his mill and store had served the sparse population of the area. In 1875, however, Bob Casey had been shot dead in Lincoln, leaving his widow, Ellen, to care for four children and the property. In May 1877 financial reverses cost her most of her cattle, which were sold at a sheriff's auction to satisfy debt. On behalf of John Tunstall, Lincoln lawyer Alexander McSween bought the cattle. Richard Brewer, who served as Tunstall's foreman in addition to tending his own ranch, drove them to the Englishman's recently acquired spread on the Rio Feliz, thirty miles south of Lincoln.[21]

Discouraged by her mounting troubles, the widow Casey decided to return to Texas. Early in October 1877 she packed her children and possessions in a wagon, rounded up her cattle, and struck down the Hondo. Late in October she paused at the Jones ranch and met Billy Bonney. He asked the widow if he could go to Texas with her. But he also coveted one of her horses and offered in trade his own, which she knew to be stolen.[22] Despite the urgings of her elder children, Robert A., sixteen, known as Add, and Lily, fifteen, Mrs. Casey firmly refused Billy's appeal.[23]

The impression that Billy projected at this time, after a month or more of exposure to Jesse Evans and his gangsters, is revealing. As Lily remembered, "The Kid was as active and graceful as a cat. At Seven Rivers he practiced continually with pistol or rifle, often riding at a run and dodging behind the side of his mount to fire, as the Apaches did. He was very proud of his ability to pick up a handkerchief or other object from the ground while riding at a run." Brother Add Casey supplied another dimension. "When I knowed him at Seven Rivers, you might call him a bum," he recalled years later. "He was nothing but a kid and a bum when I knowed him back there."[24]

In rejecting Billy's horse trade, the widow Casey had yielded less to probity than to a pragmatic qualm over getting caught with someone else's horse, as she intimated to Billy. Her own caravan, in fact, was burdened with more than a little stolen property, for it included the two hundred head of cattle that had once belonged to her but now, by virtue of the sheriff's sale of the previous May, belonged to John Henry Tunstall. Before abandoning her home, she had sent her hands to sweep Tunstall's range and run his animals into her own herd. When Tunstall learned of his loss, the elation prompted by the recovery of his stolen horses by the Brady-Brewer posse quickly dissolved. Undaunted, the worn-out Dick Brewer assembled six men and headed back down to the Pecos. Ten miles short of the Texas line, the pursuers came up with the Casey procession, faced down the Casey cowboys, and returned with all the stolen stock.[25]

Jesse Evans's coerced journey to Lincoln brought Billy Bonney for the first time to the county seat, for early in November about thirty of The Boys, together with some others interested in the liberation of the prisoners, gathered on the Ruidoso to plot an escape. Among these men was Billy Bonney.[26]

Besides The Boys, some of Lincoln's business and political elite also wanted Evans freed. In fact, he had become one of the players in the factional maneuvers that were leading inexorably to the Lincoln County War. Tunstall and his ally, lawyer Alexander McSween, had launched not only a cattle ranch on the Feliz but also a mercantile institution in Lincoln itself aimed at toppling the monopoly long enjoyed by Dolan & Co. and its predecessor, L. G. Murphy & Co.

Ambitious, smart, and ruthless, Jimmy Dolan fought back with unscrupulous cunning. He had learned well from his mentor, Lawrence Murphy, founder of "The House" and still a power in the county despite a losing bout with the bottle. Among the weapons in The House's arsenal was The Boys, who were skilled at intimidation. Indeed, the theft of the Brewer-Tunstall stock that had landed Evans in jail had been part of the program of intimidation. Dolan and his friends, therefore, wanted Evans back in business.

One of Dolan's friends was Sheriff Brady. He and Murphy had been wartime comrades and pioneer builders of Lincoln County. He tended to view matters the same as Murphy. Brady had gone to much trouble to get Evans in jail, but he probably looked on his eventual escape as fated and did little to head it off.

Even the patrician Tunstall, ambitious to supplant Dolan as economic overlord of Lincoln County, may have toyed with the idea of abetting Evans's escape. He seems to have hoped that he might win Evans away from Dolan and, if not sign him up in the coming fight, at least neutralize him. Tunstall took the prisoners a bottle of whiskey, jollied with them, and bought two of them new suits. He may also have primed Dick Brewer, his foreman, to act as courier between the jail and The Boys gathered on the Ruidoso and to set up his ranch as a source of food and mounts after the escape.

The break took place before dawn on November 17, 1877. About thirty of The Boys, including Bonney, rode over from the Ruidoso and showed up at the jail. Thanks to Brady, they found only a lone guard. They put a pistol to his head, knocked in the door to the cell with big rocks that had been helpfully assembled in advance, and rode out of town with their leader and his three lieutenants, together with another prisoner held on other charges.

On the way to Brewer's ranch, the party came on two brothers out hunting deer. They were Juan and Francisco Trujillo. The bandits surrounded Juan, but Francisco broke away. Bonney gave chase and threw down on him with his Winchester. Trujillo dismounted and threw down on Billy with his own rifle. When the others threatened to kill his brother, however, Francisco gave up. The fugitives relieved Juan of his saddle and weapons and rode on.[27]

The Boys reached Brewer's ranch after daylight. Brewer was conveniently absent, but his hands cooked breakfast for the visitors, who then saddled eight of Tunstall's horses in the Brewer corral and rode off. They left apologies for Tunstall and a promise never to steal from him again. Later, they sent back all but one of the animals. Although Tunstall may have drawn hope from this display of gallant generosity, Evans doubtless regarded it as ample return on the Englishman's investment of a bottle of whiskey and two new suits.[28]

After leaving Brewer's ranch, Evans and his men turned south to the Feliz and the Peñasco, then made their way back to the lower Pecos, where they again came to rest at the Beckwith ranch. Billy Bonney did not go with them. He remained on the Ruidoso.

Why? The most plausible answer is that he had made some new friends. In addition, he may have had some second thoughts about the life on which he had embarked. He may have wanted something better, something not so plainly outside the law.

The Ruidoso offered a setting not plainly outside the law, yet not altogether within it either. Most of the valley's residents were Anglos in their twenties, single or married to Hispanic women, who grew corn and ran a few head of cattle. They skirted the edges of the law, toiling at honest labor but not averse to rustling an occasional cow or otherwise offending the public order. They were open, friendly, and of a distinctly higher type than the ruffians with whom Billy had been consorting.

Thus the autumn of 1877 featured three distinct phases in the young life of Henry Antrim. In Arizona, he was an embryonic cowhand and occasional horse thief and cattle rustler. The Cahill killing, however, ended this life by making him, as he supposed, a fugitive wanted for murder and prompting him to return to New Mexico.

In his childhood haunts around Silver City, Henry threw in with the Jesse Evans gang. Now, Kid Antrim became Billy Bonney. For about a month, he participated in all the iniquities of that iniquitous band of desperadoes and doubtless learned much about their profession.

Finally, in a third phase, he fell back into a shadow world along the fringes of the law. It was peopled by his new friends on the Ruidoso, men who labored at an honest living but stood ready to break the law when opportunity presented or when impulse dictated. Billy Bonney thus substituted a new set of role models for the thugs who followed Jesse Evans. These new friends were soon to come together as one of the opposing armies in the Lincoln County War.

The Ranch Hand

When Billy Bonney first arrived on the Ruidoso to help plan the Evans jail break, he immediately fell in with the Coes. Of all the farmers along the Ruidoso, they were probably the hardest working and most successful. Frank Coe had a spread on the Hondo just below La Junta—the union of the Bonito and Ruidoso. His cousin George had located farther upstream, near Dowlin's Mill. Ab Saunders, whose sister had married one of Frank's brothers, helped Frank for wages. Part of a big clan of Missourians who had settled in northeastern New Mexico, these three had moved on more than a year earlier to escape the troubles simmering toward the Colfax County War.[1]

"He came to my ranch," said Frank of Billy, "wanting work. He looked so young that I did not take him very seriously about work. I invited him to stop with us until he could find something to do." On hunting excursions into the mountains in quest of deer, turkey, bear, and mountain lions, the cousins took a liking to their new friend. "He was very handy in camp," recalled Frank, "a good cook and good natured and jolly."[2]

The Kid's preoccupation with guns struck the Coes as it had Lily Casey down on the Pecos. "He spent all his spare time cleaning his six-shooter and practicing shooting," observed Frank. "He could take two six-shooters, loaded and cocked, one in each hand, . . . and twirl one in one direction and the other in the other direction, at the same time. And I've seen him ride his horse on a run and kill snow birds, four out of five shots."[3]

Will Chisum, old John's nephew, had similar memories. Billy used to while away the time, he recalled, by pitching his Winchester into the air, then catching it. "Always playing with it," said Will. Will also had vivid recollections of "those little forty-ones." Although Billy used several kinds of pistol, including the single-action Colt .44 "Frontier," he grew to favor the more compact .41-caliber Colt double-action "Thunderer," which could be fired rapidly because it did not have to be cocked manually.[4]

Billy lost no time getting to know the other farmers in the valley. "He was the center of interest everywhere he went," related George Coe, "and though heavily armed, he seemed as gentlemanly as a college-bred youth. He quickly became acquainted with everybody, and because of his humorous and pleasing personality grew to be a community favorite."[5]

One of the Kid's first acquaintances was Dick Brewer, whom he almost certainly had met at Seven Rivers when Brewer and his men forced Ellen Casey to give back Tunstall's cattle. Indeed, it is highly likely that Billy accompanied this party as it made its way back to Lincoln at the end of October. And if Brewer was mixed up in the escape of Jesse Evans, as he probably was, Billy got to know him even better as that plot unfolded. A big, handsome man of twenty-six, a fine horseman and accurate shot, Brewer managed his own spread while also acting as foreman of the Tunstall ranch on the Feliz.

Another friend was Charles Bowdre, an affable, easygoing fellow of twenty-nine with a well-developed compassion for the underdog. Born on a Mississippi plantation, according to Frank Coe, Charley was "a bookkeeper and well educated." When he could afford to, he sported a black hat and a fancy vest and went on fearsome drunks. With his Hispanic wife, he farmed a few acres on the upper Ruidoso. Billy fit in nicely, for with his fluent Spanish he could communicate with Manuela Bowdre better than could her husband.[6]

Still another friend of Billy's was Charley Bowdre's partner in

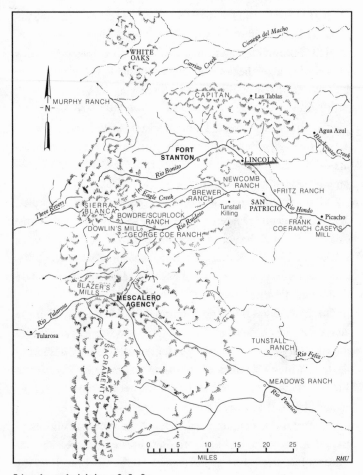

Lincoln and vicinity, 1878–81

farming, Doc Scurlock. The same age as Bowdre, Josiah G. Scurlock was a devoted family man and sensitive intellectual, with medical training somewhere in his background, but also an expert
marksman who did not hesitate to kill. He had married Antonia
Herrera and, besides farming, was busily raising what would ultimately grow to a family of ten children. Somehow he had lost his
front teeth, doubtless in a scuffle that reflected his hair-trigger temper. "He was a scrapping fool, you bet he was," remembered one
who knew him.[7]

A regular feature of life in the valley was the *baile*—exuberant dances and sings animated by the Coe cousins on the fiddle. In this setting Billy shone. "He was a mighty nice dancer and what you call a ladies' man," said Frank. "He talked the Mexican language and was also liked by the women." With the Coes belting out "Arkansas Traveler," "Irish Washerwoman," and "Fisher's Hornpipe," the revelers frolicked vigorously throughout the night. "Danced waltzes, polkas, but mostly squares," remembered Frank. Of all the tunes, Billy's favorite was "Turkey in the Straw." "He'd come over and say, 'don't forget the gaillina [turkey].'"[8]

With their typically confused sense of chronology, Frank and George Coe in later years each remembered that Billy had bunked with him through the winter of 1877–78. Billy probably did see a lot of the Coes, as well as Brewer, Bowdre, and Scurlock. They all continued to hunt together, dance together, and otherwise socialize together. Depending on where he happened to be, Billy probably bedded with each one for a night now and then. But he could not have resided with a Coe for more than a month. He arrived on the Ruidoso about the end of October 1877. He and others sprang Jesse Evans from jail on November 17. By early December at the latest, Dick Brewer had signed him on to the payroll of John Henry Tunstall.

★

John Henry Tunstall had polish. In addition to his English sophistication, he seemed open, sincere, and public-spirited. Despite his funny clothes and speech, many in Lincoln liked him. He was a youthful twenty-four, moderately wealthy in a desperately poor land, and outwardly bent on using his money to rid people of the tyranny of The House. For that alone, whatever they felt about his strange manners, his neighbors welcomed him.

Except for his family in England, however, beneficence formed no part of Tunstall's makeup. His winning ways disguised a single-minded pursuit of wealth. Beginning with a cattle ranch on the Feliz, he had moved on to a mercantile enterprise after noting the apparent prosperity of Dolan & Co. In fact, Dolan verged on bankruptcy, but Tunstall believed that a monopoly like Dolan's could be made to earn the riches he craved. Like Dolan and Murphy before him, through the judicious use of credit in a cashless economy Tunstall hoped to bind the area's farmers to his company as both producers and consumers. Controlling their crop yield, he could replace Dolan as the local supplier for government contractors at Fort Stanton and the Indian agency. His aim, therefore, was to substitute Tunstall & Co. for Dolan & Co. as the reigning monopoly. He wrote to his parents in London that he intended "to get the half of every dollar that is made in the county *by anyone.*"[9]

To further his ambitions, Tunstall had allied himself with Lincoln's only lawyer, Alexander McSween, a Scotsman ten years older than he. "Mac" harbored his own visions of wealth, and he plunged zealously into his associate's schemes. A mild-mannered, asthmatic man with an Oriental mustache framing his chin, he would engage in all manner of legal trickery to advance his fortunes, but his temperament did not equip him for a contest in which blood might flow. He was a man of peace who abhorred violence and never carried a gun.

Mac's wife, Sue, had a firmer grasp on reality and a better understanding of Jimmy Dolan. "I told Tunstall and Mr. McSween they would be murdered if they went into the store business," she later declared. "I did my best to keep McSween from entering the business, but he went in against my will."[10]

Sue McSween had accurately gauged the enemy. Discharged from the army at Fort Stanton eight years earlier, Dolan had clerked for Lawrence Murphy and absorbed from him all the crooked and devious ways of getting ahead on the frontier. In the spring of 1877, at the age of twenty-nine, he had inherited the Murphy mantle and, with Johnny Riley as partner, assumed the management of The House. Hot-tempered, quick-witted, and entirely unscrupulous, he could be expected to meet Tunstall's challenge with every weapon at his command, including violence and even murder if necessary.

Tunstall shared McSween's aversion to violence, but if he had to fight with guns, he would. By October 1877 he had begun to understand how deadly a game he had started. Thus he commissioned his foreman, Dick Brewer, to hire a small corps of men to work as hands on the Feliz ranch but also, if the need arose, to use their guns in the service of John Henry Tunstall. "It has cost a lot of money," the Englishman complained to his parents, "for men expect to be well-paid for going on the war path."[11]

By early December 1877, Brewer had recruited Billy Bonney. Legend portrays the Englishman and the youthful drifter as intimates, Tunstall taking a special interest in the Kid's latent qualities and the Kid repaying the effort with worshipful respect and intense loyalty. In his ten weeks as a Tunstall hand, however, Billy could not have spent much time with his employer. The store in Lincoln, a journey to Mesilla, and other concerns kept Tunstall away from the ranch most of the time. His letters to England never mentioned Billy.

Even so, Billy almost certainly formed an admiration and respect for Tunstall. Working for a man of such affluence, education, manners, and stature in the community was a new experience. It afforded a glimpse of a life unimagined in the world of Jesse Evans, Windy Cahill, or even William Henry Harrison Antrim. Even from a distance, and probably even unconsciously, Tunstall provided a powerful example for young Billy and added another dimension to his developing personality.

Rather than Tunstall, Billy's friends were his daily companions—Brewer and those he had recruited. Foremost among them was John Middleton. A beefy drifter off the Texas cattle trails, twenty-three years old, Middleton had a dark complexion, black eyes, black hair, and a huge black mustache. Though reserved and soft-spoken, he was fearless. He shot well, especially with the pistol. Tunstall, who thought Middleton "about the most desperate looking man I ever set eyes on," credited him with the pugnacious resolve that backed down the Casey cowboys and averted a gunfight over Tunstall's cattle.[12]

Blue-eyed, with sandy hair and mustache and a slim, wiry build, Henry N. Brown was only nineteen, a year older than Billy. He had been a buffalo hide hunter in Texas before coming to New Mexico and signing on at Lawrence Murphy's ranch thirty miles west of

Lincoln. In December 1877, after eighteen months as a Murphy cowhand, Brown quit in an acrimonious dispute over wages. At once he went to work for Tunstall. He had killed a man on the buffalo range, knew how to use guns, and, some thought, resorted to them too readily. "Nervy," judged Frank Coe, "but not smart like Kid."[13]

Frederick T. Waite had wandered into New Mexico from the Indian Territory. He was part Indian, boasting a distinguished Chickasaw lineage together with a prosperous father back home in Paul's Valley and an education that included some time in college. At twenty-five, he was considerably older than Brown and Bonney. An "OK lad," pronounced Frank Coe.[14] Billy liked Fred immensely, and the two soon became inseparable companions.

The other men in Tunstall's little army were noncombatants. One was Godfrey Gauss, the gentle, fatherly old chuck wrangler who tended the kitchen at the ranch headquarters on the Feliz. "Dutch Martin" Martz and "Old Man" William McCloskey, an experienced Texas stockman, rounded out the crew. They had been temporarily engaged to brand Tunstall's herd.

Billy surely understood that he and the others had been hired as much for their shooting skills as for their mastery of cowpunching. They spent some time at the ranch on the Feliz, where the only building, a rude two-room adobe, afforded meager shelter and no comforts. They also appeared in Lincoln and wherever else Tunstall had chores to be performed.

A place that became Billy's favorite resort was San Patricio, a tiny village of about fifteen adobe dwellings lining a single street beside the Ruidoso just above its junction with the Bonito. The residents, almost entirely Hispanic, liked Billy, and he liked them, especially their young women. Years after his death, one remembered: "The Keed was gone, but many Spanish girls mourned for him."[15]

None of Billy's new comrades were models of rectitude. Like other friends such as Charley Bowdre and Frank and George Coe, they sometimes strayed into unlawful pursuits. Even Dick Brewer, usually thought to be a law-abiding citizen, may have dabbled in

38

stolen cattle.[16] But they did not present themselves openly as out-laws who, like Jesse Evans and his followers, regarded the public contemptuously as "our oyster." With Tunstall, they had a steady job for which they drew regular wages.

Billy's new associations, and especially the model of Tunstall, exposed new sides of his character. Probably for the first time in his young life, he began to think of settling into an honest vocation and building a decent life for himself. By February 1878, he and Fred Waite had begun to lay plans for claiming a spread on the upper Peñasco and founding a farming and ranching enterprise of their own.[17]

Add Casey noted the difference in the Kid when Casey returned from Texas. The "bum" he had met at Seven Rivers in October 1877 had become a "gentleman." "After he got in with Tunstall he paid his way, and was a different man altogether," recalled Casey. "He had more sweethearts on the creek than a little."[18]

But Billy Bonney was still "the Kid," an eighteen-year-old with-out a clear adult persona. The shift from Evans to Tunstall had brought new and more appealing traits to the surface but had also showed how impressionable he remained, how susceptible he was to the influences surrounding him. Like his new friends, he had sampled both the lawful and the unlawful. Like them, he harbored the potential to turn either way—to honest toil or open outlawry. The Lincoln County War pointed some of its warriors in one direc-tion, some in the other.

Billy Bonney almost certainly had little knowledge or under-standing of the complicated legal maneuvers that moved the struggle between Tunstall and Dolan toward open war. They cen-tered on the proceeds of a life insurance policy that McSween had been engaged to collect more than a year earlier. He had succeeded, but had then withheld the money from the heirs until he could be certain of receiving his fee. Dolan, who thought he could get his hands on the money if McSween released it, persuaded one of the heirs to charge the lawyer with the criminal offense of embezzle-ment and to bring civil suit for recovery of the money. The drama reached a climax in Mesilla early in February 1878, with McSween and Tunstall present as well as Dolan and some friends. McSween managed to get the criminal trial postponed until the spring session of district court in Lincoln. But the civil proceedings required surety in the amount of the suit, ten thousand dollars. Unknown to McSween and Tunstall, who had already left for home, Judge Warren Bristol issued a writ for the attachment of enough of McSween's property to cover the amount.[19]

Billy Bonney and Fred Waite happened to be in Lincoln to observe what happened next. With the writ in his pocket, Dolan raced across mountain and desert to Lincoln, arriving on February 8, two days before McSween and Tunstall. At once, Sheriff Brady formed a posse and invaded McSween's office and home to inventory and value the furnishings. Not content with that, he moved on to the Tunstall store next door and began to list all the merchandise. Like everyone else, he erroneously assumed McSween and Tunstall to be partners and the contents of the store to be the property of both.

Tunstall had left the store in the charge of Robert A. Widenmann, a young man roughly his own age whom he had met in Santa Fe and invited to share his Lincoln adventures. A pompous blusterer, disliked by almost everyone, Rob Widenmann shouted protests and threats at Brady, to no avail. Methodically, the sheriff went about his task until his list contained property worth four times the amount stipulated in the writ.[20]

If this turn of events chagrined McSween, it infuriated Tunstall, who characteristically felt sympathy for no one but himself. He did not like Brady anyway, regarding him as a "slave of whiskey" and a tool of The House. That Brady had the gall to attach his property and to hold his store night and day like an occupying army outraged the Englishman. The day after reaching Lincoln, February 11, he and Widenmann summoned Bonney and Waite and headed for the store. While Billy and Fred stood menacingly in the door, Tunstall and Widenmann barged in and confronted Brady and his men. With pistols conspicuously displayed, they berated the lawmen and warned that all would suffer if the inventory continued. To give point to the threats, Billy and Fred brandished their Winchester rifles. Brady relented enough to release six horses and two mules from impoundment, but he continued to hold the store as if it were a fortress.[21]

That very day, Tunstall started Gauss, Middleton, and Mc-Closkey to the ranch with part of the animals, and that night Widenmann, accompanied by Bonney and Waite, followed with the rest. The two boys planned to ride on to the Peñasco and begin to put their ranching plans into effect. Whether they meant to leave Tunstall's employ is not clear; probably they intended, like Brewer, to divide their time between Tunstall's interests and their own enterprise. Arriving at the ranch on the morning of the twelfth, they spent the day and night at the Tunstall ranch building. Present now were all the Tunstall employees: Widenmann, Brewer, Middleton, Bonney, Waite, Brown, Martz, and McCloskey.[22]

Bonney and Waite apparently deferred their plan to go to the Peñasco because they thought they might be needed at the Tunstall ranch. On February 9 Sheriff Brady had decided to include the cattle on the Feliz in the attachment. As with the store merchandise, he assumed that they belonged to McSween and Tunstall as partners. Brady had therefore dispatched a posse on this mission. Widenmann and the others who drove the stock to the ranch had probably learned of the threat before leaving Lincoln, and they found that the men at the ranch had also been alerted by a passerby, who had warned that the posse came with intent to kill if necessary. Determined to defend themselves, Widenmann and Brewer had the men punch firing ports in the walls and barricade the doors with grain sacks filled with earth.[23]

To lead the posse, Brady had deputized Jacob B. "Billy" Mathews, a silent partner in Dolan & Co. With two House employees, John Hurley and Manuel Segovia (also known as "Indian"), Mathews first rode to the Indian agency and Blazer's Mills, where Dolan kept a branch store and where Mathews added two more House employees, George Hindman and Andrew L. "Buckshot" Roberts.[24]

Here too Mathews chanced across Jesse Evans and one of his henchmen, Tom Hill. Since his break from the Lincoln jail, Evans had been down to the Beckwith ranch on the Pecos and had then ridden to the far western edge of his domain. On January 19, 1878, he and two of his gang stole some horses on the Mimbres River south of Silver City. A posse overtook the thieves and in an exchange of gunfire put a bullet in Evans's groin. Two weeks later, he turned up near Mesilla and joined Jimmy Dolan, fresh from his legal coup against McSween. Still hurting from his wound, Evans persuaded Dolan to let him ride in his carriage as far as Blazer's Mills. There, on February 10 or 11, he learned of Mathews's assignment, doubtless from Mathews himself.[25]

From Blazer's Mills Mathews and his men rode up the south fork of the Tularosa and crossed to the upper Peñasco to camp at the ranch of W. W. Paul. Five miles from Blazer's Mills, Evans and Hill overtook the posse, and at Paul's ranch two more of The Boys, Frank Baker and Frank Rivers, appeared. Evans announced that he intended to accompany Mathews because he had loaned Billy Bonney some horses and wanted to get them back. If Mathews protested the presence of avowed outlaws in a sheriff's posse, he did so perfunctorily.[26]

Early on the morning of February 13, the Tunstall hands spotted the possemen and their bandit companions approaching from the south. Backed by Billy and the others with guns at the ready, Widenmann commanded the party to halt fifty yards short of the house. Mathews advanced alone, read the attachment writ, and declared that he had come to impound McSween's cattle. Widenmann answered that McSween had no cattle on the Feliz. A considerable discussion followed, in which Brewer sought to find some compromise and Widenmann stubbornly insisted that if Mathews wanted the cattle he would have to fight for them. Confused, hesitant, and probably intimidated by the firepower facing him, Mathews lamely concluded that he would have to return to Lincoln for new instructions.[27]

Brewer invited Mathews and his men to have breakfast, and while they were riding forward and caring for their horses the officious Widenmann tried to enlist his comrades in a deadly venture. Somehow, he had persuaded John Sherman, U.S. marshal for New Mexico, to give him a deputy's commission and entrust him with a warrant for the arrest of Evans, Baker, and Hill on the federal charge of stealing stock from the Indian reservation. Now Widenmann asked Brewer and the others to help him serve the warrant. With some injury to the truth, Brewer replied that all were peaceful ranchmen, and if they aided in the arrest of Evans they would all, sooner or later, be shot down in their homes by Dolan gunmen.

Evans added to Widenmann's humiliation by taunting him. Swinging his Winchester on the lever and catching it at full cock aimed at the "marshal," Evans asked if Widenmann carried an arrest warrant for him. That was his business, Widenmann bravely replied. If he ever tried to serve a warrant, Evans warned, he would catch the first bullet fired. Two could play at that game, Widenmann replied. Meantime, Frank Baker methodically spun his pistol on his trigger finger, stopping it at full cock pointed at Widenmann. Despite the tension, Widenmann's associates must have enjoyed a secret chuckle at the discomfiture of the posturing busybody.[28]

Widenmann too felt the need for fresh instructions. Accompanied again by Bonney and Waite, he rode with the Mathews party to Lincoln. Evans and his men, together with Buckshot Roberts, remained behind and soon started back to the Peñasco. That night, as Mathews worked out the next move with Sheriff Brady, Widenmann met with Tunstall and McSween. Billy and Fred probably sat in the room listening to the conversation. Widenmann had seen and heard enough to convince him that Mathews would return with a stronger posse and try to take the cattle by force. Full of indignation, Tunstall did not intend to give in without a fight. Early the next morning Widenmann and his two companions started back to the Feliz to mobilize the defenses.[29]

Brady did not intend to back down either. While Mathews signed up more men in Lincoln, a messenger rode down to the Pecos with orders for William B. "Billy" Morton, boss of Dolan's cow camp, to recruit some of the Seven Rivers stockmen and bring them up the Peñasco to Paul's ranch. By the evening of February 17, the Lincoln and Seven Rivers contingents had rendezvoused at Paul's ranch. Altogether, Mathews commanded twenty-two men, including Jimmy Dolan himself. Also on hand, not surprisingly, were Evans, Baker, Hill, and another gang member, George Davis. Evans had still not recovered his horses from Billy Bonney.[30]

By this time, February 17, Tunstall had succumbed to doubts about his defiant course. As late as the sixteenth, he had ridden the countryside enlisting men to help him in a fight with Dolan, and that night he had cursed and threatened James Longwell, Brady's chief deputy in the store. Later that night, however, Lincoln's premier gossip, the black handyman George Washington, had brought Tunstall a lurid tale of Mathews's activities. There were now forty-three possemen, Washington said, and they intended to decoy Tunstall's men out of their defenses, kill them all, and make off with the cattle. Picturing his men overrun and slaughtered, Tunstall decided that the ranch was not the place for a showdown. Without waiting for daylight, he set forth for the Feliz.[31]

The next evening, in the little house on the Feliz, Tunstall outlined his new plan. McCloskey, who had close friends in the posse, would leave at once for the Peñasco and inform Mathews that no resistance would be offered to the attachment. McCloskey was also to find "Dutch Martin" Martz, who was skilled at counting cows, and have him come with Mathews to tally the herd on behalf of Tunstall. Tunstall and the rest of his hands would pull out early the next morning, leaving harmless old Godfrey Gauss to confront the posse.[32]

At first light on February 18, the Tunstall party breakfasted and hit the road for Lincoln. They drove nine horses; six were those released by Brady on the eleventh, two belonged to Brewer, and the last was Billy Bonney's or, possibly, Jesse Evans's. Whomever that horse belonged to, it furnished the pretext for the continued presence of the outlaws with the posse. After a mile, Henry Brown, for unknown reasons, left the group and turned south to the Peñasco, en route exchanging greetings with the posse. Ten miles out, the horsemen and the horse herd veered off on a trail that afforded a mountainous shortcut to the Ruidoso while Fred Waite, driving a buckboard, continued on the road.

Back at the ranch, after a wary approach from two directions, the posse discovered conditions as McCloskey had stated. Only Gauss remained. The nine horses, however, supplied an excuse for another move. They too had to be included in the attachment. Probably at Dolan's suggestion, Mathews designated fourteen men and deputized Billy Morton, Dolan's man from the Pecos, to lead a chase after Tunstall to retrieve the horses. Evans, Baker, and Hill made ready to go too. Mathews objected mildly, but Evans declared that he and his men had a right to go after their property, that Kid Antrim had their horses and they intended to get them back. "Hurry up boys," exclaimed Morton impatiently, "my knife is sharp and I feel like scalping someone." Off the subposse clattered on the road to Lincoln, with Evans, Baker, and Hill trailing.[33]

Dusk had begun to fall when the Tunstall party crested a divide and started down a narrow gorge leading to the Ruidoso. Middleton and Bonney lagged several hundred yards in the rear. Ahead, the main group started a flock of wild turkeys, and Brewer and Widenmann veered from the trail up a steep-sided open slope on the left to see if some could be bagged. Tunstall remained on the trail with the horses.[34]

As they topped the divide, Middleton and Bonney glimpsed a party of horsemen galloping up the trail behind them. Spurring their mounts, the two raced to alert their comrades, Middleton heading for Tunstall, Billy aiming for Brewer and Widenmann, who were about two hundred yards up the hillside from the trail. Bonney had almost reached his destination when the pursuers cleared the brow of the divide and, spotting the three men to their left front, opened fire. A bullet cracked between Brewer and Widenmann and sent them hurrying for cover. The treeless slope offered none, but higher up scrub timber and scattered boulders capped a hilltop. With the possemen angling off the trail in pursuit, the three made for this cover. En route, Middleton joined them, alone.

To the rear, the possemen reined in as they reached the hillside just vacated by their quarry. They had caught sight of Tunstall and his horses on the trail below, and at once they turned down toward the new prize. Above, Billy and his friends had just reached their defensive position when they heard a burst of gunfire in the canyon below. "They've killed Tunstall," said Middleton.

Middleton had tried to save the Englishman. "I sung out to Tunstall to follow me," Middleton later recalled. "He was on a good horse. He appeared to be very much excited and confused. I kept singing out to him for God's sake to follow me. His last word was 'What John! What John!'"[35]

The killing took place in a patch of scrub timber about a hundred yards off the trail. The only witnesses were the killers themselves: Billy Morton, Jesse Evans, and Tom Hill. Morton explained to the rest of the posse that he had commanded Tunstall to surrender, only to be greeted by two shots fired from Tunstall's pistol. All three had then returned the fire. Two bullets hit the Englishman, one in the chest and the other in the head, and he fell from his horse, dead. Another shot dropped the horse.

As several of the possemen laid the body out next to the horse, they heard more shots fired. Someone brought Tunstall's pistol to place with the corpse. The cylinder contained two empty cartridges. One of the men thought Tom Hill had fired the two shots.[36]

Billy Morton's explanation to his followers stood as the official version of Tunstall's death. He had been killed while resisting arrest by a posse led by a legally designated deputy sheriff of Lincoln County. Neither Morton nor Hill got the chance to tell more about the shooting, and in subsequent testimony Evans swore that he had not even been present with the posse.[37]

None of the posse felt like testing the hilltop defenses of Tunstall's companions. Rounding up the nine horses, they returned to the Feliz. Jesse Evans or one of his sidekicks was heard to quip that Tunstall's death was small loss, that he deserved to be killed.

As night closed in, Billy Bonney and his three comrades mounted and made their way down the trail to the Ruidoso. Here they arranged for a party to come out the next day to find Tunstall and bring his body to Lincoln. Late that night they told their story to Alexander McSween and a house packed with men who had come to town in response to Tunstall's appeals for help.[38]

The killing of Tunstall touched off the Lincoln County War. None of the Englishman's supporters believed that he had been shot while resisting arrest. Rather, they were certain that he had been murdered in cold blood by Dolan gunmen masquerading as officers of the law and his pistol fired twice in order to support Morton's story.

And in truth, whatever actually happened in that thicket, the killing has to be seen as murder. Even if the posse had been required to attach the nine horses—hardly an arguable proposition—a confrontation with Tunstall need not have occurred. Morton, Evans, and Hill rode past the horses to reach Tunstall, then chased him a hundred yards off the trail. Even if he pulled his pistol, even if he fired it, even if his assailants had not premeditated a killing, Tunstall was murdered.

Billy Bonney's role in this prelude to war was minor. He was a witness and a participant in momentous events but exerted little influence on their course or outcome. Other men, chiefly Widenmann and Brewer, did the thinking, the deciding, and the leading. Billy followed. He did what he was expected to do, as when he and Fred Waite backed Tunstall and Widenmann in the confrontation with Sheriff Brady on February 11. But Billy did nothing to make himself conspicuous and played no other part than simply one of the boys. With them as with the Evans gang, he was the Kid—if no longer a green adolescent, still no more than an apprentice adult.

With the outbreak of war, the Kid would mature swiftly.

The Avenger

The slaying of John Henry Tunstall profoundly affected Billy Bonney. Frank Coe recorded a revealing scene in a back room of the Tunstall store, as the dead man's body was laid out on a table for embalming. "Kid walked up," related Coe, "looked at him, and said, 'I'll get some of them before I die,' and turned away."[1]

Billy's actions in the few days following the killing betrayed the depth of his feeling. No longer was he the unobtrusive bystander. Suddenly he displayed a boldness, a truculence, and an initiative that made him one of the more conspicuous of the men operating out of the McSween house during the cold February days after the murder. Although still a follower, he took the first steps toward leadership.

The top leader now was Alexander McSween. On the night of February 18, 1878, forty to fifty men had responded to Tunstall's call. About midnight, however, Widenmann, Brewer, Middleton, Bonney, and Waite arrived with news of the Englishman's fate, and the mantle passed to McSween.

The lawyer had no stomach for an armed contest with Dolan. He preferred legal stratagems. The district judge, the district attorney, and the county sheriff had already shown their partiality for Dolan, and McSween could expect no cooperation from them. But Lincoln contained other officers of the law: the justice of the peace and the town constable. John B. Wilson, an easily influenced, barely literate old man of marginal intelligence, served as justice of the peace.

Atanacio Martínez, of firm enough fiber but skeptical of the role McSween marked out for him, was constable. McSween's scheme was to obtain warrants for the arrest of Tunstall's killers from "Squire" Wilson and use the men in the McSween house, acting under Martínez's authority, as a posse to serve the warrants.[2]

Arrest warrants could not be issued unless supported by affidavits alleging crime. The next morning, therefore, McSween accompanied Dick Brewer, John Middleton, and Billy Bonney to Squire Wilson's office. There the three men swore that on the day before William S. Morton, Jesse Evans, and a list of other offenders had "wounded & killed J. H. Tunstall contrary to the statute in such case made and provided and against the Peace & dignity of the Territory." Named on the list of murderers were James J. Dolan, who in fact had remained with Mathews and other possemen at the Tunstall ranch, and the outlaw Frank Baker, whose worn-out horse had kept him out of the action.[3]

While at Wilson's office, McSween prepared an affidavit of his own to support still another warrant. Brady's continued occupation of the Tunstall store rankled, and the lawyer had found a clever way to strike back. The previous day, probably alarmed by the gathering of men at the McSween house, the sheriff had called on Captain George A. Purington, the commanding officer at Fort Stanton, for a detachment of soldiers to protect him from harm. Thoughtlessly, Brady then authorized his men in the Tunstall store to provide a small amount of hay for the troopers' horses. The hay belonged to Tunstall, not the county, and McSween charged Brady and his men with larceny.[4]

While Wilson labored with the paperwork, Billy and as many as forty other McSween men found opportunity to express their rage. Sam Wortley, who ran a hotel and restaurant at the western edge of town, afforded a pretext for browbeating the occupiers of the Tunstall store. At noon on the nineteenth, he made his way down the street with dinner for the five men in the store. Billy Bonney and Fred Waite stepped forward to bar the way and ordered Wortley to return without delivering the meal. Seeing James Longwell watching from the door of the store, Billy then turned and threw down his

Winchester on the posseman. "Turn loose you sons-of-bitches, we will give you a game," shouted Billy. Longwell retreated inside, and he and his men barricaded the doors and windows. Billy and Fred, however, drew off without provoking a fight.[5]

Thanks to Justice Wilson's helpful cooperation, Constable Martínez received warrants for the apprehension of five outlaws and twelve members of the Mathews posse for murder and of Sheriff Brady and the five men in the Tunstall store for larceny. The constable had some understandable reservations about the task assigned him, particularly the arrest of the county sheriff and twenty-two men acting under his legal authority as officers of the law. But McSween's formidable and determined throng supplied a powerful impetus to cooperate.

Unexpectedly, Rob Widenmann came to the rescue. He had ridden to Fort Stanton to break the news of Tunstall's death. During the night of the nineteenth someone brought word to the fort that Jesse Evans was thought to be in Lincoln. Still a deputy U.S. marshal and still bearing the federal warrants for Evans and others for stealing Indian horses, Widenmann thought he could now make a better showing than he had at the Tunstall ranch on the thirteenth. Captain Purington had standing orders to furnish military aid for this purpose if Widenmann asked for it. Before dawn on the twentieth, therefore, Rob showed up in Lincoln with Lieutenant Millard F. Goodwin and a posse of thirty black cavalrymen.[6]

Martínez had meanwhile already organized his own posse from among the men at the McSween house. It numbered at least eighteen, including Bonney, Brewer, Waite, Middleton, and the Coe cousins.[7]

Widenmann's little army provided a convenient screen for Martínez's posse. Before dawn on the twentieth, looking for Evans, the soldiers invaded the Dolan store and conducted a thorough search. Martínez and his men followed and carried out their own search. Finding nothing, the two posses proceeded down the street to the Tunstall store to repeat the operation.

Alerted by a commotion in front of the store, Jim Longwell looked out to see both soldiers and civilians gathering in the predawn gloom. He noticed Widenmann, rapped on the window to catch his attention, and asked what was up.

"You will find out damn quick," Rob replied.

Longwell then recognized Lieutenant Goodwin, leaned his Winchester against the wall, and went outside. The officer explained that the soldiers had come to town to help the deputy U.S. marshal find Jesse Evans and his cohorts, who were thought to be hiding in the Tunstall store. Longwell denied that Evans had been in the store and invited Goodwin to search it. The search turned up no sign of Evans.

As the soldiers filed out of the store, Martínez and his men burst in. Surprised, facing an imposing array of Winchesters pointed at them, Longwell's men quickly surrendered. Martínez produced his larceny warrant, had the prisoners disarmed, and marched them down the street to the cellar jail. Later, after Brady had arrived from his home east of town, the posse seized him too and hauled all six before Justice Wilson for arraignment. Wilson discharged Longwell and his companions but bound over Brady for appearance before the district court, with bond set at two hundred dollars. The McSween forces now had possession of the Tunstall store, and they never relinquished it.[8]

Sometime during the twentieth, Captain Purington rode down from Fort Stanton to investigate the crisis in Lincoln. A huge man with white hair and mustache that made him look two decades older than his thirty-nine years, he was a plodding mediocrity. He talked with McSween and Brady and quickly sized up the McSween crowd as a mob, maddened by the killing of Tunstall and unrestrained by legal niceties in seeking vengeance. The lives of Brady, Dolan, and Riley, he decided, "would not be worth a farthing if turned over to the McSween party." As he admitted the next day in a letter to Judge Warren Bristol, "I hardly know what to do." He left Lieutenant Goodwin and his troopers in Lincoln with the delicate mission of trying to keep the peace without interfering with the civil authorities.[9]

Goodwin, who also regarded the Martínez posse as no better than a mob, felt that he had been duped into using his soldiers for an improper purpose. He complained bitterly to Widenmann, who apologized. Goodwin also reproached Martínez, who replied, according to the lieutenant, that he did not want to serve the warrants, "but was told by Antrim 'Kid' and others at McSween's house that if he did not serve them they would kill him."[10]

Dolan, Mathews, and others whose names appeared on Martínez's murder warrant had gathered with Brady in the Dolan store. Caught up in the frenzy, Widenmann asked Goodwin to take his soldiers back to the fort and let the two sides fight it out. Goodwin refused. Widenmann then inquired what the lieutenant would do if an attempt were made to arrest the culprits in the Dolan store. Goodwin answered that he could not interfere with civil authorities but that he considered McSween's followers a mob whose actions would lead to bloodshed. Therefore, he would have to post his soldiers between the two factions, which he did by deploying them at the Dolan store.[11]

Widenmann probably came up with the solution to this dilemma: attempt the arrest without the backing of the "mob." If only Martínez and a couple of men entered the Dolan store, the soldiers could not meddle without opening themselves to charges of obstructing a civil officer in the discharge of his duty. The constable could not have had much enthusiasm for this daring scheme, but once again threats against his life probably spurred him to his duty, as suggested by his deputizing Billy Bonney and Fred Waite to accompany him into the enemy's lair. The presence of soldiers outside the store could be expected to restrain Brady and his men from extreme measures, but even so, considering the temper of both sides on this day, the plan bordered on the foolhardy. It shows how staunch was the Kid's determination to avenge the death of Tunstall.

Fearlessly, Martínez and his two deputies barged into the Dolan store. Inside, they confronted the same spectacle that had greeted Longwell and his men at the Tunstall store earlier in the day: a battery of Winchester rifles trained on their chests. Relieving the invaders of their arms, Brady asked their business. Martínez pulled out his warrant and began to read it. The sheriff interrupted to declare that the men named happened to be his posse, that no one was going to arrest them, and that anyway he did not recognize the authority of Justice Wilson to issue arrest warrants. Thereupon the men in the store "cursed and abused" the three interlopers. After a few hours they released the constable and, without returning his arms, sent him away. But Bonney and Waite remained prisoners. Widenmann's grand design had collapsed, as he might have expected.[12]

With the Dolan forces holding two of McSween's men, tensions remained high through the night and into the next day. But the presence of Lieutenant Goodwin and his cavalrymen kept the conflict from exploding. Even so, during the night someone fired a shot that killed a cavalry horse. The next day, Captain Purington sent an infantry detachment to Lincoln to bolster the cavalry.[13]

February 21 passed quietly, as the townspeople gathered to bury John Henry Tunstall in the vacant lot east of his store. Reverend Taylor F. Ealy, a Presbyterian divine who had arrived only two days earlier to bring the true word to heathens and Catholics, preached the funeral sermon. Squire Wilson translated for the Hispanics. In the absence of Sue McSween, who was in the East, Mrs. Ealy played Sue's organ, carried to the gravesite for the occasion.

After the funeral, the citizens gathered in a public meeting to discuss the tribulations that had overtaken their community. Probate Judge Florencio Gonzalez headed a committee of four charged with calling on Sheriff Brady to learn why he had seized Martínez, Bonney, and Waite without legal process and to see if some way could be found to end the law's harassment of McSween. At once, the four men trooped down the street to the Dolan store and confronted Brady, who had no difficulty recognizing them as spokesmen for the other side. Curtly, the sheriff dismissed the question about the constable and his two aides with the answer that he had taken them prisoner because he had the power. The committeemen, who included merchants José Montaño and Isaac Ellis, then offered their own property in an amount double the bond specified by the court if Brady would call off the attachment that had produced the crisis. Brady refused, but after they left he did free Billy

Bonney and Fred Waite, after thirty hours of imprisonment, though without returning their arms. Billy would not quickly forget, or forgive, his humiliation at the hands of Brady and his associates.[14]

The attachment process, a civil action, was the least of McSween's troubles. The criminal charge of embezzlement underlay a much more immediate danger. Judge Bristol had required him to post bond for his appearance at the spring term of district court to answer the charge. But District Attorney William L. Rynerson, a friend and ally of Dolan's, refused to accept McSween's bondsmen on the spurious ground that they were not worth the amounts pledged. The plot, of course, was to force McSween to spend six weeks in Brady's jail while awaiting his court hearing. Once there, as a report that reached Mac on February 24 indicated, Dolan would bring in Jesse Evans "to do his part." Plainly a fugitive from the law after Rynerson sent back his bond disapproved, McSween made out his will and fled Lincoln.[15]

McSween thus relinquished control of his little army. Neither he nor Martínez had managed it very well anyway. If it were to function at all, it demanded more aggressive leadership. A new chief materialized in the person of Dick Brewer. When Martínez returned his warrant unserved on February 22, Justice Wilson wrote out a new warrant, appointed Brewer a "special constable," and empowered him to arrest the men named as Tunstall's murderers.[16]

Under the captaincy of Dick Brewer, the Martínez posse emerged as the "Regulators." For the next five months, claiming the sanction of the law, they fought McSween's battles. Tunstall had promised them four dollars a day to ride in his cause. McSween could pay nothing; by February 1878, he was as bankrupt as Dolan and Riley. But the lawyer held forth the prospect of monetary reward by Tunstall's father, and he seems occasionally to have provided food and ammunition. Thus the Regulators were not mere mercenaries. Although they hoped to be paid, they also felt genuine outrage over the slaying of Tunstall and the tyrannies of The House. With an odd mix of sincerity and cynicism, they portrayed themselves as an arm of the law contending with other arms of the law that had been corrupted.

Although *regulator* was another word for *vigilante*, McSween's men were not typical vigilantes. Like vigilantes, they saw themselves as a force organized to "regulate," or set right, an intolerable situation. Like vigilantes, also, they elected their officers and bound themselves by an oath. Unlike vigilantes, however, they had not formed in the absence or breakdown of the regular law enforcement and judicial machinery. The machinery had not broken down but rather had been captured by the other side. The McSween Regulators presented themselves as agents of the law—the justice of the peace court—and not as extralegal friends of the law. Although displaying some characteristics of typical vigilantes, the Lincoln County Regulators did not ride in the mainstream of the American vigilante tradition.[17]

The strength of the Regulators ranged in number from ten to about thirty, and in the big shootout in Lincoln in July it reached sixty. Sometimes Hispanics rode with the Regulators, but the core group consisted of about a dozen Anglos. Billy Bonney served faithfully and participated in every major operation and armed encounter. Other former Tunstall hands who signed up were John Middleton, Fred Waite, and Henry Brown. Billy's old friends Charley Bowdre and Frank and George Coe were members, as was Doc Scurlock. A particularly formidable warrior, recently on Chisum's payroll, was "Big Jim" French. Others of the faithful included John Scroggins, Steve Stanley, and Sam Smith.

Still another Regulator was Frank McNab, a "cattle detective" from the Texas Panhandle who now worked for Hunter, Evans & Co. John Chisum had sold all his herds to this firm but continued to manage them in behalf of the company. Thus McNab's interest focused on the rustlers who preyed on the former Chisum holdings. Since the rustlers were chiefly Seven Rivers stockmen, including Dolan's hands on the Pecos, the Regulators offered McNab a way of pursuing his mission. His ties to Chisum, of course, made him anathema to the Seven Rivers crowd.[18]

In time the dozen Anglos who formed the heart of the Regulator force forged close personal bonds and took on a powerful sense of mission. They subscribed to an oath they called the "iron clad." It bound each, if caught, not to bear witness against any of the others or to divulge any of their activities.[19]

Thus the factions that fought the Lincoln County War both claimed to be instruments of the law. On the one side stood the county sheriff, backed by the district judge and the district attorney. The sheriff's posse consisted chiefly of men who worked for Jimmy Dolan or had strong reasons for supporting him. On occasion the Dolanites were joined by Seven Rivers cowboys, who favored Dolan because John Chisum had lent his name to the Tunstall-McSween cause. On the other side stood the Regulators, led by a "special constable" appointed by the justice of the peace and carrying an arrest warrant issued by his court. Under color of law, both sides were about to engage in a great deal of unlawful activity.

The most wanted man named on the warrant in Dick Brewer's pocket was Billy Morton, head of the subposse that had cut down Tunstall and one of the three men who had fired the fatal shots. Twenty-two years old, the offspring of a prominent southern family, Morton boasted a quick mind and a good education. A sister remembered him as "wild and reckless, but brave, tender and generous." He had worked for Dolan for a year or more, and as foreman of the Seven Rivers cow camp his principal mission was to enlarge the Dolan herds by converting the long rail brand of John Chisum into the arrow brand of Jimmy Dolan.[20]

The first important operation of the Regulators was therefore to ride down to the Pecos and look for Billy Morton. On March 6 they spotted him in a group of five horsemen about six miles up the Peñasco from the Pecos. A stirring chase followed. The pursued split, but the Regulators kept after two men who turned out to be Morton and Frank Baker. As a Jesse Evans henchman, Baker's name also occupied a prominent place on the arrest warrant, although he had taken no part in the Tunstall slaying.

For five miles Brewer and his men raced in pursuit, firing some

56

one hundred shots in a vain attempt to bring down the quarry. At almost the same moment, the horses of Morton and Baker gave out from exhaustion, and the two men took cover in a prairie depression. A shouted parley ended in Brewer's promise to guarantee their safety, and they yielded their arms and surrendered. "There was one man in the party who wanted to kill me after I had surrendered," Morton wrote two days later, "and was restrained with the greatest difficulty by others of the party." This man was probably Billy Bonney.[21]

With their prisoners, the Regulators made their way up the Pecos to John Chisum's South Spring ranch. En route, they fell in with William McCloskey, Tunstall's former employee at the Feliz ranch and a friend of Morton's. Brewer distrusted McCloskey. He had been altogether too close to Mathews's possemen and in fact had even ridden with Morton's subposse. Only a tired horse had kept him from the scene of Tunstall's killing.

Morton feared that he would never see Lincoln. He had good reason for anxiety. Aside from the Regulators' appetite for vengeance, what to do with the captives posed a problem for Brewer and his men. Already, rumors reached them that Dolan was forming a rescue party, and even if they made their way safely to Lincoln, Sheriff Brady could hardly be trusted to ensure that the prisoners remained in custody until court convened, especially since he denied the validity of Justice Wilson's warrant. Brewer had betrayed his misgivings at the time of the surrender. "The constable himself said he was sorry we gave up," wrote Morton, "as he had not wished to take us alive."[22]

On March 8 the party stopped at John Chisum's South Spring ranch. Here Billy fell in with Will Chisum, John's fourteen-year-old nephew, who was tending the ranch's milk cows. Billy asked if Will had any fishhooks. Will said he did and got out his fishing gear. The two went to the banks of the South Spring River and, as Will remembered, "hauled them in."[23]

While the two boys hauled them in, Billy Morton penned a letter to a friend in Richmond, Virginia. He described his predicament, recounted his capture, speculated that he might be murdered en route to Lincoln, and asked that if his fears proved correct the circumstances be investigated.

The next morning, March 9, the Regulators rode over to Roswell and reined in at Captain Lea's store, which also housed the post office. Morton entrusted his letter to Postmaster Ash Upson. McCloskey, who shared Morton's fears, told Upson that he had decided to stick with his friend. Threats had been made to kill the prisoners, he said, but it would not be done as long as he lived.[24]

Upson provided a glimpse of Frank Baker at this time. "His countenance was the strongest argument that could be produced in favor of the Darwinian theory," he wrote to his niece a few days later. "Brutish in feature and expression, he looked a veritable gorilla."[25]

That evening a traveler arrived in Roswell with word that the Brewer party had left the main road and taken the little-used trail up Blackwater Creek and through the Capitan foothills. This tended to reinforce the foreboding Morton had expressed, although it could also have signified a tactic to avoid tangling with a Dolan rescue party.

At dusk the next evening, March 1, Frank McNab rode into Roswell with a report of what had happened. On the Blackwater, Morton had suddenly leaned over, grabbed McCloskey's pistol from its holster, and shot him dead. "Although mounted on a poor slow horse, he put him to his best speed closely followed by Frank Baker," said McNab. "They were speedily overtaken and killed." At the same time, in Lincoln, Brewer told the same story to McSween.[26]

McSween happened to be in Lincoln because he had decided to come out of hiding and face whatever Sheriff Brady might offer. He had arrived on the afternoon of March 9, however, to find his cause a shambles. Only hours earlier, New Mexico Governor Samuel B. Axtell had been in Lincoln to investigate the troubles. His visit attested to Dolan's continuing success at outmaneuvering his opponents. Dolan enjoyed cordial relations with most of Santa Fe's political and business establishment, most notably United States District Attorney Thomas B. Catron, the most powerful man in the

58

territory. Catron, in fact, held a mortgage on The House and all its property, which gave him a stake in the Lincoln County War. Axtell thus came predisposed to Dolan and remained deaf to all explanations by the other side.

The governor's three-hour stay in Lincoln shredded McSween's blueprint. In a formal proclamation, Axtell declared Squire Wilson to be occupying the office of justice of the peace illegally and named Judge Bristol and Sheriff Brady as the only instruments of the law in the county. With a few strokes of the pen, Axtell knocked the supports from McSween's strategy. Without the authority of the justice of the peace, McSween and the Regulators could not claim to be enforcing the law.[27]

In addition, as McSween had to explain to Dick Brewer the next day, if Wilson's tenure had been illegal all along, that meant that his arrest warrants and his appointment of a special constable were likewise illegal. If the Regulators had never had any authority to act as officers of the law, they opened themselves to charges of false arrest and, however the killings on the Blackwater happened, murder as well. Already, according to McSween, Dolan had taken steps to have the Regulators run down and arrested. The only solution seemed to be for the Regulators and McSween alike to take to the hills and hide until district court convened and untangled the legal snarl.[28]

When the killings of Morton, Baker, and McCloskey became known, the Dolan forces hurled the charge of murder back on their opponents. As with the slaying of Tunstall, the only witnesses were the killers themselves. No one could dispute the official version, but as Ash Upson observed, "This tale was too attenuated. Listeners did not believe it."[29] They did not think that Morton could have been so foolhardy as to attempt a break or that he would have killed the only friend he had in the group. That the bodies of both Morton and Baker each bore eleven bullet holes, one for each Regulator, looked suspiciously like deliberate assassination.

And such it probably was. Although no participant ever admitted to any but the official version, just as plausibly the Regulators could have agreed among themselves to do away with their captives. When McCloskey objected, one of the group simply blew him off his horse. The shot signaled Morton and Baker to attempt a desperate break, and they were indeed gunned down while attempting to escape. The exact truth can never be known, but the holes in the official story are big enough to entitle one to believe that Morton, Baker, and McCloskey were as surely murdered as was John Henry Tunstall.[30]

The Blackwater shootings gave Billy Bonney his second recorded experience with homicide. In his first, he alone had shot and killed Windy Cahill. In his second, he had shared the deed with others. Although Ash Upson credited Billy with the marksmanship that dropped both Morton and Baker, who fired the fatal rounds cannot be known. For a virtual certainty, however, at least one of Billy's bullets wound up in Morton and one in Baker.

For Billy Bonney, alias Kid Antrim, the three weeks following the death of Tunstall were packed with action and adventure and replete with new experiences. For the first time, he had a cause to which he could dedicate himself wholeheartedly—revenge for Tunstall. In the Regulators he had congenial comrades with whom to share adventures, hardships, and dangers; men he liked and respected and learned from; men who must have given him a richer sense of belonging and mission than did the shallow, shoddy, and evil thugs who made up the Jesse Evans gang. By their example and the task they had set for themselves, the Regulators lifted Billy Bonney from anonymity and provided the conditions and opportunity for his progress toward adulthood. In the confused maneuvers that marked the days after the slaying of Tunstall, Billy showed himself among the most willing, daring, and brave of the McSween followers. If not yet officer caliber, he had grown into a tough, energetic soldier with plenty of potential for leadership.

As George Coe remarked, "Billy the Kid wasn't known then as a warrior. We just knew him as a smart young lad and we named him Kid. But he grew bigger and bigger."[31]

The Assassin

Unlike most of the young bravos locked in combat for supremacy in Lincoln County, William Brady was a mature man of forty-eight. He had lived a full and useful life. Born in Ireland, he had emigrated at age twenty and, in common with many countrymen, adapted to his new nationality in the hard school of the regular army. During the 1850s he had put in two five-year enlistments in the Regiment of Mounted Riflemen, rising to the rank of sergeant and becoming an experienced Indian fighter on the frontiers of Texas and New Mexico. Discharged in 1861, on the eve of the Civil War, he had promptly won a commission in the New Mexico Volunteers. His wartime service, chiefly against Indians, revealed him to be a firm, seasoned, able combat leader, and he was mustered out in 1866 as a captain with a brevet of major.[1]

A tour of duty at Fort Stanton had introduced Brady to the Bonito country, and he returned to homestead a farm east of Lincoln, then called La Placita del Rio Bonito. Over the next decade he emerged as one of the valley's most respected citizens, a family man and a leader in building the fledgling community. He served variously as sheriff, U.S. commissioner, and first elected representative of Lincoln County in the territorial legislature. He also became a close friend and associate of Lawrence G. Murphy's; they were both Irish immigrants, both former sergeants in the regular army, both wartime officers in the volunteers, and both prominent citizens of Lincoln County. To cement the connection, for years Brady was heavily in debt to Murphy. Understandably, the relationship with Murphy predisposed Brady to favor Dolan in the troubles that broke out early in 1878.

As county sheriff, Brady dispensed a brand of law enforcement typical of first-generation frontier communities all over the West. Personal, pragmatic, capricious, physical, and final, it expressed the fine points of the law less than the instincts of the man behind the badge. Because of vast distances and nonexistent transportation, it prevailed mainly in the county seat and the immediate vicinity, and only there when Brady came to town from his farm three miles down the valley. Ash Upson sized up the sheriff of Lincoln County with acute insight:

Major Brady was an excellent citizen and a brave and honest man. He was a good officer too, and endeavored to do his duty with impartiality. The objections made against Sheriff Brady were that he was strongly prejudiced in favor of the Murphy-Dolan faction—those gentlemen being his warm friends—and that he was lax in the discharge of his duty through fear of giving offense to one party or the other.[2]

Except for pressing the attachment process to absurd extremes, Brady had in truth pursued McSween with a laxity that probably irritated Dolan. Occasionally Brady even let slip a word of sympathy for the beleaguered attorney. His pocket contained a writ of attachment signed by Judge Bristol, yet he did nothing to recapture the Tunstall store after being evicted by the Martínez posse on February 20. His pocket also contained an arrest warrant signed by Judge Bristol, yet he showed little disposition to track down McSween and throw him in the cellar jail. Brady's seeming lethargy probably signified an inclination simply to procrastinate until district court met and settled the issues one way or another.

To McSween, however, Brady was almost as villainous as Dolan. His handling of the attachment had enraged the lawyer, and the very existence of the arrest warrant in the sheriff's possession kept McSween on the run. If he had to spend any time in the Lincoln jail awaiting the opening of court, he was certain that Brady would look the other way while Dolan brought in Jesse Evans to "do his part."

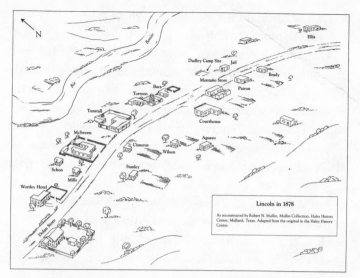

Lincoln, New Mexico, in 1878

Some of McSween's followers, moreover, had special reasons for hating Brady. He had physically mistreated George Coe and Charley Bowdre, and he had "cursed and abused" Bonney and Waite, held them prisoner for thirty hours, and then turned them loose without giving back their arms.

Throughout the last three weeks of March, the Regulators lay low. Most of them probably remained quietly in their homes. Bonney and Waite seem to have passed the time in the congenial surroundings of San Patricio. Late in March, however, Billy, Fred, and the rest of the faithful gathered for a meeting with McSween. His wife, Sue, had returned from the East, and the two had been living at John Chisum's South Spring ranch.

From that meeting sprang a plot to rid the county of William Brady. Whether McSween stated that he wanted Brady out of the way, implied it, or unintentionally left that impression with his listeners is not known. At least one heard him offer a reward to anyone who killed the sheriff. In any event, as they rode up the trail to Lincoln the Regulators laid plans for assassinating Brady. On the Blackwater the party split, the Anglos sending the Hispanics off to

San Patricio because their sensibilities might be injured by the slaying of a man who had a Hispanic wife.[3]

That McSween could have urged such a foolish act seems preposterous. It would undermine his contention to be acting in behalf of the law, and almost certainly it would offend the substantial body of public opinion that had so far supported him. Moreover, Brady himself visited the Chisum ranch on March 28, about the same time as the Regulators, and let it be known that he felt confident of McSween's appearance at court and would not try to find and arrest him.[4]

But McSween had no confidence in Brady's assurances. Court convened on April 1, and McSween feared that before he could even reach the courthouse Brady would arrest him if given the chance. In Brady's jail, McSween felt certain, the arrest warrant would turn out to be a death warrant.[5]

McSween's state of mind may well have produced such fevered imaginings. The civil suit, the criminal charge, the murder of Tunstall, the crisis in his finances, and his plight as a fugitive from the law had left him demoralized and distraught, possibly muddying his thinking and impairing his judgment. Sue McSween, a tough and determined woman, may also have urged forceful measures.

During the night of March 31, the assassins prepared their ambush. Six Regulators posted themselves in the corral behind the Tunstall store. An adobe wall with a gate for wagons projected eastward from the rear of the building, hiding the corral from the street. The executioners were Billy Bonney, Frank McNab, John Middleton, Fred Waite, Jim French, and Henry Brown. Rob Widenmann would come out the back door shortly before the fatal moment—to feed Tunstall's dog, as he later explained. Most people believed that he was part of the group too, and anti-McSween newspapers later contemptuously labeled him "the dog-feeder."

About nine o'clock on the morning of April 1, Sheriff Brady walked down the street from the Dolan store, accompanied by deputies Billy Mathews, George Hindman, George Peppin, and John Long. Mathews, of course, had headed the attachment posse, and Hindman had ridden with Morton's subposse. Peppin was one of the men who had occupied the Tunstall store in February. Reverend Ealy and his family, living temporarily in the McSween house, watched the party make its way down the street. Brady paused to talk briefly with a woman, then hurried to catch up with his companions.[6]

The sheriff and his aides were going to the courthouse to post notice that a clerical error had fixed the wrong day for the convening of district court. The appointed day was not April 1, as had been announced, but April 8. After accomplishing this purpose, Brady and the deputies turned back up the street to the west and headed for the Dolan store.[7]

When the lawmen drew opposite the Tunstall corral, the concealed gunmen rose from behind the wall, leveled their Winchesters, and opened a rapid fire. A storm of bullets swept the street, striking down Brady and, behind him, George Hindman. At least a dozen bullets ripped through the sheriff. One struck Hindman, who fell wounded and crying for water. As Mathews, Peppin, and Long raced for the cover of a house across the street, Ike Stockton emerged from his saloon, pulled Hindman to his feet, and started to help him to safety. Another bullet finished the deputy. Still farther across the street, Justice of the Peace Wilson lay hurt and bewildered in his garden. While hoeing onions, he had caught a wild round through the fleshy part of both buttocks.

After a few moments of silence, Billy Bonney and Jim French leaped the corral wall and sprinted into the street. Backed by French, Bonney stooped over Brady and picked up his Winchester rifle. At this moment Billy Mathews, watching from the window of the Cisneros house beyond, took aim and fired. The bullet punched through Billy's thigh and zipped through French's thigh as well. The Kid dropped the rifle, and the two hobbled back to the protection of the corral.

This reckless deed has usually been seen as no more than an attempt to steal Brady's rifle. That may indeed have been part of the purpose, for Billy would have wanted to retrieve the rifle Brady had taken from him on February 20 or at least get a replacement. More likely, considering McSween's preoccupation with the arrest warrant and attachment writ, the daring dash was aimed mainly at recovering these documents. Frank Coe later declared that the Kid "ran to get the papers from Brady." If so, Mathews's bullet intervened, and the papers remained in the sheriff's pocket.[8]

Although the firing alerted the entire town, an eerie solitude fell over the scene. Citizens cowered in their homes while the assassins and the deputies remained warily behind cover. Carlota Baca, the young daughter of Saturnino Baca, had been playing with dolls on the top floor of the *torreon*. She looked into the street below, then hurried next door to tell her mother.

"Oh God, run and see, it may be papa," screamed Juanita Baca.

Carlota darted into the street and bent over Sheriff Brady, probably the first to venture into the open after the shooting.[9]

Billy's wound did not immobilize him, but Jim French's was serious enough to require medical attention. Reverend Ealy was not only a preacher but also a doctor—a "medical missionary," as he styled himself. French therefore slipped out of the back of the corral and made his way next door to the McSween house, where the Ealys admitted him.

"He came walking into our back door," Ealy remembered. "The ball passed through his left thigh. I drew a silk handkerchief through the wound, bound it up and he was taken charge of by Sam Corbet [Tunstall's former clerk]."[10]

The Regulators seemed in no hurry to leave town, and Brady's deputies showed little interest in provoking a gun battle. Finally the murderers rode leisurely off to the hills while the deputies loosed a long-range fire at them. Almost nonchalantly, John Middleton dismounted, seated himself on the ground, took deliberate aim with his elbow resting on his knee, and returned the fire.[11]

With the departure of the Regulators, the deputies grew bolder. George Peppin took charge and, hardly knowing what to expect, sent an appeal for help to Captain Purington, who showed up in the afternoon with a cavalry detachment.

Meantime, Peppin and his men followed a trail of blood to McSween's back door. Three times they searched the house without finding Jim French. As Reverend Ealy later explained, "I learned that Sam Corbet had sawed a hole through the floor under a bed and as there was not any cellar under the house laid him on a blanket on his back with 2 revolvers in his hands."[12] That night, after the excitement died down, French slipped out of town, possibly with Billy's help.

Lincoln boiled with shock and excitement. Adding to the turmoil, shortly after the shooting, Mac and Sue McSween arrived, as expected, with John Chisum in his carriage. Learning that he was a week early for court, McSween went to the home of Isaac Ellis, at his store on the eastern edge of town. There, backed by a squad of soldiers, Peppin produced the arrest warrant that Brady had carried. More fearful than ever of falling into the toils of county lawmen, McSween answered that Brady's death deprived Peppin of his authority as a deputy. Finally, however, McSween agreed to place himself in military rather than county custody, and the officer with Peppin, Lieutenant George W. Smith, assented. Later, Captain Purington proved less anxious to interfere with Peppin, but at length, possibly perceiving that McSween would not survive for a week in the Lincoln jail, he agreed to hold McSween at Fort Stanton until court convened.[13]

Whatever had led to the Brady assassination—McSween's wishes, a Regulator plot, simply an opportunity of the moment—the deed could hardly have been more damaging to McSween's interests. The code sanctioned killing for cause, but here there seemed insufficient cause. To gun down a generally respected lawman from ambush disgusted people inclined to tolerate almost any measure of violence or homicide that could be rationalized. Heretofore, public opinion had largely favored McSween. Now, it held both sides to be equally evil, lawless, and murderous.

In the Brady slaying, Billy Bonney again demonstrated the daring and aggressiveness that had marked his part in the exploits of the Martínez posse on February 20. Tradition credits Billy with taking the lead in firing on Brady, whereas McNab is generally thought to have put the first bullet into Hindman, against whom he supposedly bore a grudge. The second and fatal shot to Hindman almost certainly was fired by Fred Waite.[14] Though unprovable, the tradition, so far as it touches Billy, is consistent with his rash bolt into the street to Brady's body. Despite an occasional flamboyant feat of this kind, however, he remained essentially one of a group of rugged, heedless warriors—by now a peer but hardly a chieftain.

Following on the execution of Morton, Baker, and McCloskey, the slaying of Brady revealed another truth about Billy and his friends: they were willing to take human life in circumstances that violated even the lax ethical code of the time and place. Even more than the killing of Morton, Baker, and McCloskey, even more indeed than the slaying of Tunstall, Brady's death was cold-blooded murder.

Yet the assassins looked on themselves as soldiers in a righteous war and on the slaying as justified by the code of war rather than the code of the frontier. Years later Eugene Manlove Rhodes, a gifted writer who traced his origins to the New Mexico frontier, perceived the distinction. "It has at last penetrated my thick old head that the Lincoln County War was WAR," he wrote. "Ghastly but no worse than any war." Billy the Kid and his friends had gunned down Brady and Hindman from ambush. "In war this would have been brilliant strategy, generalship, fame-building." All war, he noted, was murder. "Chisum and Murphy men were doing exactly what the Allies and the Germans did; what the damyanks and johnnyrebs did—nothing more or less."[15]

Although overstated, the parallel captures the state of mind with which Billy and his comrades approached both the ambush of Brady and their further campaigns against the enemy.

The Shootout

Like most of his neighbors on the Ruidoso, Andrew L. Roberts had a murky past. It may have included a stint as a hunter for Buffalo Bill Cody, and it may have involved a shootout with the Texas Rangers. He rarely talked of his past and minded his own business, but the load of buckshot he carried in his right shoulder suggested that he could be a scrapper if pressed. The wound prevented him from raising his arm above the waist, which forced him to do his firing, rifle and pistol, from the hip. He was short and stocky and preferred a mule to a horse. He ran a few cows on the upper Ruidoso, where he had made friends with Frank Coe, and also worked occasionally for Jimmy Dolan at his branch store at South Fork, near Blazer's Mills.

As Dolan employees, Buckshot Roberts and George Hindman had been tapped by Billy Mathews for posse service when Mathews arrived at the South Fork store on February 12, 1878. They rode with him to the Tunstall ranch on the next day and again on February 18. Roberts had been at the ranch with Mathews and others when Morton's subposse cut down Tunstall, but his name had wound up on the arrest warrant issued by Justice Wilson. That Governor Axtell had in effect invalidated that much-worn document, as well as Dick Brewer's commission as special constable, had not discouraged the Regulators from their self-appointed mission.

Roberts wanted no part of the troubles that had engulfed Lincoln County and had singled him out as a target for the other side. He sold his ranch to someone in Santa Fe and awaited only the arrival of the payment before clearing out of the county altogether. That the check might be in the mail carrier's pouch brought him over the mountain to South Fork on the morning of April 4.[1]

Cradled by forested slopes rising on both sides of a narrow valley, Blazer's Mills spread along the north bank of the upper Tularosa River, here a mountain stream about ten feet wide. Over the span of a decade, Dr. Joseph H. Blazer, a former dentist, had emerged as the leading citizen of the little frontier community. The surrounding Indian reservation had come later, and whether Blazer's property belonged to him or the U.S. government remained an unresolved issue. Despite the standoff, Blazer got along reasonably well with the Indian agent, Frederick C. Godfroy. Indeed, Blazer had leased his big house to the government for use as the agent's residence.

This house, a two-story adobe fortress surmounted by a cupola, faced the river about two hundred yards upstream from the sawmill and gristmill. Agent Godfroy and his family occupied the house and occasionally took in lodgers. Mrs. Godfroy cooked meals for travelers. Blazer, who lived with his family in another dwelling immediately to the east, maintained an office in one room on the northwest corner of the big house. A shed tacked to the rear housed the Blazer store.

Mounted on his mule and trailing a packhorse, Buckshot Roberts showed up at the big house on the morning of April 4. He hoped to receive his money from the mail carrier due that day, he explained to Dr. Blazer, then continue to Las Cruces. He had best move on, Blazer said. An Indian had just reported a band of men on the road to the west. They had killed a steer from the agency beef herd the night before, said the Indian, and were headed east. Suspecting these men to be Regulators and wanting no gunplay on his property, Blazer urged Roberts to leave.

Why the Regulators had come west of the divide, beyond the theater of war, remains unclear. They themselves dropped some vague explanations about men they wanted to arrest being reported on the Tularosa. Lawrence Murphy furnished another explanation when he alerted the military at Fort Stanton that the Regulators had ridden west to ambush the judicial party traveling from Mesilla to hold court in Lincoln. A massacre of the judge, the district attorney, the clerk of the court, and other officials would have been as reckless as the murder of Sheriff Brady, but the tip was taken seriously enough to prompt dispatch of a cavalry escort to meet the supposed victims.[2]

Whatever the Regulators' mission, there they were on the Tularosa only two days after the murder of Sheriff Brady. Dick Brewer had fourteen men, including the Coes, Middleton, McNab, Scurlock, Brown, Waite, and Bowdre. Even Billy Bonney and Jim French, surely sitting their saddles in pain as a result of the bullet Billy Mathews had drilled through their thighs, rode with their fellow subscribers to the "iron clad."[3] They reined in at Blazer's Mills late on the morning of April 4, herded their mounts into a corral surrounded by a high board fence across the river from the big house, and asked Mrs. Godfroy to fix them dinner.

Roberts, meantime, had heeded Dr. Blazer's appeal and headed west, following a mountain trail rather than the main road to avoid the Regulators. He saw them riding back up the road but later also spotted the mail buckboard laboring up the grade toward Blazer's Mills. Turning back in hopes of getting his check, he scouted the little settlement from a distance. He saw no sign of the Regulators, whose horses were hidden behind Blazer's corral fence, and assumed that they had ridden on to the east. Tying his packhorse to a tree, he prodded his mule across the valley to pick up his mail.

John Middleton lounged on guard outside while the Regulators ate inside. Seeing Roberts approach, he went in and reported a "mighty well-armed man" riding up on a mule and said he had heard the man give his name as Roberts. Brewer said, "I have a warrant for Roberts." Frank Coe, who knew Roberts, went outside alone to talk with him.[4]

Too late Roberts discovered his blunder. He had tied his mule at the southwest corner of the house and, respecting a rule of Dr. Blazer's, draped his pistol belt over the saddle horn. Winchester carbine in hand, he was making his way toward the front door when Frank Coe emerged. The two shook hands, then walked around the corner of the house to the west to have a talk. Impatiently, Brewer and his comrades waited to see if Frank could persuade Roberts to surrender.

Frank found Buckshot as stubborn as reputed. Sitting on an uncovered plank porch in front of the door to Dr. Blazer's office, Coe tried to talk his friend into giving up.

"No," answered Roberts, "never alive. The Kid is with you and he will kill me on sight."[5]

"No," said Coe, "give me your gun and we'll walk around to the crowd. I'll stand by you."

"We talked for half an hour," remembered Coe. "I begged him to surrender, but the answer was no, no, no. I think he was the bravest man I ever met—not a bit excited, knowing too that his life was in his hands."

Brewer could contain his impatience no longer. He sent a handful of his men storming around the house to end the stalemate. Backed by Middleton and George Coe, Charley Bowdre appeared immediately in front of the pair.

"Roberts, throw up your hands," he yelled.

"No," replied Buckshot, as he rose to his feet and brought his carbine up to his hip.

Both fired at the same time. Roberts's bullet smashed Bowdre's buckle and dropped his pistol belt to the ground, then ricocheted into George Coe's right hand, mangling his thumb and trigger finger. Bowdre's bullet punched through Roberts's stomach just above the hips. "The dust flew from his clothes from both sides," noted Frank Coe, who had leapt to get out of the line of fire.

Brewer's other men dashed into the fray as Roberts, grievously wounded, backed into the doorway of Dr. Blazer's office while pumping his carbine from the hip. "I never saw a man that could handle a Winchester as fast as he could," marveled Frank Coe later. A bullet thudded into John Middleton's chest and lodged in a lung. Another hit the barrel of Doc Scurlock's holstered pistol and coursed down his leg, "burning him like a hot iron."[6] Still another almost got Billy Bonney. "The Kid slipped in between the wall and a wagon," recalled Frank Coe. "Roberts took a shot at him, just shaved his arm. Kid backed out as it was too hot there for him."[7]

Billy had seen Roberts's cartridge belt and pistol on his saddle and knew how many rounds the magazine of his carbine held. When Roberts had emptied his weapon, therefore, the Kid dashed to the porch and, thrusting his Winchester at Roberts, pulled the trigger. At the same instant Roberts shoved the muzzle of his empty carbine into the Kid's midriff, knocking him breathless and deflecting his aim. The bullet smashed the doorjamb. Quickly, once again, the Kid backed out.[8]

Roberts did not remain weaponless for long. Although in searing pain from his stomach wound, he stumbled into the room behind him. On a wall mounting he spotted Dr. Blazer's single-shot Springfield rifle and found a box of cartridges that fit it. Dragging a mattress from a bed, he barricaded the door, lay down with the rifle, and made ready to continue the fight.

Brewer was furious over the intransigence of Roberts and the casualties incurred in trying to arrest him. "He ordered me to go into the room to put the man out," recalled David Easton, "which I refused to do. I begged Brewer to take his men and go off. Brewer replied that he would have that man out if he had to pull the house down." Brewer next turned on Dr. Blazer and Agent Godfroy, who had come in for dinner, and commanded them to get Roberts out of the house. When they also balked, Brewer threatened to burn it down. Finally, he set off to try to get Roberts himself.[9]

Crossing the river on a footbridge, Brewer circled around the corral and made his way down the valley toward the mills. About 125 yards west of the big house, he came across a pile of logs, assembled for Blazer's sawmill. Crawling in behind the logs, he discovered that his rifle covered the entire west side of the big house, including the open door to Blazer's office. Taking careful aim on the door, Dick fired.

Inside Blazer's office, Brewer's bullet slammed into the wall behind Roberts, blowing particles of adobe onto the floor. Glancing down the valley, Roberts saw smoke from Brewer's rifle drifting away from the logs. Propping Blazer's rifle on the mattress, he sighted on the log where the smoke had been and waited. Soon the top of Brewer's head appeared. Buckshot squeezed the trigger. The big Springfield blasted. The bullet hit Brewer in the left eye, leaving a tiny blue mark, then blew the back of his skull into fragments.

"After that no one tried to get Roberts," observed Frank Coe. They knew he would die, and three of their own were hurting badly. Middleton had taken a severe chest wound that all thought would prove fatal. Dr. Blazer did what he could for the wounded, and Agent Godfroy provided a government wagon to transport them over the mountain.

En route the Regulators met Dr. Daniel Appel, Fort Stanton's military surgeon, who had already been summoned by a courier from Blazer's Mills. He gave some first aid, then hurried on to minister to Roberts.

The bullet in Middleton's lung did in fact prove fatal, but not for another seven or eight years. Almost miraculously, he continued to fight with the Regulators. As for George Coe, the Reverend Doctor Ealy recalled that "I took off a thumb and finger for him after that fight."[10]

Back at Blazer's Mills, no one dared approach Roberts's little fortress. He would not believe that his assailants had left. Finally Dolan storekeeper John Ryan made his way warily up the slope from the west with a white flag. A little old man and a friend of Roberts's, he managed to get close enough to be recognized. Dr. Blazer tended Roberts until Dr. Appel arrived that night, but the wound was plainly fatal.

Buckshot Roberts died the next day. A carpenter nailed together two coffins, covered them with black muslin and lined them with white, and the two dead men were given a Christian burial on the hillside behind Dr. Blazer's big house.

On the heels of the Brady murder, Blazer's Mills cost the McSween faction still more public sympathy. Even the death of the popular Brewer—"one of nature's noblemen," McSween called him—did not offset the feeling that Buckshot Roberts had fallen before an overwhelming and somehow unfair onslaught. His courageous defense, moreover, earned the admiration of people who set high store on skilled gunfighting. And the reports, however untrue, that the Regulators had plotted to kill Judge Bristol and his fellow travelers angered people who saw the courts as the only hope of ending the warfare in Lincoln County.

Once again, Billy Bonney had cemented his bonds to his comrades of the "iron clad" and had demonstrated his dedication to the Regulator mission. By rushing Roberts in the doorway of Blazer's office, he had also once again shown the brand of reckless bravery that had sent him into the street, under fire, after the killing of Brady. Neither their purpose nor their performance at Blazer's Mills gave the Regulators much to brag about. But for Billy it was one more exciting experience in the education of a gunfighter.

The Warrior

CHAPTER 8

Jimmy Dolan and his friends had good reason to expect the district court to revive their flagging fortunes. Judge Warren Bristol, a timid man easily frightened by guns and gunmen, had for years tended to sustain Murphy and then Dolan in their legal undertakings. The judge usually affected an air of impartiality, but not so the prosecuting attorney for the district, William L. Rynerson. A great hairy giant with a turbulent past in New Mexico politics, he unblushingly sided with Dolan against McSween.

The partiality of Bristol and Rynerson, however, failed to make the spring 1878 term of district court turn out well for Dolan. The grand jury, although demoralized by conditions in Lincoln County and intimidated by gunmen of both sides, found the courage to back McSween personally. Despite a long lecture from Judge Bristol in which he abandoned judicial detachment altogether and virtually commanded the jurors to indict the lawyer for embezzlement, they steadfastly refused. "We fully exonerate him of the charge," they insisted, "and, regret that a spirit of persecution has been shown in this matter."[1]

The grand jury dealt less resolutely with the violence that had racked the county since February. The jury heard many witnesses, few of whom could have offered any but hearsay evidence, and ended by returning indictments that fell indiscriminately on guilty and innocent while omitting men everyone knew to be guilty.

The indictments showered on both factions. In the Tunstall kill-

76

ing, both Billy Morton and Tom Hill had gone to their reward, but murder indictments named Jesse Evans and also three of his gang who were not even at the scene. At the same time, indictments as accessories to the murder accused Dolan himself, together with Billy Mathews.

For the murder of Sheriff Brady, the Kid was indicted along with John Middleton and Henry Brown, and for Hindman's death Fred Waite was indicted, but the others in the Tunstall corral that morning drew no mention. Alone among the Regulators at Blazer's Mills, Charley Bowdre stood charged with murdering Buckshot Roberts. The killing of Morton, Baker, and McCloskey eluded the official notice of the grand jury altogether.

Other setbacks afflicted Dolan. For one, Jesse Evans was no longer available "to do his part." On March 9, the very day of the demise of Morton, Baker, and McCloskey, Evans and Tom Hill had tried to rob the camp of a sheep drover near Tularosa, west of the mountains. In an exchange of gunfire with a camp attendant, Hill had been killed and Evans so badly wounded in the wrist that he had gone to Fort Stanton for medical treatment. Here, Rob Widenmann at last succeeded in serving the federal warrant he had carried for months, and Evans once more found himself behind bars, this time those of the more secure lockup at the fort.[2]

Far worse for Dolan, he and Riley finally plunged into bankruptcy. Tom Catron foreclosed on the mortgage he had held since January. He sent his young brother-in-law, Edgar Walz, to take charge of the Dolan firm's assets. The big store in Lincoln closed its doors.[3]

If all this were not enough, Dolan hobbled around on crutches with a leg in splints. On March 11, in Lincoln, he had dismounted before his horse came to a halt, and he wound up with a broken leg.[4]

Dolan sustained still another reverse of fortune in the appointment of a new sheriff. To replace Brady, the county commissioners named John Copeland, post butcher at Fort Stanton. A hulking man of thirty-seven, he moved and thought slowly, and he could be influenced by almost anyone of stronger will. One such was McSween, and Sheriff Copeland quickly fell under his domination.

Particularly galling to the Dolanites, Copeland carried arrest warrants for the Kid, Middleton, Brown, Waite, and Bowdre, the Regulators indicted by the grand jury, yet he failed to serve them.

The Regulators made their headquarters at the McSween house, now reoccupied, following the dismissal of the embezzlement charge, by Mac and Sue. The gunmen elected Frank McNab their new captain, replacing the dead Brewer. With Squire Wilson still sidelined pending another election, McNab obtained a commission as deputy constable from Gregorio Trujillo, justice of the peace at San Patricio. Despite this new cloak of legality, the Regulators launched no new operations. Elated over the advent of a friendly sheriff, they spent their days carousing. Copeland shared freely in the festivities with the very men for whom he carried arrest warrants.[5]

A pastime that especially appealed to Billy Bonney was singing. Mary Ealy played Sue's piano (she boasted both piano and organ) as the men gathered around to sing. "And how they did sing," Mary remembered. "They stood behind me with their guns and belts full of cartridges; I suppose I was off tune as often as on it as I felt very nervous, though they were very nice and polite."[6]

While the Regulators partied, the Dolanites plotted a comeback. The new sheriff needed some help, they decided, in understanding his responsibilities, especially in recognizing his obligation to arrest the killers of Brady, Hindman, and Roberts. Billy Mathews and George Peppin, still claiming to be deputies by appointment of Brady, gathered a few men and rode down to the Pecos to organize a posse. They signed up about twenty Seven Rivers cowboys, most of them veterans of the posse that had attached Tunstall's cattle in February, and headed for Lincoln.[7]

On the afternoon of April 29 the posse paused for a rest at the Fritz ranch nine miles below Lincoln. Here they learned of the approach of three of the enemy. Regulator chief Frank McNab, Frank Coe, and Ab Saunders, Coe's in-law and hired hand, were on their way to the Coe ranch. At the Fritz ranch the three men rode squarely into an ambush. A volley of gunfire dropped their horses.

78

Saunders took a slug in the hip that would ultimately prove fatal. McNab ran up a gully pursued by Manuel Segovia ("Indian") and was shot and killed. Coe sprinted up another gully but surrendered when he saw that he was trapped.[8]

During the night the possemen took positions in the timber on the east edge of Lincoln, opposite the Ellis store. A few, with Coe as prisoner, moved up the river on the north side, crossed, and slipped into the Dolan store. Although closed in bankruptcy, it was in charge of Catron's agent, Edgar Walz.

The Regulators learned of their peril the next morning, April 30, when a messenger brought word to Sheriff Copeland in the McSween house that a force of deputies had come to help him arrest the Kid, Middleton, Bowdre, Waite, and Brown. Quickly, the Regulators fanned out through town and took up firing positions. George Coe, on the roof of the Ellis store, spotted one of the enemy sitting on a cow skull several hundred yards distant, hunched over and unrecognized even as a man.

"I'll lift whatever it is out of there with this old Sharp's rifle," said Coe to Henry Brown. He took careful aim and fired.

As Coe remembered, "My bullet cut through the flesh of both the man's legs—they were crossed in front of him—and cut a gash nearly six inches long through his hip, about 440 steps away." The victim was "Dutch Charley" Kruling, the only casualty of the Battle of Lincoln.[9]

Firing erupted from both sides. The men in the Dolan store rushed into the street and ran toward the Ellis store, leaving Frank Coe to walk away a free man. At once they encountered a hot fire from rooftops and behind adobe walls. Pulling back, they turned north, crossed the Bonito, and made their way downstream to unite with their confederates. For four hours the two sides exchanged fire without hurting anyone.

Meantime, a confused Copeland had sent to Fort Stanton for military aid. About 3:30 in the afternoon Lieutenant George W. Smith arrived with twenty black cavalrymen. Gesturing wildly with his pistol, Copeland led them to the lower end of town. Smith rode between the battle lines and waved his uniform cap. Several of the enemy came forward for a parley. Which men did he want arrested? the lieutenant asked the sheriff.

"I want the whole damn business," replied Copeland.

Fearing assassination, none of the attackers would surrender to Copeland, but at length agreed to give up to the army. Smith sent them around town on the north side of the river to avoid more shooting, then conducted them to Fort Stanton.

Billy Bonney did not stand out among the defenders of Lincoln. Presumably he simply fired at the Dolan men from a rooftop. With Bowdre, Middleton, and others, he then left Lincoln. They tarried in and around San Patricio while McSween and Dolan indulged in legal sparring that made almost everyone look like buffoons.

Caught in the middle was a new presence at Fort Stanton. On April 4, the day of the shootout at Blazer's Mills, Lieutenant Colonel Nathan A. M. Dudley had assumed command of the fort. A handsome, soldierly figure, he was also vain, pompous, quarrelsome, and bibulous. His stormy temperament did not equip him for the subtle role his superiors expected him to play in the troubles besetting Lincoln County. Military involvement in civil affairs, although common, rested on shaky legal foundations, and army meddling in southern elections and eastern railroad strikes had given the issue political sensitivity as well.

Reflecting Captain Purington's prejudices, Colonel Dudley quickly formed a dislike for McSween and his allies. When Sheriff Copeland called for help on April 30, however, the colonel dutifully dispatched Lieutenant Smith to the rescue. As a result, Dudley wound up with a small army of Dolanites whom the sheriff wanted detained. McSween moved swiftly to produce the legal grounds for the request, for Copeland soon appeared with a warrant, issued by the compliant justice of the peace at San Patricio, for the arrest of eighteen of the Mathews-Peppin posse for the murder of Frank McNab.

Dudley thought Copeland less than impartial and told him so. To give force to this sentiment, he had three of the Dolan men swear affidavits against McSween and the Regulators for "riot" and sent a messenger across the mountain to obtain a warrant for their arrest from the justice of the peace at Blazer's Mills. Presenting it to Copeland, together with a cavalry detachment, Dudley delivered a stern lecture and sent the baffled sheriff forth to do his duty.

This warrant, of course, contained Billy Bonney's name besides about twenty others, including McSween's. With Bowdre and Middleton, the Kid almost got caught in the net. On the evening of May 2, McSween bought them dinner at Dow's store in San Patricio. Afterwards, they headed back for the mountains just as the military posse rode into town. Sheriff Copeland shrank from serving his warrant on McSween, but the escort commander, Lieutenant Goodwin, insisted. Once again McSween found himself in the toils of the law.

But not for long. On May 4, worried about the legal requirement for a speedy examination of prisoners, Copeland asked Dudley to release them to his custody. Dudley complied. With thirty men on his hands, most of them unruly, Copeland did not know what to do next. Bewildered, he simply turned them loose with the injunction to go home and quit feuding. "Both parties seem to have had a scare," Dudley commented dryly.[10]

The Regulators now elected their third captain, Doc Scurlock, who promptly planned an operation to the Seven Rivers country. Most of the Dolanites released at Fort Stanton on May 4 had gone down to the Pecos to help Johnny Riley meet a beef contract by bringing a herd up to the Indian agency. Their names were on the warrant issued by Justice Wilson in February, and in addition Scurlock presumably carried the warrant for Mathews stemming from the grand jury's accessory indictment in April. With a deputy's commission from Copeland, Scurlock rode with a more substantial cloak of legality than had shielded any previous Regulator campaign.

Besides the usual "iron clads," including Billy Bonney, Scurlock also led a contingent of Hispanics that augmented his force to more than twenty gunmen. The Hispanics followed their own deputy, Josefita Chavez. An unkind critic thought this a shrewd gambit of McSween's, a "master stroke to draw the Mexican population of this county into the fight." Copeland, he charged, was "ordered to take Mexicans on his next posse, get a few of them killed and thus rouse the whole county against Dolan & Co."[11]

On May 15 the Regulator force stormed into the Dolan cow camp near Seven Rivers. They seized twenty-five horses and two mules and did all they could to scatter the cattle in every direction. They also seized the camp cook, who turned out to be Manuel Segovia ("Indian"). He had been with the Mathews posse in February, as well as the bunch that bushwhacked Coe, Saunders, and McNab. He was believed, probably correctly, to be the man who had killed McNab.

Mindful of the fate of Morton, Baker, and McCloskey, "Indian" felt himself certain to be executed.

"Don't let them kill me," he implored of Francisco Trujillo.

While riding up the river, Trujillo overheard Scurlock, Chavez, and Bonney talking about killing the prisoner. Trujillo observed to Chavez that the law ought to be allowed to run its course.

Charley Bowdre rode up and said, "Come on, Francisco, let us be running along." The two spurred ahead.

"When Charley and I had gone about fifty yards we noticed that the Indian had gotten away from his captors and was riding away as fast as he could. Billy the Kid and Jose[fita] Chavez took after him and began to shoot at him until they got him." Thus another Regulator captive had fallen while trying to escape.[12]

All this activity, surprisingly, took place within a mile of Johnny Riley, Billy Mathews, and the Seven Rivers bravos. Rather than risk an open battle, they hung back and did not even challenge the aggressors. Riley contented himself with complaining to Colonel Dudley and hinting that if a military escort were not sent to his aid the Indians might not get fed. Dudley knew that beef could be obtained locally, however, and thought Riley had enough well-armed men to take care of himself. Thus the Regulators returned unmolested to Lincoln.[13]

The raid on the Dolan cow camp turned out to be a heavy-handed blunder, less damaging to Dolan's interests than to those of

Thomas B. Catron. All of Dolan's property now belonged to that unforgiving potentate, and when he learned two weeks later that his cattle had been scattered across the Pecos Plains, he erupted in fury. He complained to Governor Axtell, who complained to Colonel Edward Hatch, commander of the District of New Mexico. Hatch ordered troops to the Pecos, but had to cancel the order when his superiors decreed that he had overstepped his authority. Even so, the Regulators' grubby little victory and the execution of "Indian" scarcely balanced the enmity of the territory's most powerful politician.[14]

The cow-camp operation marked the beginning of more than a month's lull in hostilities. For one thing, Jimmy Dolan had left Lincoln to help Lawrence Murphy, fearful of assassination by the Regulators, settle in a new home in Santa Fe, where he died from the effects of alcoholism five months later. For another, a federal investigation was under way, and the two factions tried to stay on good behavior. Distressed over the murder of one of Her Majesty's subjects, the British foreign office had stirred up Washington officialdom, and Frank Warner Angel had come west to look into the matter on behalf of both the Justice and Interior departments.

Although his sentiments ran to the McSween side, Angel dutifully gathered depositions from almost everyone involved in the outbreak of the war. Even young Bonney told his story under oath certified by Squire Wilson, once more justice of the peace. This took place on June 8 in Lincoln, where the Regulators had again taken up residence at the McSween house. Centering on the events of February 11–18 that culminated in the murder of Tunstall, Billy's deposition, in Rob Widenmann's handwriting, bore a suspicious resemblance to Rob's own deposition. How much of it represented Rob's prompting may be wondered.[15]

Meanwhile, Jimmy Dolan had not been idle in Santa Fe. He wrote complaining letters to the *New Mexican* and surely unburdened himself to Governor Axtell and U.S. District Attorney Catron. Who else but Dolan would have brought to the governor's attention the obscure legal technicality that Sheriff Copeland had failed to post bond within thirty days of his appointment? Citing this transgression, on May 28 Axtell removed Copeland as sheriff and three days later named George W. Peppin as his successor.[16]

Except in his firm allegiance to Dolan, the new sheriff was a virtual clone of the old. Thirty-nine, a Frenchman and a stonemason, "Dad" Peppin was amiable, well intentioned, weak of intellect, and easily dominated. He gave promise of serving Dolan as loyally as Copeland had served McSween.

Badly outmaneuvered, the Kid and his friends faded into the mountains as Peppin stormed into Lincoln on June 19. He led a formidable force: not only Dolan himself and the usual posse of Dolanites but also a cavalry detachment and, to Colonel Dudley's disgust, a dozen deputized gangsters from the Mesilla Valley under Jesse Evans's old partner John Kinney. They seem to have been recruited to the cause by Johnny Riley with promises of booty. As Frank Coe recalled Riley's part in the war, he was The House's "confidence man"—"smooth talker and make you believe anything, worked in Santa Fe, Albuquerque, and Las Cruces and sent in men to help them. Was a damned coward but gave us more dirt than any of them."[17]

Peppin also brought with him still another arrest warrant to add to the bewildering collection that already existed. Drawn up by U.S. Marshal for New Mexico John Sherman, almost certainly with the collaboration of Dolan, Peppin, and District Attorney Rynerson, it was a federal rather than a territorial document, commanding the apprehension of Billy and his comrades who had fought at Blazer's Mills—even the dead Brewer. The schemers behind this ploy reasoned that since the slaying of Roberts had occurred on an Indian reservation, it fell under federal jurisdiction. When the fugitives failed to appear before the U.S. District Court in Mesilla on June 22 (Judge Bristol served as both federal and territorial judge), the U.S. grand jury indicted them all for murder. Thus Billy now found himself wanted by the territory for the murder of William Brady and by the United States for the murder of Buckshot Roberts.[18]

After fleeing Lincoln, the Regulators took refuge in the familiar haunts of San Patricio. At night they hid in the mountains, with the ubiquitous George Washington serving as camp cook. Even McSween joined his troops in the field—"clean shaved and with a very large hat," according to Washington. By day the fugitives consorted with the congenial people of the town, with whom Billy, in particular, was popular. He spoke their language, never patronized, loved their *bailes,* and captivated their damsels.

Peppin lost no time in launching his offensive. He named as field commander Jack Long, a garrulous, hard-drinking deputy who, like Peppin, had been with Brady on the fatal April 1. At dawn on June 27 Long and five possemen, bolstered by "Colonel" Kinney and his dirty dozen, rode into the plaza of San Patricio. They found no Regulators, but flushed George Washington, who sprinted across a wheat field in an attempt to escape. Kinney's Winchester tore up the ground around his feet and brought him to a halt. Dropping his rifle, Washington promptly poured out all he knew about his friends.

While Kinney held San Patricio, Long and his men rode up the Ruidoso Valley to search John Newcomb's ranch. Finding nothing, they returned. Two miles west of San Patricio, they spied a dozen horsemen across the river and, supposing them to be Kinney's squad, rode in their direction.

Long was mistaken. Eleven Regulators had come down from the mountains and, probably accidentally, stumbled into the six deputies. Present, besides the Kid, Waite, Bowdre, and others, were McSween and former sheriff Copeland, who had promised Peppin to go home and mind his own business.[19] At a range of seventy-five yards, Billy and his friends let fly a fusillade of rifle fire. They saw two horses drop and the rest scamper out of range.

The firing brought Kinney charging to the rescue. Sighting the reinforcements, the Regulators turned and ascended a ravine-scored mountaintop, where they dismounted and spread out in strong defensive positions. The enemy shrank from a direct assault, but Kinney and six men tried to work into positions from which to dislodge the defenders. A heavy fire held them a full five hundred yards distant.

The standoff lasted for four hours, when Billy and his companions slipped off to the south, made their way through the mountains to Frank Coe's ranch, then lost themselves north of the Hondo in the Capitan foothills. The cavalry command summoned by Long followed the trail but never overhauled the quarry.[20]

Imitating McSween, Peppin decided to get Hispanics involved on his side too. Stimulated by the sheriff's command, fortified by legal summonses, fifteen found themselves enlisted in a posse under Deputy José Chavez y Baca and dispatched on another foray against San Patricio. They reached the town shortly before dawn on July 3.

This time the Regulators were waiting, posted on the rooftops. "Those dobes had little breastworks around the tops," said George Coe, "and we got behind those and punched out loopholes." Riding into the plaza in the early morning gloom, the attackers encountered a storm of bullets. "We were scattered around all over town," related Coe. "Two or three of us got on top of every house. It was too dark to see to shoot accurately, but we killed a horse or two and think we wounded a man." They had. Julian López had his arm shattered as the posse retreated.[21]

Expecting the enemy to return in greater strength, the Regulators abandoned San Patricio and made their way down the Hondo. A stronger force soon appeared in their rear—Jack Long, Kinney and his crowd, and Jimmy Dolan himself. Pressed closely, Scurlock dismounted his men and posted them in firing positions along the crest of a steep ridge four miles east of town. When the pursuers ran into a burst of rifle fire that cost them two horses, they abandoned the mission and fell back. Foiled a second time in less than a week and irate over the sympathies of the citizens of San Patricio, they tore up the town and terrorized the residents before returning to Lincoln.

The Regulators continued down the Hondo to the Pecos and put in at Chisum's ranch. "We went down to visit Old John and to rest on the Fourth," recalled George Coe. Chisum was not there, but the ranch hands prepared a big dinner, and everyone made ready to celebrate Independence Day.

If the chief was absent, Sallie Chisum was not. Athletic and strong-willed, Old John's niece was a pretty sixteen-year-old with long, straw-colored hair. Billy Bonney found her fascinating, and she returned the favor.[22] During the morning, accompanied by Frank and George Coe and several others, Billy rode over to Captain Lea's store to buy candy for Sallie from clerk Ash Upson. On the return, twelve Seven Rivers possemen galloped to the attack. In a running fight, the two groups of horsemen exchanged fire all the way back to the ranch.

They "fought around the ranch most of the day," remembered George Coe, "but the ranch was a good defensive work and no harm was done." The feast proceeded as planned, while the posse sent to Lincoln for help. By the time reinforcements arrived, grumbled one, "McSween's mob had escaped."[23]

Inexorably, the Lincoln County War escalated toward a climax. The Battle of Lincoln on April 30 marked the first armed clash between opposing forces. The two fights at San Patricio and the one at the Chisum ranch also represented open warfare between the two factions. Except for slain horses and slight wounds, these skirmishes had been virtually bloodless. The genuine bloodshed had occurred earlier, in homicides rather than battles. But by July, battle had become the accepted form of conflict, and tempers on both sides flared ominously. At the same time, the only restraining influence had been neutralized. A congressional ban on military involvement of any kind in civil affairs had withdrawn the army from the equation altogether. Now the issue rested with Dolan and McSween, and both seemed ready to have it out once and for all.

The Fire

Four months into the Lincoln County War, Billy Bonney had become an accomplished fighter, rash at times, but confident in his abilities, trusted and liked by his comrades.

He had also grown callous toward human life and stood ready to kill, without hesitation and by means fair or foul, when the cause seemed to require it. In this he was not unique. He shared the attitude and instinct with his companions. However barbarous, the mindset is at least understandable in terms of a feud that had escalated into a war.

Of those who rode with Billy at this time, only Frank Coe has left a full and convincing portrait. Allowing for his unabashed partisanship, Frank's appraisal is to be taken seriously. He recalled that as a fighter, Billy

stood with us to the end, brave and reliable, one of the best soldiers we had. He never pushed in his advice or opinions, but he had a wonderful presence of mind; the tighter the place the more he showed his cool nerve and quick brain. He was a fine horseman, quick and always in the lead, at the same time he was kind to his horses and could save them and have them ready and fresh when he needed to make a dash.

Frank also touched on other traits:

He never seemed to care for money, except to buy cartridges with; then he would much prefer to gamble for them straight. Cartridges were scarce,

88

and he always used about ten times as many as anyone else. He would practice shooting at every thing he saw and from every conceivable angle, on and off his horse. He never drank. He would go to the bar with any-one, but I never saw him drink a drop, and he never used tobacco in any form. Always in a good humor and ready to do a kind act for some one.[1]

Sometime in May or June 1878, the Regulators picked up an-other recruit, destined to grow even closer to Billy than Fred Waite. More than six feet tall, red-headed, younger by two years than Billy, "Big Foot" Tom O'Folliard had come up from Texas and, like Billy before him, asked Frank Coe for work. "The Kid came in and said he could make a real warrior out of him," related Coe. "He did this." With a big, long-range buffalo gun, Billy taught Tom how to shoot. After that, "he followed the Kid everywhere he went," said Coe. "He was the Kid's inseparable companion and always went along and held his horses. He held his horses when the Kid would pay his attentions to some Mexican girl. It mattered not that he was gone thirty minutes or half the night, Tom was there when he came out."[2]

Tom O'Folliard idolized Billy and constantly fed his self-esteem. So did the other Regulators, who admired his abilities and achieve-ments and said so. Aside from such reinforcement, Billy could not have been oblivious to his expanding talents. Since leaving the Ev-ans gang, he had made much progress in the skills that frontier so-ciety valued highly and that found frequent expression in the op-erations of the Regulators. As the Lincoln County War moved toward its fiercest battle, Billy Bonney took on a self-assurance that would lift him into the front ranks of the Regulators.

After the bloodless battle at the Chisum ranch on July 4, Mc-Sween resolved to run no more. Dashing about on horseback, ex-changing gunfire with the enemy, and bedding down in mountain hideaways was not his style of conflict. He had been led into this kind of fighting, said Sue McSween, by the "foolhardy boys" he rode with, among whom she numbered Billy Bonney in the fore-front. "I never liked the Kid," she later wrote, "and didn't approve of his career." She thought him "too much like Dolan, did not think it amounted to much to take a man's life."[3]

A strange mix of defiance and despair drove McSween back to his home in Lincoln. On the one hand, he clearly intended to fight if pressed, for he brought with him nearly sixty men, including a large contingent of Hispanics under Martín Chavez of Picacho. "He had been out in the hills long enough," Dr. Daniel Appel, the Fort Stanton surgeon, quoted him as explaining. "As he had now returned to his house they would not drive him away again alive." On the other hand, Reverend Ealy's wife remembered, "He seemed to think he was doomed. He was Scotch and had some superstitions."[4]

The expanded Regulator force slipped into Lincoln on the night of July 14 while most of Sheriff Peppin's possemen were out scouring the countryside. Peppin, Dolan, and a handful of men bunked at the Wortley Hotel, across from the old Dolan store, and Jack Long and five deputies held the *torreon*. Heavily outnumbered, they made no move to contest the occupation. Some of the Regulators climbed to the rooftops of McSween's house and José Montaño's store, a short distance beyond the *torreon*, and knocked firing ports in the parapets. They then divided themselves among the Montaño store, the home of Juan Patrón immediately to the east, and the Isaac Ellis store on the far edge of town. Billy stationed himself at the Montaño store.

The five-day battle for Lincoln opened on the afternoon of July 15. With high winds kicking up clouds of dust, Peppin's posse clattered into town from the west. Reining their mounts at the Wortley Hotel, the Peppin-Dolan headquarters, they aimed a volley of rifle fire at the McSween house, splintering slats on the drawn shutters. Hearing the firing, Billy and a dozen others emerged from the Montaño store and dashed down the street to the rescue. From the *torreon* Jack Long shouted for them to halt. They gave him a blast of gunfire, which Long and his men answered in kind. At the McSween house, the Regulator squad fired off a fusillade that spattered the Wortley and its corral and sent the posse scurrying for cover.[5]

The odds favored the McSween forces, sixty to forty. Almost equally divided among the McSween, Montaño, and Ellis buildings, however, they formed separate islands of strength, beyond communication with one another at the enemy's discretion. About twenty, including Frank Coe, Middleton, Bowdre, and Scurlock, held the Ellis store. Another twenty, mostly Chavez's Hispanics, defended the Montaño store and the Patrón home. The rest posted themselves in the McSween house.

A spacious, U-shaped adobe, the McSween residence housed two families. The Ealys had moved next door, to the living quarters in the Tunstall store, leaving the McSweens to reoccupy the west half of their house. The east half sheltered the David Shield family. David, Mac's law partner, was in Las Vegas, but Elizabeth, the sister of Sue McSween, and her five children remained at home, together with Susan Gates, Reverend Ealy's assistant. Regulators crowding the house, besides Billy Bonney, were Tom O'Folliard, Jim French, George Coe, Henry Brown, Joe Smith, Tom Cullens, Harvey Morris (a tubercular Kansan reading law with McSween), Florencio Chavez, José Chavez y Chavez, Yginio Salazar, Ygnacio Gonzalez, Vicente Romero, Francisco Zamora, and José María Sanchez.[6]

Peppin's group counted only about forty gunmen. Most were veterans of the Mathews posse of the previous February, both Dolan adherents and the ubiquitous Seven Rivers warriors. The posse also included John Kinney and his dozen bandits from the Mesilla Valley, and once again Dolan had Jesse Evans present "to do his part." He had stood trial for stealing Indian horses and won acquittal, and Judge Bristol had freed him on bail to await trial for the murder of Tunstall.[7]

Although outnumbered, Peppin could bring all his force against any one of the Regulator strongholds without danger from the others. His principal dilemma, rather, was how to seize them without exposing his men to a murderous fire from strong defenses.

Neither side had much idea how to break the stalemate without getting someone killed. They contented themselves with firing an occasional shot and jockeying for position. Sometime in the next three days a stray shot punched into the McSween house and killed Tom Cullens. After dark on the eighteenth Ben Ellis, feeding a mule in the corral of his father's store, caught another stray in the neck. The Reverend Doctor Ealy tried to go to his aid, but a blast of gunfire from the *torreon* drove him in panic back to the Tunstall store. The next morning he got through and patched up the severely wounded young man.[8]

On July 16 the McSween house defenders committed a major blunder. At dusk men on the rooftop squinted into the setting sun and spied a rider approaching from the west. They opened fire and saw him fall from his horse, then recover and sprint to the cover of the Wortley Hotel. The rider was a cavalryman bearing a message from Colonel Dudley informing Peppin that he could not have the howitzer he had asked to borrow. The trooper had been thrown by a frightened horse and had not been hit, but firing on a U.S. soldier was not a politic thing to do. Colonel Dudley called it "this infamous outrage."

The next day the Regulators compounded the mistake. Peppin had sent two marksmen to the hills south of town to clear the Regulator rooftops. Somehow the pair concluded that the enemy had fled, and they walked down the mountainside. From the Montaño store, Doc Scurlock's father-in-law took careful aim and fired. The ball hit one of the men in the stomach and smashed his spine. "Fernando Herrera shot Charlie Crawford with a 45–120–555 Sharpes," recalled a contemporary, who ranked the shot "among the great examples of marksmanship." Accompanied by another officer and two soldiers, Dr. Appel, who was in town to investigate the previous day's firing on the trooper, went to Crawford's succor. Although clearly recognizable by their uniforms, the party drew further fire from the Montaño store. As bullets tore up the hillside, they retrieved the fatally wounded man and returned to cover without being hit.[9]

These insults to the federal uniform scarcely helped to keep Colonel Dudley out of the fray. His orders barred him from lending any aid to either side and enjoined him to remain aloof from civil affairs. But for a week he had been bombarded by the pathetic pleas of terrorized citizens. When the fight settled in the heart of Lincoln, innocent people came under immediate threat of injury or death.

"All possessed of terror," said José María de Aguayo. "You could not see in the town any person except Nigger Joe [Dixon] and myself," he related, "because my children were crying, because they were hungry and I had to go about and look for milk."[10] To stand by while women and children were imperiled by a senseless war over money and power sorely tested the officers at Fort Stanton.

Not until the fifth day did the impasse break, and then only because Colonel Dudley, disobeying explicit orders, could no longer resist rushing to the aid of helpless citizens. He went for worthy and defensible motives, but his elaborate show of neutrality in fact favored Peppin and Dolan. Representing the most credible institution of law, the sheriff had Dudley's sympathies, besides which Dudley disliked McSween and all his friends, especially after the two Regulator attacks on blue uniforms. Despite good intentions, Dudley displayed the same bad judgment in Lincoln that had marked his career for more than twenty years.

About midmorning on July 19, Billy Bonney and his friends looked out the front door of the McSween house on an ominous scene. Astride his mount, the erect colonel led a blue column down the street. With him rode four officers, followed by eleven mounted troopers of the black Ninth Cavalry and twenty-four white footmen of the Fifteenth Infantry. In the rear, tended by infantry, rattled a small twelve-pounder mountain howitzer and a rapid-fire Gatling gun.[11]

A short time later the defenders of the McSween house saw three mounted soldiers return to the Wortley, then head back east accompanied by Peppin. The sight of the sheriff riding the street with military escort led to an obvious conclusion: Dudley had come to help Peppin. "We all became alarmed," said Sue McSween.[12]

McSween hastily scribbled a note addressed to Dudley and handed it to Billy to read:

Would you have the kindness to let me know why soldiers surround my house. Before blowing up my property I would like to know the reason. The constable is here and has warrants for the arrest of Sheriff Peppin and posse for murder and larceny. Respectfully. A. A. McSween

Billy handed the note back, and McSween passed it to the Shields' little daughter to carry to Dudley. Soon she returned with Dudley's reply, signed by his adjutant. It said that no troops surrounded McSween's house and added that if he wanted to blow up his own house, the colonel had no objection provided soldiers were not endangered.[13]

In fact, no soldiers surrounded McSween's house, although the alarm of the occupants is understandable. Dudley had pitched camp on the north side of the street, just beyond the Montaño store. Except for details of soldiers such as were sent for Peppin, he kept his troops well in hand. He made a big show of neutrality, informing everyone that he had come solely to protect women and children and would not take sides. If either side endangered his camp, he vowed, he would respond with force.

"God damn you understand me," he exploded at Peppin, "if one of your men wound one of my men I will blow you above the clouds."[14]

However neutral in intent, Dudley's actions wrought disastrously unneutral consequences for McSween. Immediately on reaching his campsite, supposedly as a defensive measure, Dudley unlimbered his howitzer and turned it on the front door of the Montaño store. Frightened, the Regulators there poured out and ran down the street to join their cohorts in the Ellis store. Dudley then had the howitzer aimed at the Ellis store. The combined force evacuated that bastion and, amid a scattering of shots from Peppin deputies, crossed the river into the hills beyond. Later in the day they made a halfhearted attempt to join McSween, but Dudley had his Gatling gun turned in their direction, and Peppin fired a few rifle shots at them from the top of the *torreon*. They faded back into the hills.[15]

Dudley's "defensive" measures cost McSween two-thirds of his men, giving Peppin a two-to-one numerical superiority and freeing him to concentrate his entire force on the McSween house. Moreover, Dudley's warning to blow above the clouds anyone whose fire came his way favored Peppin. He could fire at the McSween house without coming close to soldiers; McSween could not fire back without risk to soldiers. As Jack Long later remarked, "There was a more confident bunch inside the McSween house than was to be found outside it, until after the soldiers arrived."[16]

Late in the morning, the people in the McSween house heard a commotion at the southwest window, which fronted the street. They had closed the shutters and piled up adobe bricks there as a barricade. Several possemen, however, had crept along the front wall, pried loose the shutters with butcher knives, and ripped them from their fastenings. The men then used their rifles to smash the glass and to push over the adobe barricade. From the cover of the outside wall, Deputy Marion Turner shouted that he had warrants for McSween's arrest. McSween answered that he would not surrender, that he had warrants for the posse's arrest. Turner demanded to see them.

"Our warrants are in our guns, you cock-sucking sons-of-bitches," yelled Jim French.

Turner and his men decided not to face the guns and pulled back.[17]

Early in the afternoon Sue McSween announced her determination to have a talk with Dudley. En route down the street, she saw preparations being made to set fire to her house. At the *torreon* she had a spirited argument with Sheriff Peppin, who told her that if she wanted to save her house from flames she had to persuade the men inside to surrender. At the military camp, she quickly fell into a shouting contest with Dudley, alternately denouncing him for siding with Peppin and imploring him to intervene to save her husband. Dudley stubbornly refused to interfere in any way with a sheriff in the lawful discharge of his duty.[18]

Back in her home, Sue found efforts well advanced to set it afire—not an easy task with an adobe structure. The house had two kitchens, one at the end of each wing. Billy Bonney had gone to the rear of the Shield wing, to the room next to the kitchen. Mrs. Shield was removing furniture and other valuables in anticipation of the fire. Billy watched through the door as Jack Long and a deaf-mute known only as "Dummy" piled kindling on the kitchen floor, doused it with coal oil, and set it afire. Incredibly, Billy made no move to interfere, possibly out of concern for Mrs. Shield.

The kitchen opened onto a small backyard enclosed by an adobe wall with a door on the north and by a board fence on the east. A privy stood in the corner, its vault dug into a slope and uncovered in the rear. A gate at the northeast corner afforded passage to an open space separating the McSween house from the Tunstall store.

Unknown to Long and Dummy, George Coe, Henry Brown, and Joe Smith had slipped into the Tunstall store and taken positions at windows in the west wall. When the two possemen emerged from the gate, the Regulators let fly with their Winchesters. The two men dove for the nearest cover, which happened to be the privy vault. Another deputy jumped in at the same time. They dared not leave. As Coe remarked of the "little house," when no other target appeared, "we riddled it from top to bottom." Until after dark, Long and his friends stood in the sink. "It was not a good place to set down," he explained.[19]

Long and Dummy failed, for the fire in the northeast kitchen sputtered for a time and then went out. Possibly Billy Bonney put it out. He would have been remiss indeed if he had done nothing after the two possemen left the kitchen.

Andy Boyle had more success. After watching Long and Dummy for a time, he went out the northeast gate, had his neck grazed by a bullet from Coe or one of his comrades, and ran around the adobe wall to the north. Aided by other deputies, he collected the makings of another fire at the McSween stable and slipped into the northwest kitchen. "I set it on fire with a sack of shavings and chips," he said, "and used what timber there was on top of the stable to make it burn. It burned very slowly all afternoon from one room to another turning in a circle around the house."[20]

Boyle's fire took hold about 2:00 P.M. As it made its way from room to room, a thick column of smoke rose from the house. Room by room, the defenders retreated as the flames advanced. What transpired as their plight grew increasingly hopeless can only be guessed. The survivors told almost nothing. Elizabeth Shield and her children, and Miss Gates, left during the afternoon and sought refuge with the Ealys in the Tunstall store. Sue McSween stayed until 5:00 P.M., when she too went next door.

As Sue recalled the scene in the burning house, "The boys talked to each other and McSween and I were sitting in one corner. The boys decided I should leave. They were fighting the fire in my sister's house [the east wing]. McSween said he guessed that was better. . . . The Kid was lively and McSween was sad. McSween sat with his head down, and the Kid shook him and told him to get up, that they were going to make a break."[21]

This tantalizing glimpse, together with Billy's statement that McSween showed him his note before dispatching it to Colonel Dudley, is the only firsthand testimony to Billy's role in the McSween house on July 19, 1878. It suggests that he either assumed command or had it thrust on him by the others. In light of Frank Coe's assertion that Billy rarely volunteered his opinions (p. 88), the latter seems the more likely. Their situation was desperate, McSween had sunk into helpless despair, and someone needed to produce a solution and the leadership to carry it out. All probably looked to Billy, only eighteen but a veteran.

As darkness fell, the flames drove all the men into the northeast kitchen, cluttered with the debris of Long's abortive attempt to kindle a bonfire. "The house was in a great blaze lighting up the hills on both sides of the town," recalled Dr. Appel. Firing intensified. Captain Purington remarked that "if the poor devils in that house could live through such a fire and get away they were certainly entitled to freedom."[22]

The men in the house had only one avenue of escape: out the back door, across the little yard, through the northeast gate, along the back of the vacant lot between the fence and the Tunstall store, and into the timber lining the river to the north. The flames lit the night sky and the vacant lot, but the backyard, enclosed by the board fence and adobe walls, lay in shadows. The possemen at the door in the back wall, only a few steps from the kitchen door, could make out almost nothing in the yard.[23]

With the kitchen beginning to catch fire, the breakout came

shortly after 9:00 P.M. One by one, the men slipped out the door into the gloom of the yard and crept to the gate in the fence. In single file they started into the open. Jim French went first, followed by Harvey Morris, Tom O'Folliard, José Chavez y Chavez, and Billy Bonney.

Not until the escapees were in the middle of the space between the fence and the Tunstall store did the light of the flames fall on them and alert the possemen. From behind the north wall and from the street, they opened a hot fire. At the first volley, said José Chavez y Chavez, "I went with all my might," and so did the other four. A fatal ball struck down Harvey Morris, but the rest dodged through the leaden storm and lost themselves in the darkness of the river and its sheltering trees.

Only these five made it out of the gate before the heavy fire of the deputies sealed off the escape route. McSween and the others fell back into the shadows, some crouching against the adobe walls, others taking refuge in a chicken house in the northwest corner of the yard. After about five minutes, a few of the trapped men tried to break through the gate but were again driven back.

Ten minutes passed. Then McSween called out, "I shall surrender."

Robert Beckwith, old Hugh's son from Seven Rivers, replied, "I am a deputy sheriff and I have got a warrant for you."

Accompanied by John Jones (son of Heiskell and Ma'am Jones), Joe Nash, and Dummy, Beckwith entered the yard through the door in the wall and walked to the kitchen door, where he faced McSween.

Suddenly McSween yelled, "I shall never surrender."

Andy Boyle was standing in the door in the adobe wall. "When McSween said he would not surrender," Boyle related, "every one of them commenced to shoot." He called the wild and confused melee "the big killing." In the darkened yard, both sides fired blindly and at close range. Bob Beckwith caught the first ball in the corner of his left eye and died instantly. Five bullets cut down McSween. Vicente Romero and Francisco Zamora fell dead next to McSween. Young Yginio Salazar crumpled with a bullet in the back and one in the shoulder. Later he crawled to safety. His arm smashed by a bullet, Ygnacio Gonzalez got away in the confusion, as did Florencio Chavez and José María Sanchez.

In the river bottom, Billy and his friends joined George Coe, Henry Brown, and Joe Smith. Taking their cue from the men in the McSween house, the three had abandoned the Tunstall store at the same time. Slipping into the corral behind the store, they had confronted an eight-foot adobe wall. Tunstall's bulldog, chained in a corner, charged at Brown, who threw down his rifle on him.

"Henry," shouted Coe, "let that old dog alone and let's get out of here."

Beer bottles had been thrown in a mound against the wall. The three men leaped to the top of the pile, then vaulted over the wall and ran to the river.[24]

Billy and the other escapees made their way down the river and crossed to the Ellis store.

"For God's sake, get out of here," said Ike Ellis, who had sampled enough danger and excitement for one day.

"Keep your shirt on," replied George Coe. "We have got out of something worse than this."

One of the family rustled some grub for the hungry men, and they left. Sleeping on a hilltop near town, they walked down the valley the next morning and stopped at the home of a Hispanic farmer for coffee. He balked, protesting that the other side would kill him. "We told him he would die just a little sooner if he did not get us some coffee," related Coe. He did. All the Regulators rendezvoused at the ranch of Frank Coe on the Hondo.[25]

★

None of the principals in the Five-Day Battle for Lincoln could find much to boast about. It was not an especially mismanaged battle but rather an almost altogether unmanaged battle. Having sought a decisive test at arms, both sides then lost their nerve and let it run its course without direction.

Sheriff Peppin provided virtually no leadership. He spent the first four days indecisively idle in the Wortley Hotel and the fifth day observing from the top of the *torreon*. His sole contribution to the course of events was to order the McSween house set afire, a task then accomplished on the initiative of others.

Jimmy Dolan played an even smaller role. Still slowed by his broken leg, he watched the attack on the McSween house from one of the little adobe residences across the street.

Of all the factors influencing the outcome of the battle, Colonel Dudley's mindless combination of action and inaction proved most decisive. He came to Lincoln to protect women and children, then refused to take the only action that would have protected women and children—stop the fighting and let the courts decide. Simply by entering Lincoln he had disobeyed orders; to have gone a step farther in behalf of humanity could not have brought him any more censure. As Sue McSween's tirade made clear to him, the McSween house itself contained three women and five children, and still he would not interfere. Yet his handling of the artillery, combined with his very presence in town, changed the equation of the battle and ensured Peppin's victory.

And finally, the Regulator leadership failed. McSween came to Lincoln with a stubborn resolve and a formidable army but with no plan of how to use it. Scattered among several strongholds around town, it lost the advantage of numbers and was fatally crippled by an inability to communicate.

Far worse, the men in the Montaño and Ellis stores allowed themselves to be stampeded by Colonel Dudley's bluster and ran from battle without firing a shot. Doc Scurlock, the Regulator captain, faltered badly. With forty men at his command, he made one halfhearted effort to relieve the McSween house but turned tail when a scattering of rifle shots came his way. The most charitable explanation is that these men feared getting into a fight with Dudley's soldiers. Their timidity left McSween and his men to their fate.

The escape from McSween's blazing home gave Billy Bonney a modest notoriety in New Mexico. The territorial newspapers named him as one of the defenders of the McSween house and at first reported him among the dead. So far, however, neither the public nor the press perceived him in any larger dimensions than warranted by strict fact. He was simply one of about a dozen face-less Regulators who got their names in the papers whenever they fought a skirmish or shot one of the opposition. He had done nothing to give him any more prominence in the public eye than the men with whom he rode and fought. Even the daring breakout, which he probably engineered, was successfully shared with three other men. However highly regarded by his comrades, Billy had yet to gain a public reputation.

Yet the Five-Day Battle gave Billy a baptism of fire far more searing than any in his earlier experience. Trapped in a predicament that seemed hopelessly fatal, he had kept his head, risen to a position of leadership, plotted an escape, and for himself and three others at least, carried it out with all the boldness and bravery for which he had come to be admired by his fellow Regulators.

The Drifter

The Lincoln County War should have ended in Alexander Mc-Sween's backyard on the night of July 19, 1878. The war was a struggle to decide whether an existing monopoly or an aspiring monopoly would dominate Lincoln County. Neither would achieve that distinction, for both collapsed in the rubble of war. McSween's death and Dolan's bankruptcy left nothing to fight about.

Although now lacking a purpose, the Regulators did not disband. The dozen "iron clads" had shared danger and hardship for five months. The momentum of past rivalries and conflicts kept them together even as their cause crumbled. After the Five-Day Battle, they embarked on a period of uncertain drifting.

For rootless Billy Bonney, the Regulators had furnished the first feeling of belonging since the death of his mother. He not only had been accepted by the older men but had risen to a position of respect and, finally, moderate leadership. Although Doc Scurlock remained captain, his interest increasingly turned to his family and farm. Billy, who had never enjoyed satisfactions such as the Regulators provided, had better reason to want to keep the band together, and more and more he determined the direction of the aimless drifting, if not the ultimate purpose of the drifters.

The first need of the Regulators was horses. Theirs had been left in the Ellis corral on July 19 and had been confiscated by Peppin's men. "Brown met some fellow and took his saddle and horse," said George Coe, and over the next few days the others mounted themselves in the same way. Efforts focused on the old Casey ranch below Frank Coe's place. The Casey boys tied their horses at the front door and ran the ropes inside the house. Billy tried to take one of these. "The horse was snuffy and he failed to get him," recounted George Coe. "I was a better horseman than the Kid," he claimed. "He was a fighter but did not understand horses like I did."

Even so, Billy stole a horse before George, who was the last to remain afoot. Finally, the entire group returned to the Casey ranch to get George a mount. While his friends stood at the ready in the darkness, Coe crept up to a tethered horse. "I had a sharp knife, got hold of the rope, and he never made a move. I got six or eight feet of the rope, whacked it off, throwed a loop over the horse's nose, jumped on him, hit him with my old hat and left there. The boys commenced shooting, whooping, and laughing."[1]

For a few days the Regulators hung around Lincoln, menacing people thought to be friends of Dolan's. The posse had dissolved, and Peppin, mindful of the fate of Brady, had holed up at Fort Stanton. The Regulators terrorized Saturnino Baca, who more than anyone had prompted Colonel Dudley's decision to come to Lincoln, and he too sought haven at the fort. They even hurled threats of assassination at Dudley himself, whom they held responsible for McSween's death.[2]

Among those who felt endangered was Frederick C. Godfroy, agent for the Mescalero Apaches. In February McSween had tried to get his job for Rob Widenmann (who subsequently, in June, had left Lincoln forever) and had also engineered an official investigation that ultimately got the agent fired. Notwithstanding this background of friction, the animosity of the Regulators is hard to understand, for others had given greater cause for malice. But Godfroy himself, asking Dudley for soldiers to escort him between the fort and the Indian agency, declared that he knew positively that the Kid intended to kill him.[3]

For this or other reasons, about twenty Regulators showed up at the Indian agency at South Fork on August 5. Frank Coe said that they went to visit Dick Brewer's grave, though other evidence suggests a plundering foray against the Indian horse herds. Among the band were Bonney, Scurlock, Middleton, Bowdre, Brown, French, and other of the "iron clads," together with about ten Hispanics, including Fernando Herrera, Ygnacio Gonzalez, and Atanacio Martínez.

As the horsemen approached the agency, the Anglo contingent veered off the road to the left and headed for a spring on the valley floor. The Hispanics continued on the road. No sooner had Billy and his friends dismounted to drink than they heard a burst of firing from the road.

The Hispanics had encountered a party of Indians, and firing had at once broken out. Who fired the first shot or why was never discovered.[4] At the agency issue house, Godfroy and his clerk, Morris Bernstein, were doling out rations to some Indian women when they heard the gunfire. Hastily mounting, they galloped out to investigate. Bernstein, in advance, rode into the midst of the battle and was shot down by Atanacio Martínez. With bullets zipping around him, Godfroy turned and raced back to the agency. A few soldiers happened to be there, and they joined Godfroy in a counterattack.

Back at the spring, Billy had dropped the reins of his horse and was drinking. Startled by the firing, the horse reared and bolted. Then both the Indians and the soldiers spotted the men at the spring and opened fire on them. George Coe swung into his saddle and pulled the Kid up behind him, then with the others spurred across the open glade to the timber-screened road. "I'll bet they shot fifty times at us," remembered Coe. "We were having to ride on the sides of our horses but they never touched a hair of us."[5]

Working their way across the wooded hillside north of the road, the Regulators crept up on the agency corral, which was full of horses and mules. Not only Billy but also three of his comrades had been dismounted, and they doubtless looked on the tempting prize as a fair trade. Opening the gate, they made off with all the agency's stock. The Kid roped an Indian pony and rode him bareback all the way to Frank Coe's ranch.[6]

The killing of Bernstein stirred great excitement and brought public censure on the Regulators. He had been shot four times, his pockets turned out and emptied, and his rifle, pistol, and cartridge belt taken—presumably by his slayers, though Indians could as well have been guilty. Although more accidental than deliberate, the shooting had all the marks of a brutal murder. "This wanton and cowardly affair," declared Dudley, "excels the killing of Sheriff Brady, inasmuch as the attacking party was ten to one." Even though he had been drinking at a spring several hundred yards distant, the Kid came to be looked on as Bernstein's murderer.

The theft of government stock gave Colonel Dudley an excuse to put a detail of troopers on the trail of the culprits. But they easily escaped. Indeed, they vanished from the Lincoln area altogether.

With their stolen stock, Billy and a handful of Regulators turned up on the Pecos River at Bosque Grande on August 13. Bosque Grande had been the first Chisum ranch headquarters, and here they met up with some Chisums. John Chisum had been in St. Louis for several weeks, but his brothers Jim and Pitzer were taking themselves and a big herd of cattle northward out of the war zone.

The meeting may not have been coincidental, for present with the caravan was Sallie Chisum. She and Billy had been exchanging letters, and he may have known about her family's plan to leave South Spring ranch. Indeed, he wrote her a letter from the McSween house during the siege, and she received it on July 20. On August 13 she recorded in her diary: "The Regulators (Bonney and friends) came to Bosque Grande."

As the Chisum caravan moved up the Pecos, Bonney and friends went along. When the Chisum caravan laid over at Fort Sumner on August 17, so did Bonney and friends. At both Bosque Grande and Fort Sumner, Billy paid court to Sallie: "Indian tobacco sack presented to me on the 13th of August 1878 by William Bonny [sic]." "Two candi hearts given me by Willie Bonney on the 22nd of August."[7]

For Billy and his friends, Fort Sumner offered other attractions as well. Some of the "iron clads" who had tarried around Lincoln after the agency raid joined Billy at Sumner. "When we got there," recalled Frank Coe, "Kid and others had a baile for us. Got George and I to fiddle. . . . House was full, whiskey free, not a white girl in the house, all Mexican, and all good dancers . . . polite, never say much upon the floor, but start off when the tunes started. Danced all night. Boys swinging them high."

After a week of fun at Fort Sumner, the Regulators rode up the Pecos River. Laying over two nights at the adobe hamlet of Puerto de Luna, according to Frank Coe, "We had another big dance there. Mexicans sociable there and had respect for white people." Farther up the valley, they stopped at Anton Chico, "the best of the towns this side of Las Vegas."[8]

On the first night at Anton Chico, word came that a posse from Las Vegas, under San Miguel County Sheriff Desiderio Romero, had lined up at the bar of Manuel Sanchez's saloon inquiring about the "Lincoln County War party" reported to be in town.

"Let's go down and see what they look like," said the Kid, "and not have them hunting us all over town."

Trooping down to the saloon, the Regulators entered and confronted the posse. There were "about eight big burly Mexicans," recounted Frank Coe, and "of all the guns and pistols you ever saw in your life they had them, as they had come down to take us dead or alive."

"Always in the lead," according to Coe, Billy identified the sheriff and asked his business.

When told, Billy replied: "This is the Lincoln County War party I guess you are looking after, right here. What do you want to do about it? Now is the time and you'll never get us in a better place to settle it than right here."[9]

Surveying the Regulator firepower, the sheriff backed down.

"Come up here and take another drink on the house," said the Kid, "and then we want you to leave town right now."

The posse gulped the drinks and rode out of Anton Chico. The Regulators stayed about two days longer and had a dance each night.

But a time for decision had come. Several nights after facing down the posse, the group rode about three miles below town, kindled a big bonfire, and had a "war pow-wow." Frank Coe announced that it was all over, that he and George were pulling out for Colorado.

"It's not all over with me," declared Billy. "I'm going to get revenged." Striding to one side, he said, "Who wants to go with me?"

All but the Coes gathered around him. "We are going the other way," said George Coe.

At the "war pow-wow" at Anton Chico the Kid emerged as chief of the Regulators. Although signifying the measure of his growth and the esteem of his comrades, it was an empty honor. The war was over and the "iron clads" were verging on dissolution.

Parting with the Coes, Billy and his followers rode toward Lincoln. He intended to steal some horses and drive them over to the Texas Panhandle for sale, he explained.

Billy's "revenge" fell on Charles Fritz, whose ranch nine miles below Lincoln had provided the setting for the killing of Frank McNab on April 29. Less from sympathy than fear, Fritz followed the lead of Jimmy Dolan. If revenge were the true motive, more fitting targets could have been found. In fact, revenge was more a rationalization than a purpose. On September 7 Regulators fell on Fritz's horse remuda, grazing on a mesa above his ranch house, and made off with fifteen head.[10]

Even before Fritz rode into Fort Stanton to complain of his loss, the blustering Colonel Dudley had recorded the return of the "McSween ring." The Kid, Jim French, Fred Waite, and others, he wrote, had taken over Lincoln. "Stock stealing is a daily matter, the animals being taken toward the Pecos and Seven Rivers."[11]

In returning to Lincoln, the Regulators had another purpose besides revenge. Doc Scurlock and Charley Bowdre had remained at home when the others had gone to Fort Sumner after the killing of Bernstein. In war's aftermath, however, they felt insecure and had decided to leave. Driving the stolen horses, Billy and his friends now helped the Scurlocks and Bowdres move their possessions to Fort Sumner, where Charley and Doc obtained employment with Pete Maxwell. Thus, like the Coes, these two pulled out of the dwindling band of war veterans.[12]

Others had defected too, and as Billy set forth from Fort Sumner for the Panhandle in late September 1878, he had with him only Tom O'Folliard, Henry Brown, Fred Waite, and John Middleton. Approaching the Texas line, they once more overhauled the Chisum outfit. "Regulators come up with us at Red River Springs on the 25 Sept 1878," recorded Sallie Chisum in her diary. It was the last time she would ever see Billy Bonney. Considering the uninhibited and free-spirited nature of both, one may guess that the brief romance had achieved a greater intimacy than condoned by the conventions of the time.

The Texas Panhandle, overlaid with the grassy sweep of the Staked Plains, was the last frontier of the cattlemen's empire. Less than two years before Billy's arrival, it had been exclusively the domain of Kiowa and Comanche Indians. In the spring of 1877, Charles Goodnight had established his JA-branded longhorns in Palo Duro Canyon, and other outfits had worked down the Canadian River to found such pioneer enterprises as the LX and LIT. Tiny but booming Tascosa served the entire region.[13]

Billy Bonney chose his market well. Panhandle stockmen needed horses and did not inquire too closely where they came from. "We knew those horses had been stolen over in New Mexico," recalled one of Tascosa's reigning belles, "Frenchie" McCormick, "so we didn't care." Of Billy she added: "He was the best natured kid and had the most pleasant smile I most ever saw in a young man."[14]

With one Tascosa resident Billy struck up a firm friendship. Henry Hoyt, a young physician adventuring in the West before embarking on a distinguished medical career, socialized regularly with the Kid and his friends. He fell in with Billy because, almost alone of the men who frequented Tascosa, the two did not drink. "Billy was an expert at most Western sports," he wrote, "with the exception of drinking." In the other sports—poker and monte, horse racing, target shooting, and the ever popular *bailes*—they participated vigorously.[15]

Pedro Romero's weekly *bailes* proved especially merry, although Romero required everyone to leave his firearms outside. One evening Hoyt and the Kid stepped outside for a stroll. At the far edge of the plaza Hoyt challenged Billy to a footrace back to the dance hall. Tearing across the plaza, Billy failed to check his pace as he neared the doorway. He tripped on the threshold and sprawled in the middle of the crowded floor. "Quicker than a flash," said Hoyt, "his prostrate body was surrounded by his four pals, back to back, with a Colt's forty-five in each hand, cocked and ready for business." No one knew where the guns had been hidden, but for the Kid and his friends embarrassment turned to disappointment when, having broken the rules, they found themselves barred from Romero *bailes*.[16]

Dr. Hoyt portrayed Billy Bonney at this time. He was

a handsome youth with smooth face, wavy brown hair, an athletic and symmetrical figure, and clear blue eyes that could look one through and through. Unless angry, he always seemed to have a pleasant expression with a ready smile. His head was well shaped, his features regular, his nose aquiline, his most noticeable characteristic a slight projection of his two upper front teeth.

"He spoke Spanish like a native," added Hoyt, "and although only a beardless boy, was nevertheless a natural leader of men."[17]

As the time for departure neared, Hoyt presented Billy with a gold watch he had admired, and Billy returned the favor with a sorrel horse that Hoyt had admired. That there be no later question of ownership, Billy stepped to the bar in Howard and McMasters' store and wrote out a bill of sale. The date, October 24, 1878, marked the approaching end of Billy's sojourn in the Panhandle.[18]

Having disposed of their stolen horses, the gang discussed the next move. Middleton, Waite, and Brown wanted to turn their backs on New Mexico, where they felt that constant danger, if not death, awaited them. They urged Billy and Tom to come east with them. But Billy insisted on returning and could not be dissuaded. They ended the argument by going their separate ways, Billy and Tom heading back to Fort Sumner. Thus did the last of the Regulator band disintegrate.[19]

For the next two months Billy and Tom seem to have been at

loose ends. They spent several weeks at Fort Sumner, frequenting the *bailes*, gambling, and visiting with Doc Scurlock and Charley Bowdre. Then they drifted westward, back to the familiar haunts around Lincoln. Billy had many friends here, and he had once wanted to settle on his own spread nearby. Like thoughts may have drawn him again to Lincoln.

His presence did not long remain unnoticed. By mid-December Colonel Dudley was lamenting the return, "in the last month," of such "murderers and rustlers" as the Kid and others of the old band of Regulators. On December 20 he issued an order placing Fort Stanton off limits to ten named men and "other parties recognized as the murderers of Roberts, Brady, Tunstall, Bernstein, and Beckwith."[20]

Most of the men named in Dudley's proscription were nowhere near Fort Stanton. French, Scurlock, Bowdre, Brown, and the Coes had fled to safer realms. But "Antrim alias Kid" had come back, with his sidekick Tom O'Folliard, and they promptly got caught up in the old rivalries of the Lincoln County War. As Dudley's order betrayed, the Lincoln cauldron had started bubbling anew.[21]

1. Billy the Kid. Of half a dozen or more pictures that may be Billy the Kid, this is the only one that is indisputably Billy the Kid. It is one of two almost identical tintypes taken at the same time at Fort Sumner in 1880. The original of the first disappeared years ago, and most reproductions are indistinct. This is taken from the original of the second, which was preserved for years in the Sam Diedrick family and came to light only in 1986. Since tintypes are reversed images, this picture led to the myth of the left-handed gun. Here the reversed image has been reversed to show the Kid as he actually posed, with a Winchester carbine in his left hand and his holstered Colt single-action on his right hip. (Reproduced by special permission of the Lincoln County Heritage Trust)

2. Main Street in Silver City, New
Mexico, in the 1870s. Young
Henry Antrim spent two years
here, 1873–75, before falling afoul
of the law, squirming up the chimney and out of the local jail, and
vanishing into Arizona. (Mullin
Collection, Haley History Center)

3. Lincoln, New Mexico, scene of Billy's coming of age in the Lincoln County War. Although taken about 1885, this view portrays the town much as it appeared in 1878. The Dolan store, later the county courthouse, is in the foreground, the Wortley Hotel is hidden in the trees across the street, and the Tunstall store is the building with the pitched roof in the right center. (Museum of New Mexico)

4. The U.S. Army post of Fort
Stanton sprawled on the banks of
the Rio Bonito nine miles above
Lincoln. Although maintained to
keep watch on the Mescalero
Apache Indians, it played an important role in the Lincoln County
War. On July 19, 1878, Colonel
Dudley's Fort Stanton troops intervened decisively in the climactic
battle for Lincoln. (National Archives)

5. Frederick T. Waite. A Chickasaw from Indian Territory, Fred Waite was the Kid's closest friend during the Lincoln County War. The two had planned to take up farming on the Peñasco, but the outbreak of war prevented the partnership. Later, Waite returned to the Indian Territory and led a quiet and useful life. (Special Collections, University of Arizona Library)

6. Left: Charles and Manuela Bowdre. With Doc Scurlock, Charley farmed on the Ruidoso until getting caught up in the Lincoln County War. At Blazer's Mills he fired the fatal bullet into the groin of Buckshot Roberts. After the war Bowdre rode with the Kid out of Fort Sumner but also tried to break his outlaw ties and lead an honest life. At Stinking Springs, Pat Garrett's bullet ended Charley's dilemma. (Museum of New Mexico)

7. Right: Thomas O'Folliard. At sixteen, Tom came up from Texas in time to participate in the final scenes of the Lincoln County War. With the Kid he escaped from the burning McSween house and then became his worshipful sidekick, happy even to hold his horse during nocturnal adventures with eager paramours. Tom died in front of Pat Garrett's Winchester at Fort Sumner in December 1880. (Museum of New Mexico)

8. John H. Tunstall (top left) and Alexander A. McSween (below). The young Englishman, Tunstall, teamed up with Scotsman McSween, Lincoln's only lawyer, to challenge the mercantile monopoly imposed on Lincoln County by Lawrence Murphy and his protégés, James J. Dolan and John H. Riley. (Special Collections, University of Arizona Library)

9. Top right: Jimmy Dolan stands beside his mentor, Murphy. Johnny Riley (below left) shrank from gunfire but was adept at devious dirty work. Dolan henchman Jacob B. Mathews (below right) led the posse that killed Tunstall. Mathews also shot the Kid in the thigh during the Brady assassination and testified in his murder trial. Understandably, Billy had no love for Mathews. (Mullin Collection, Haley History Center)

10. A veteran soldier and competent lawman, Sheriff William Brady favored the Murphy-Dolan side in the Lincoln County War. On April 1, 1878, Regulators gunned him down in the center of Lincoln's only street, escalating the war and ultimately gaining the Kid a murder conviction. (Special Collections, University of Arizona Library)

11. Blazer's Mills, scene of the classic Old West shootout that took the lives of Dick Brewer and Buckshot Roberts. The house in the right center was the focus of the battle. This picture was taken in 1884. (Special Collections, University of Arizona Library)

12. Left: Tunstall's foreman, Richard Brewer, served as first captain of the Regulators, until Buckshot Roberts blew his brains out at Blazer's Mills. (Special Collections, University of Arizona Library)

13. Below: Iowa dentist Joseph H. Blazer established a sawmill and gristmill at South Fork at the close of the Civil War. His big house on the Tularosa River provided the battleground for the gunfight between Dick Brewer's Regulators and Buckshot Roberts. (Special Collections, University of Arizona Library)

14. Right: Lieutenant Colonel Nathan A. M. Dudley, Fort Stanton's pompous and bombastic commanding officer, steered an erratic course in the Lincoln County War. His appearance in Lincoln on July 19, 1878, led to the defeat of the McSween forces. (Collections of the Massachusetts Commandery, Military Order of the Loyal Legion, U.S. Army Military History Institute, Carlisle, Pa.)

15. Robert Beckwith, son of patriarch Hugh Beckwith of Seven Rivers, led sheriff's possemen into McSween's backyard on the night of July 19, 1878, only to fall with a fatal bullet in his left eye. (Mullin Collection, Haley History Center)

16. Governor Lew Wallace, sent to New Mexico to end the Lincoln County War, proved more interested in completing his novel, *Ben-Hur*. His unfulfilled bargain with the Kid contributed to the boy's drift toward outlawry. (Museum of New Mexico)

17. Judge Warren Bristol presided over the Third Judicial District Court. Although partial to the Dolan cause in the Lincoln County War, he was easily frightened by the gunmen of both sides. In April 1881 he sentenced the Kid to be hanged for the murder of Sheriff Brady. (Museum of New Mexico)

18. John Simpson Chisum, the "cattle king of New Mexico." Chisum favored the McSween cause in the Lincoln County War but did not, as the Kid later insisted, promise Billy wages for his service as a McSween gunman. Nonetheless, Billy blamed Chisum for all his troubles. (Special Collections, University of Arizona Library)

Toscoso Texas

Thursday Oct 24th
1848

Know all persons by these presents
that I do hereby Sell and deliver
to Henry F. Hoyt one Sorrel
Horse Branded BB on left hip
and other indistinct Branded on
Shoulders. for the Sum of Seventyfive
Dollars. in hand received

W H Bonney

Witness
Jas McMasters
Geo F Howard

The above is The handwriting of the
outlaw known as "Billy the Kid"

19. Left: In the Texas Panhandle in the autumn of 1878 the Kid formed a close friendship with Dr. Henry Hoyt, later to pursue a distinguished medical career. This bill of sale, in the Kid's handwriting, legalized his gift to Hoyt of a sorrel horse. (Panhandle-Plains Historical Museum, Canyon, Texas)

20. Below: One of Billy's outlaw associates was Dave Rudabaugh, shown here (below) in 1886 after citizens of Parral, Mexico, separated his head from the rest of his body. (Mullin Collection, Haley History Center)

21. Right: A big, muscular bully, Bob Olinger fought against the McSween forces in the Lincoln County War. As a deputy sheriff, he died when Billy the Kid, escaping from confinement, blasted him in the face and chest with his own shotgun. (Special Collections, University of Arizona Library)

22. Below: The Kid became acquainted with Godfrey Gauss when the fatherly old German was cook at the Tunstall ranch. On April 28, 1881, Gauss was in the courthouse yard in Lincoln and helped Billy make good his escape. (Mullin Collection, Haley History Center)

23. Top left: Lincoln County Courthouse, formerly the Dolan store, scene of Billy the Kid's spectacular breakout on April 28, 1881. Bob Olinger entered the gate to the left of the balcony and was shot by the Kid from the upstairs side window. Later, Billy harangued townspeople from the balcony in front, then rode out of town. In February 1878, at the outbreak of the Lincoln County War, Billy and Fred Waite were held here for almost two days by Sheriff Brady and his possemen. (Mullin Collection, Haley History Center)

24. Right: Pat Garrett and John William Poe (seated) pose with a later deputy, Jim Brent. On July 14, 1881, Garrett and Poe, with Tip McKinney, ended the outlaw career of Billy the Kid. The shooting took place in the Maxwell house at old Fort Sumner (bottom left). Garrett was in Pete Maxwell's bedroom, the corner room in the foreground, when the Kid entered and was gunned down. (Mullin Collection, Haley History Center)

25. Marshall Ashmun Upson. A wandering journalist who became acquainted with the Kid while serving as Roswell postmaster, Ash Upson ghosted Pat Garrett's *Authentic Life of Billy the Kid* and thus contributed enormously to the legend that bloomed after Garrett killed Billy. (Special Collections, University of Arizona Library)

The Bargain

CHAPTER 11

Billy Bonney returned to Lincoln early in December 1878 with a vague notion of squaring himself with the law and going straight. Only ten months earlier he and Fred Waite had almost settled on their own spread on the upper Peñasco, but Tunstall's murder had intervened. Now that the Regulators had fallen apart, Billy had no close personal attachments beyond Tom O'Folliard. Constantly dodging the law was nerve-wracking, and after the danger and tumult of war a quiet farm of his own may have held momentary appeal. No one else had been punished for the excesses of the Lincoln County War, so why should he be? As he told his friend Sam Corbet, he was tired of fighting, wanted to stand his trial, and did not want to have to run from the Dolan outfit and the civil officers any longer.[1]

In Billy's absence from Lincoln, however, the old McSween-Dolan hostilities had not been laid to rest. In November, in fact, they had flared anew with the return of Sue McSween from a two-month stay in Las Vegas. With her came Huston Chapman, an excitable, one-armed lawyer who saw every issue in apocalyptic form. Together, they set out to bring Colonel Dudley to justice for the death of Alexander McSween. This crusade, acting on Dudley's volcanic temperament, stirred dread of new outbreaks of violence. Chapman in particular bred anxiety. He was "a 'rule or ruin' sort of fellow," said Ben Ellis, "whom nobody liked."[2]

Other developments had occurred during Billy's Texas sojourn

111

that bore on the new tensions. The federal investigator, Frank Warner Angel, had turned in a report damning to the administration of Governor Axtell. To restore order in the territory and credibility to its government, President Rutherford B. Hayes had named a new governor. He was Lew Wallace of Indiana, Civil War general, lawyer, politician, philosopher, musician, artist, sportsman, and rising literary star.

Governor Wallace had taken two steps toward ending the troubles in Lincoln County. Although he wanted the president to proclaim martial law, he had to settle for a proclamation of insurrection. This laid the constitutional groundwork to employ the army in suppressing the "insurrection," and for the first time since June, Colonel Dudley's soldiers could act as military posses for the civil authorities. Wallace had followed with a proclamation of his own, declaring an end to the disorders in Lincoln County and extending a "general pardon" to all offenders not already indicted by a grand jury.

Both documents contained flaws. The president's proclamation, while making policemen out of soldiers, stopped short of martial law and left the courts in civil hands. Witnesses, jurors, and indeed the judge himself remained in terror of both factions and shrank from forceful measures. Why arrest anyone, asked army officers, if the courts would not convict? The governor's proclamation declared a peace that did not exist, and his amnesty invited the return of dangerous men who had fled the country rather than risk military arrest.

While aggravating the stresses in Lincoln County, Wallace's proclamation did not lift the cloud from Billy Bonney. The "general pardon" applied only to men who had not been indicted. Billy stood under two indictments—territorial for the murder of Sheriff Brady and federal for the murder of Buckshot Roberts.

For the time being, Billy ran little risk of arrest. Peppin had ceased to function as sheriff months earlier and had been defeated in the November election. The new sheriff, George Kimball, did not immediately qualify to replace Peppin, which left law enforcement incapacitated until early in 1879.

With Chapman keeping up a ceaseless agitation, tempers ran high, and people feared another explosion. Except for Billy and Tom O'Folliard, most of the "iron clads" had left the country, but many who had ridden as Regulators remained. On the other side were Dolan, Billy Mathews, the ubiquitous Jesse Evans, and a newcomer, Billy Campbell. A wandering cowboy, Campbell was a fierce-looking man with a huge brown mustache. His disposition, ill-tempered and thoroughly mean, matched his appearance.

As Billy had told Sam Corbet, he did not want to fight Dolan and the law both, a sentiment given special force by the advent of the steady, competent Kimball as sheriff. Early on February 18, 1879, exactly a year after Tunstall's death, Billy put out a peace feeler, sending a message to a Dolan adherent at Fort Stanton asking whether the Dolan people proposed war or peace. The reply came back that they would come to Lincoln for a parley.[3]

That night the two sides faced each other from behind adobe walls on opposite sides of the street. Fifteen or twenty men had gathered, but only about half came as belligerents. Backing Billy were Tom O'Folliard, Joe Bowers, and Yginio Salazar, now recovered from the wounds received in McSween's backyard on July 19. Dolan headed the opposition, backed by Campbell, Evans, and Mathews.

Hard words from Jesse Evans almost provoked a gunfight. He declared that the Kid could not be dealt with and would have to be killed on the spot. Billy replied that they had met to make peace, and he did not care to begin the negotiations with a fight. As tempers cooled, the men left their barricades and gathered in the street. A few minutes of dickering produced agreement: no one on either side would kill anyone on the other, or testify against him in court, without first withdrawing from the treaty; and anyone who violated the agreement would be executed. Amid general handshaking, they reduced the terms to writing and signed the document.[4]

With peace declared, the uneasy friends embarked on a boozy celebration. Noisily, and growing drunker with each stop, they staggered from one drinking place to another. About 10:30 P.M., lurching up the dark street in front of the courthouse, they chanced to meet Huston Chapman, unarmed and his face swathed in bandages to ease the pain of a severe toothache. Billy, coolly sober in contrast to the others, watched the scene unfold.

Campbell challenged the lawyer and asked his name.

"My name is Chapman," was the reply.

"Then you dance," commanded Campbell, drawing his pistol and shoving it against Chapman's chest.

He did not propose to dance for a drunken crowd, answered the lawyer, adding, "Am I talking to Mr. Dolan?"

"No," interjected Jesse Evans, "but you are talking to a damned good friend of his."

Dolan, standing about ten feet behind Chapman, drew his pistol and drunkenly fired a shot into the street. At the report, Campbell's trigger finger jerked and the revolver's muzzle exploded into Chapman's chest.

"My God, I am killed," he exclaimed as he slumped to the ground, his clothing ablaze from the powder flash.

Chapman's killing did not dampen the revelry. Leaving his body burning in the street, the celebrants made for Cullum's eatery. Over an oyster supper, Dolan and Campbell decided that someone should return to place a pistol in Chapman's hand so that the killing could be explained as self-defense. Billy, anxious to part with the group, volunteered. Taking Campbell's pistol, he went outside, found his horse, and rode out of town.[5]

Aside from getting implicated in still another murder, Billy had good reason to leave town. Sheriff Kimball had spotted him earlier in the day and had gone to Fort Stanton for a military posse to aid in his arrest. Accompanied by a lieutenant and twenty cavalrymen, Kimball returned to Lincoln shortly before midnight. They searched the town without finding Billy, but they did come across Chapman's corpse, his clothing in ashes and his upper body severely burned. They carried it to the courthouse.[6]

Whether Chapman's death was deliberate murder or simply a drunken accident stirred heated debate at the time and has yet to be definitively resolved. Years later one of the bystanders recalled it in terms that ring true for the time and place. When ordered to dance, he said, Chapman refused, "so one of the boys shot him through the heart and he fell over against me, dead. There was really no malice in this shooting. Life was held lightly down there in those days."[7]

The killing of Huston Chapman whipped up intense excitement among Lincoln's residents, who feared that it signaled a fresh burst of violence. They applauded Colonel Dudley's prompt response to their appeal for protection and drew comfort from the presence of a detail of soldiers that he stationed in Lincoln. With even more relief they greeted the news that the governor himself was finally coming to Lincoln.

Lew Wallace had no sooner taken the oath of office the previous October 1 than he had vowed to go to Lincoln and investigate in person. He had procrastinated ever since. He put forth unconvincing excuses to explain the delay, but the truth probably lay in a literary project in which he had become deeply immersed. It was a sweeping saga of biblical times, and night after night he withdrew to the inner recesses of the governor's palace to spin the fictional adventures of a hero he had named Ben-Hur. Not until the blazing corpse of Huston Chapman nudged aside Ben-Hur did Lew Wallace make good on his promise.

Once in Lincoln, which he reached on March 5, the governor moved swiftly to reestablish public confidence in the government. As a first step, he got rid of the troublesome Colonel Dudley. Colonel Edward Hatch, military commander in New Mexico, had accompanied Wallace from Santa Fe and now yielded to his insistence that Dudley had become so enmeshed in local factionalism as to destroy his usefulness. On March 8, triggering a predictable cry of outrage, Hatch relieved Dudley of the command of Fort Stanton.[8]

The new commander, Captain Henry Carroll, proved much more compliant. On March 11, after quizzing Justice Wilson at length, Wallace furnished Carroll with a list of thirty-five names of men who should be arrested and brought into court. Most could go free simply by pleading the governor's amnesty, but not Bonney, Waite, Bowdre, and other "iron clads" who had already been indicted. "Push the 'Black Knights' without rest," Wallace urged Carroll, who probably puzzled over the governor's medieval romanticism.[9]

The governor especially wanted the men involved in the Chapman killing. This had occurred after the amnesty proclamation, and their conviction would go a long way toward reviving public faith in the law and the courts. He had heard that Billy Bonney and Tom O'Folliard were at Las Tablas—"Board Town"—some twenty miles north of Lincoln and that Dolan, Evans, and Campbell were at Lawrence Murphy's old ranch thirty miles west of Lincoln. At Wallace's request, Colonel Hatch sent detachments to find the culprits. Las Tablas failed to yield the Kid and O'Folliard, but the troopers returned with Evans, Campbell, and Mathews. Dolan too fell into military hands, and the four were confined at Fort Stanton.[10]

Meanwhile, Captain Carroll pushed the "Black Knights" without rest. With methodical persistence, he kept his patrols scouring the country and rounding up wanted men. By the end of March he had a dozen in custody, and a week later a newspaper reporter observed that the fort's lockup had become "a 'Bastille' crowded with civil prisoners."[11]

Wallace squirmed over a painful dilemma. On the one hand, until citizens acted fearlessly as witnesses and jurors, the courts could not convict. On the other, until the courts convicted, citizens would not act fearlessly. In dread of retribution, witnesses to crimes refused to swear the affidavits that were legally required as a basis for the issue of arrest warrants. "The truth is," confessed Wallace, "the people here are so intimidated that some days will have to [pass] before they can be screwed up to the point of making the necessary affidavits." Bowing to the governor's pleas, Colonel Hatch authorized the troops to make arrests without warrants, and some of the prisoners loudly protested their unlawful detention by the military. Lincoln's only lawyer was kept busy preparing writs of habeas corpus.[12]

Secure in their haven near San Patricio, Billy and Tom kept abreast of Wallace's campaign with an absorption rooted in self-interest. Billy's quick mind instantly focused on Wallace's need. On March 13 he sat down to pen the first of several letters that one of his San Patricio friends carried to the harried governor.

"I was present when Mr. Chapman was murdered and know who did it," Billy wrote. "If it was arranged so that I could appear at court, I could give the desired information, but I have indictments against me for things that happened in the late Lincoln County War, and am afraid to give up because my enemies would kill me." "If it is in your power to annul those indictments," Billy suggested, "I hope you will do so, so as to give me a chance to explain."

Billy then concluded: "I have no wish to fight any more, indeed I have not raised an arm since your proclamation. As to my character I refer you to any of the citizens, for the majority of them are my friends and have been helping me all they could. I am called Kid Antrim, but Antrim is my stepfather's name."[13]

Those may have been hollow words contrived to win the governor's sympathy. More likely, as confirmed by his avowal to Sam Corbet, they expressed his true feeling at the moment. And a great many citizens would indeed have vouched for his character.

Billy Bonney had embarked on a risky venture. In exchange for lifting the indictments against him, he offered himself as the one thing Wallace needed most: an eyewitness to murder who would testify in court. Billy hated Dolan, Evans, Mathews, and Campbell and would have enjoyed seeing them locked behind bars. In openly testifying against them, however, he placed his life at peril, the more so because he broke the peace accord concluded on the night of Chapman's murder. That document specified death for any violator. That the other signatories were confined at Fort Stanton afforded some comfort, but not much.

Not above bargaining with a nineteen-year-old outlaw, Wallace responded immediately. "Come to the house of old Squire Wilson," he wrote on March 15, "at nine (9) o'clock next Monday night alone." Billy should steal into town from the foothills on the south, Wallace instructed, and knock on the east door of Wilson's jacal. The governor also touched on the two assurances Billy needed to enter into a bargain: immunity from prosecution and protection from reprisals. "I have authority to exempt you from prosecution if you will testify to what you say you know," Wallace wrote. "The object of the meeting at Squire Wilson's is to arrange the matter in a way to make your life safe. To do that the utmost secrecy is to be used. *So come alone.* Don't tell anybody—not a living soul—where you are coming or the object. If you could trust Jesse Evans, you can trust me."

After dark on March 17, the governor and the justice of the peace sat tensely expectant in the candle-lit gloom of Wilson's little dwelling near the courthouse. At the appointed hour the door vibrated with a firm knock.

"Come in," said Wallace.

Billy entered warily, a Winchester in his left hand, a pistol in his right. "I was to meet the governor here," he said. "Is the governor here?"

Wallace rose, extended his hand, and invited the boy in. The three sat at a table, and Wallace explained his plan.[14]

"Testify before the grand jury and the trial court and convict the murderer of Chapman," Wallace proposed, "and I will let you go scott-free with a pardon in your pocket for all your own misdeeds."

"If I were to do what you ask," replied Billy, "they would kill me."

No, answered Wallace, he would contrive a fake arrest that would look genuine to the world, then keep Billy in protective confinement. With the bargain sealed, Billy slipped out into the night.

Billy could hardly have received more unsettling tidings than reached him at San Patricio the very next day, March 18. Jesse Evans and Billy Campbell had persuaded their guard to desert and, with his help, had broken out of the Fort Stanton lockup and lost themselves in the mountains. Even in protective custody, the Kid could readily visualize himself shot down by these two before he could relate his story to the grand jury. "Please tell you know who that I do not know what to do, now as those Prisoners have escaped," he wrote to Squire Wilson on March 20.[15]

On the same day, however, Billy followed this letter with a long message assuring Wallace that he would keep his part of the bargain. "But be sure to have men come that you can depend on," he beseeched. "I am not afraid to die like a man fighting but I would not like to be killed like a dog unarmed."

He then offered detailed counsel on where to look for Evans and Campbell. "It is not my place to advise you," he concluded, "but I am anxious to have them caught, and perhaps know how men hide from Soldiers, better than you."

The next day, March 21, Sheriff Kimball and a posse surrounded the house of one of San Patricio's many Gutierrezes, a mile below town, and arrested Billy Bonney and Tom O'Folliard. Escorted to Lincoln, they were placed under guard in the home of Juan Patrón, next door to the Montaño store where Wallace lodged.

That the Kid had not exaggerated in assuring Wallace that many citizens would vouch for him became clear several days later. In reporting the incident to Secretary of the Interior Carl Schurz, however, the patrician governor betrayed the condescension with which he looked not only on his prisoner but on the entire territory. "A precious specimen nick-named 'The Kid,'" he wrote, "whom the Sheriff is holding here in the Plaza, as it is called, is an object of tender regard. I heard singing and music the other night; going to the door, I found the minstrels of the village actually serenading the fellow in his prison." [16]

Billy not only stood ready to testify in the Chapman case but also proved willing to explain the outlaw scene in general. In a long meeting with Wallace, he poured out explicit details of outlaw trails, hiding places, techniques, and above all personalities ranging all the way from Seven Rivers to Silver City. Once again he had broken the terms of the peace treaty of February 18. [17]

Billy was soon joined in his "prison" by an old friend. Wallace had formed a militia company, the Lincoln County Rifles, and had sent it out with his list of culprits. Early in April the unit rode over to Fort Sumner to search for Charley Bowdre and Doc Scurlock, both under federal indictment in the Roberts killing. Bowdre got wind of the threat and fled, but Scurlock was seized, brought back to Lincoln, and confined with Billy Bonney. [18]

Exactly what Wallace promised Billy seems to have been left

vague in both their minds. In his letter to Billy, Wallace said that he could exempt him from prosecution, whereas in his memory of the meeting in Squire Wilson's dwelling he offered a pardon. A pardon could have been granted at any time before or after trial. An exemption demanded more immediate action, before court convened.

An exemption, moreover, did not lie within the governor's power unless agreed to by the prosecuting attorney. As it turned out, Billy had more to fear from William L. Rynerson than from Evans and Campbell, who prudently disappeared into Texas. A Dolan ally throughout the Lincoln County War, an overt partisan who thought nothing of subverting the law to his private interests, Rynerson could hardly be expected to view the Kid with compassion.

To make matters worse, Wallace did not even remain in Lincoln for the spring term of court but instead returned to Santa Fe and, doubtless, Ben-Hur. A Las Vegas attorney, Ira Leonard, represented Wallace as an aide to Rynerson, who neither needed nor wanted an aide.

Judge Bristol opened the proceedings on April 14. Fear and intimidation stalked witnesses, jurors, and even the judge. Partisans on both sides championed the old Dolan and McSween interests. Judge Bristol, anxious to get out of town, pushed the grand jury hard. He showed "the timidity of a child," Leonard complained, "and stood in fear of the desperate characters."[19]

True to his word, Billy Bonney took the stand to name the slayers of Chapman. So did Tom O'Folliard, who had also witnessed the killing. The testimony identified both Campbell and Dolan as the killers and described the role of Evans, in court legalese, as to "incite, move, procure, aid, counsel, hire and command" them to commit the deed. Based on this testimony, the grand jury indicted Dolan and Campbell for murder and Evans as an accessory. Mathews escaped notice.[20]

Apparently District Attorney Rynerson had allowed Governor Wallace to believe that, in exchange for turning state's evidence, the Kid would be released from prosecution in the Brady killing. Rynerson reneged, however, prompting the *Mesilla Independent*'s comment that "considering the character of the man [Billy] the action was right in the premises."[21]

"He is bent on going for the Kid," Ira Leonard wrote to Wallace of Rynerson's posture, and "he is bent on pushing him to the wall. He is a Dolan man and is defending him by his conduct all he can." Far from dropping the prosecution of Billy, the district attorney pressed the case vigorously. On Rynerson's motion, Judge Bristol granted a change of venue to Doña Ana County, where jurors would be less likely to sympathize with the likable young fellow.[22]

Despite Rynerson's obstructionism, the grand jury spewed out indictments—some two hundred falling on fifty men. Dominated by former McSween followers, the jury took note chiefly of the offenses of Dolanites. Even Colonel Dudley, target of Sue McSween's vendetta, found himself charged with arson in the burning of the McSween house.

Only two people actually came to trial, and they went free. Judge Bristol had already released fifteen of the Stanton prisoners on writs of habeas corpus. Others who had been indicted, such as Evans and Campbell, were nowhere near Lincoln, and those who were in town pleaded the governor's amnesty and had the charges quashed. A few who chose to fight, such as Dudley, Dolan, and Peppin, obtained changes of venue from Judge Bristol. All ultimately won acquittal or had the charges dropped by friendly prosecutors. Jimmy Dolan, a prime author of the war, slipped easily into a new life of respectability and became one of Lincoln County's most honored citizens.

Billy Bonney enjoyed no such official favor. By bearing witness against Dolan and his friends, the Kid had planted in Rynerson and even Bristol a fierce resolve to see him hang for the Brady killing. Even the favor of the governor could not offset the implacable hostility of these two pillars of the law.

With Doc Scurlock, Billy "perambulated at leisure" around Lincoln, as the *Independent* complained. Technically under arrest, the Kid was allowed considerable latitude by a tolerant Sheriff Kimball, who knew the circumstances under which he had been taken into custody. "Kid and Scurlock are expected to walk off at any time," observed the *Mesilla News*, "as little restraint is placed on these favorites of the governor."[23]

Billy tarried in Lincoln to aid in Sue McSween's continuing crusade against Colonel Dudley, a cause in which he could participate wholeheartedly. The army had appointed a court of inquiry to look into Dudley's actions in Lincoln on July 19, 1878, and Sue was busily assembling witnesses who would swear that soldiers bolstered Peppin's posse in the siege of the McSween house and even helped set the house afire.

The court began taking testimony at Fort Stanton on May 12, 1879. Governor Wallace led off as the first of more than sixty witnesses. Several, including Sue McSween, swore to the active participation of soldiers in the fighting. In testimony given on May 28, Billy Bonney described the breakout from the McSween house and contended that soldiers posted at the southwest corner of the Tunstall store fired at him and the others as they dashed to safety. A parade of witnesses dissented, and Dudley's counsel, Henry Waldo, persuasively discredited the allegation, as well as the motives of those who had conceived it.[24]

In particular he tore into Billy. Waldo was a master at sarcasm, and in his summation he wielded it brutally to demolish both the character and the testimony of Billy Bonney.

"Then was brought forward," he said contemptuously, "William Bonney, alias 'Antrim,' alias 'the Kid,' a precocious criminal of the worst type, although hardly up to his majority." Billy was the perpetrator of the "cowardly and atrocious assassinations" of Sheriff Brady and Andrew Roberts, Waldo pointed out, and "there were warrants enough for him on the 19th of July last to have plastered him from his head to his feet, yet he was lugged in to do service as a witness."

With allowance for hyperbole, that came close to the truth. Just as he signed the affidavit that Rob Widenmann probably composed for the Angel investigation, Billy now told the army judges what Sue McSween wanted them to hear.

As the Dudley Court ground on through June to its conclusion—exoneration of Dudley—Billy Bonney faced another danger.

Early in June, Judge Bristol convened the United States District Court in Mesilla. The U.S. marshal for New Mexico, John Sherman, received instructions to produce both the Kid and Scurlock to answer the charge of murdering Buckshot Roberts within a federal jurisdiction. Sherman procrastinated, but finally took steps to have the two "prisoners" escorted to Mesilla.[25]

Billy Bonney could not have looked with optimism on the prospect of facing Judge Bristol again. He had every reason to feel disillusioned and disgruntled. He had struck a bargain with the governor of the territory, had risked his life to carry out his promise, yet had received nothing in return. The spring session of territorial court had left no doubt in his mind that Rynerson and Bristol intended to convict him of the murder of Sheriff Brady. Now he confronted the more immediate threat of a murder trial in federal court for the Roberts killing. However sincere the governor's intentions, he had not lived up to his promise. He had not persuaded Rynerson to drop the territorial charges against Billy, and he had made no move to grant a pardon. The law seemed forgiving of everyone except Billy Bonney.

On the night of June 17, 1879, with a sense of betrayal, Billy simply rode out of Lincoln. Doc Scurlock went along, while Sheriff Kimball looked the other way.[26]

Billy spent the next few weeks in Las Vegas. According to charges later filed in district court there, on July 1 a person known only as "Kid" operated an unlawful monte gaming table. Billy Bonney loved monte and dealt it expertly, but neither the charges nor the arrest warrant ever caught up with the accused. He may have been Billy Bonney or another of the many "Kids" who peopled the frontier West.[27]

In July 1879 Las Vegas offered an appealing setting for gamblers and every other variety of adventurer, confidence man, and criminal. On Independence Day the first train on the Santa Fe Railroad steamed into the "New Town" where the depot was located. Night and day Las Vegas throbbed with the raucous hilarity that marked the advance of all the transcontinental lines. Billy would have been drawn by the excitement and opportunity.

Other testimony to Billy's presence in Las Vegas came from his old friend Dr. Henry Hoyt. Now tending bar in one of the railhead community's many saloons, Hoyt took Sunday dinner in late July at a popular hotel associated with the hot springs six miles northwest of town. Here, to his astonishment, he found himself seated next to Billy Bonney, who in turn introduced him to a companion, a "Mr. Howard." Later, Billy confided that Mr. Howard was none other than the notorious outlaw Jesse James, traveling incognito.[28]

By early August Billy was back around Lincoln, provoking Sheriff Kimball into halfhearted efforts to arrest him. On August 9, with an officer and fifteen men from Fort Stanton, Kimball tracked Billy down the Bonito Valley and cornered him in a cabin six miles below Lincoln. Surrounding the cabin in the darkness, they settled down to await daylight. But the resourceful Kid recalled a similarly desperate predicament in his past. As the Fort Stanton commander reported, "he escaped by climbing up a chimney, leaving his arms behind, and escaping under cover of night." If he learned of the feat, Sheriff Whitehill of Silver City must have enjoyed a chuckle.[29]

On another occasion, Billy slipped into Lincoln and went to Sue McSween's house. He had heard that Frank Coe had come down from Colorado to retrieve his hay-cutting machine and was staying there. While Tom O'Folliard held the horses outside, Billy went to the door. Inside, Frank sawed his fiddle while Sue and a sergeant from Fort Stanton danced. Billy entered, confronted the soldier, and asked what he was doing there.

"I guess you ought to know," the soldier replied.

"Well," said the Kid, "why don't you do something?"

"We're sent out," the sergeant answered lamely, "but don't have to do anything."

To break the tension, Frank began to fiddle again. "Kid went dancing around with his carbine in hand," Coe remembered. "Had the whole room to dance in, but kept dancing around and over the Sergeant's feet and Sergeant kept drawing them up under him. I thought there was going to be a kill and stopped playing, and said 'Come here, Billy, I want to talk with you.'" As they stepped out the front door, a frightened sergeant quickly let himself out the back door and vanished.

"I told Kid that they were looking for him," Frank remembered. "He said he knew it, but he was tired of dodging and had run from them about long enough."[30]

In truth, Billy Bonney had scarcely begun his career of dodging. With both federal and territorial murder charges hanging over him, he had no choice but to continue dodging unless Governor Wallace came to his aid. That seemed increasingly unlikely. Wallace had failed to deflect District Attorney Rynerson's relentless pursuit at the April term of territorial court and apparently had done nothing to interfere with the effort to bring Billy before the federal court in June. Billy could conclude only that the governor had forsaken him.

As Billy later explained his reasoning, "I went up to Lincoln to stand my trial on the warrant that was out for me, but the territory took a change of venue to Doña Ana, and I knew that I had no show, and so I skinned out."[31]

The Rustler

As he had done more than once in the past, when Billy Bonney "skinned out" of Lincoln, he headed for Fort Sumner.

For Billy, the old fort turned frontier town held many attractions. The most important, in the closing months of 1879, was an almost total absence of law. Fort Sumner lay along the southern margin of San Miguel County, one hundred miles from the county seat at Las Vegas. The sheriff and his deputies had more than they could handle in that booming railroad town. They did not often get to Anton Chico or Puerto de Luna, much less to distant Fort Sumner. Billy did not need to worry that a lawman with a posse of soldiers and a handful of arrest warrants would disturb his sleep.

Another attraction was a wide circle of friends—or, increasingly, men who professed friendship rather than give offense. The Hispanic sheepherders who drifted with their flocks across the grassy plains were authentic friends. At the sheep camps Billy could always count on hospitality and any help he needed in evading the law. The Anglo cattlemen would help too, though less genuinely and more in apprehension than true fellowship.

And here, in addition, Billy counted at least one old comrade from the Lincoln County War. Doc Scurlock had gone to Texas, but Charley Bowdre remained. He worked for wages for Thomas G. Yerby, a respected stockman who had bought Lucien Maxwell's blooded cattle and established a ranch at Las Cañaditas, twenty miles northeast of Sumner. Besides Charley, Billy could, as always, count on "Red Tom" O'Folliard, the strapping youth who had clung to him like a shadow ever since the breakout from the Mc-Sween house.

Fort Sumner boasted a lively social scene that appealed to Billy. The saloons of Beaver Smith and Bob Hargrove rocked with hilarity as cowboys, sheepmen, and outlaws congregated to carouse and gamble. Billy passed many hours dealing monte, especially in Smith's place. Beaver Smith operated the town's most popular drinking hole. A former chuck wrangler for John Chisum, Smith's chief distinction was the Chisum brand, unwillingly acquired when he chose the wrong side in a cowboy strike. As an acquaintance explained it, "the boys got drunk one day and branded him—put a rail on his side and jinglebobbed his damned ears."[1]

A powerful appeal, as Billy well remembered from his sojourn at Fort Sumner in the fall of 1878, lay in the frequent and spirited *bailes*. As Pete Maxwell's sister Paulita reminisced,

Fort Sumner was a gay little place. The weekly dance was an event, and pretty girls from Santa Rosa, Puerto de Luna, Anton Chico, and from towns and ranches fifty miles away drove in to attend it. Billy the Kid cut quite a gallant figure at these affairs. He was not handsome but he had a certain sort of boyish good looks. He was always smiling and good-natured and very polite and danced remarkably well, and the little Mexican beauties made eyes at him from behind their fans and used all their coquetries to capture him and were very vain of his attentions.[2]

"Billy the Kid," Paulita continued, "fascinated many women." "In every *placeta* in the Pecos some little señorita was proud to be known as his *querida*." Although she later denied it, Paulita herself was one of the *queridas*. Another was Celsa Gutierrez, whose sister was married to a tall, lanky, former buffalo hunter named Pat Garrett. A third, Abrana García, bore Billy two daughters, who later succumbed to diphtheria. Gossip also connected him to Nasaria Yerby and Charley Bowdre's wife, Manuela. Nasaria was Tom Yerby's eighteen-year-old "housekeeper," whose year-old daughter was commonly believed to have been fathered by Billy.[3]

Billy's intentions as he took up residence in Fort Sumner are ob-

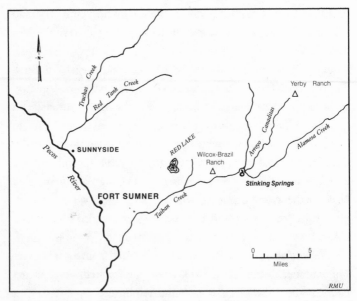

Fort Sumner and vicinity, 1880–81

scure. Disillusioned with the system of justice, he may have decided to get back at his persecutors by turning to open outlawry. More likely, since he did not give up his efforts to have the charges against him set aside, he simply drifted ambivalently into a life of more and more frequent crime.

In 1880 Fort Sumner afforded an ideal incubator for crime. Criminals abounded, drawn into New Mexico by the Santa Fe Railroad, driven into New Mexico by the Texas Rangers. Perhaps fifty or sixty hard cases descended on Fort Sumner, strategically situated on the western edge of a burgeoning cattle empire and under almost no risk from law officers. Consorting with these men in Beaver Smith's saloon, Billy Bonney, Charley Bowdre, and Tom O'Folliard easily fell in with their schemes.

Billy's travels in the Texas Panhandle in the autumn of 1878 had provided him with a glimpse of the possibilities. The big ranches—the LIT, the LX, and others—lay along the northern edge of the Staked Plains, a vast table of grass stretching south from the Canadian River for almost three hundred miles and on the west shouldering into New Mexico to the borders of the Pecos Valley. In winter, fierce "northers," checked by barely a single tree, drove the scattered herds south across this level plateau. Enterprising New Mexican rustlers had only to ride up the western scarp of the caprock, round up drifting strays, and drive them off the range before the cowboys from the north could complete their spring sweep.[4]

An ideal place to assemble and hide drifted cattle was Los Portales, a hollow in the plains about seventy miles southeast of Fort Sumner where a spring issued from a rough rock formation. The rocks reminded Hispanics of porches, hence "Portales." Here, outlaws hid their booty. Here, as Billy later admitted, he and Charley Bowdre had a "ranch."

Markets for Panhandle beef lay to the west, in Billy's old retreats amid the mountains of Lincoln County. One was the U.S. government at Fort Stanton and the Mescalero Apache Indian Agency, reached indirectly through a middleman based on the far side of the Sierra Blanca. Here Pat Coghlan reigned as the "King of Tularosa." A six-foot, ruddy-faced Irishman, powerfully built and athletic despite his nearly sixty years, Pat had settled at Tularosa in 1874, opened a saloon and hotel, and built up an extensive ranching enterprise. Acquiring rustled cows for twelve dollars a head and selling them to government contractors for twice that, Coghlan earned substantial profits. "Coghlan was stealing every way he could," recalled one of his cowpunchers. "He was a pretty hard old thief."[5]

A second market was the booming new mining town of White Oaks. Sprawling across a narrow, mountain-girt valley forty-five miles by wagon road northwest of Lincoln, White Oaks had blossomed almost overnight after gold was discovered there in 1879. Increasingly, White Oaks rather than Lincoln became Billy's home away from Fort Sumner. The town's ten saloons vibrated with life, the gaming tables stoked his fondness for monte, and a ready market existed for almost anything one had to sell, including illicit beef.

★

"I wasn't the leader of any gang," Billy later told reporters.[6] Contrary to legend, he probably spoke the truth. The outlaw temperament did not lend itself to the discipline and structure of an organization commanded by a single chief. Rather, impromptu gangs formed for particular operations, then dissolved and reformed in differing strength and composition.

Of the names generally assigned to Billy's "gang" in 1880, only O'Folliard and Bowdre recur consistently. Three other men frequently worked with Billy, Tom, and Charley: David Rudabaugh, Thomas Pickett, and William Wilson. That they also ran with men not associated with Billy and engaged in exploits of which he was not a part indicates that they were not members of an organized gang headed by the Kid. When they came together for particular undertakings, Billy's quick mind and forceful personality probably gave him a controlling influence. But the older and fiercely independent Rudabaugh, for one, would not have tolerated any hint of command.

Dave Rudabaugh was a stocky man about forty years of age, with long brown hair curling at the tips, a square-jawed face, a big mustache and, in the field, a shaggy beard. He had rustled cattle in Texas, held up trains in Kansas, and robbed stagecoaches in New Mexico. With others of the "Dodge City gang," he had plagued Las Vegas for six months with theft and confidence games while City Marshal John J. Webb gave covert support. In return, when Webb found himself in jail convicted of murder, Rudabaugh tried to break him out. A shootout erupted, and Dave or his accomplice gunned down the jailer. The killing of a Hispanic lawman by an Anglo outlaw so enraged the Hispanic population of Las Vegas that Rudabaugh fled down the Pecos to Fort Sumner, where in the late spring of 1880 he cast his lot with the other rustlers who hung out at Beaver Smith's saloon. For unadulterated evil, Rudabaugh far outshone Billy.[7]

Another who fell in with Billy was Tom Pickett, the black sheep of a prominent Texas family, who had followed Rudabaugh from Kansas to New Mexico. Roughly Billy's age, the erect, powerfully built youth had served briefly as a Texas Ranger, then made himself so unpopular as a Las Vegas policeman that he had to flee because, as a local editor later recalled, "a 'job' was put up to kill him." Like Rudabaugh, he found his way into the Fort Sumner area, where

Charley Bowdre hired him to help on the Yerby ranch. When Bowdre rode with the Kid, so did Pickett.[8]

A third who became closely identified with the Kid during 1880 was Billy Wilson. An Ohioan, he reached Fort Sumner by way of Dodge City, White Oaks, and Lincoln. He was two years younger than the other Billy, was stouter, and had a light complexion, sandy hair, and a serious disposition.[9]

Although Billy ramrodded no formally organized gang, as the months of 1880 passed he grew more and more prominent in the outlaw circles of Fort Sumner, and the people of White Oaks and Lincoln came to regard him as a leader in the rustling fraternity. Several events spotlighted his name.

One was the second killing with which the Kid can be solely and incontestably credited.[10]

This feat grew out of the reappearance in the Pecos Valley of the Chisum herds, which had been moved to the Texas Panhandle in the autumn of 1878 to escape the ravages of the Lincoln County War. At that time the cows belonged to Hunter, Evans and Company, with John Chisum simply acting as manager. Subsequently, the firm sold them back into Chisum ownership—not to Old John but to his brothers James and Pitzer. Back on the Pecos, the Chisum stock suffered repeated depredations during the last months of 1879. Justly or not, much of the suspicion fell on Billy Bonney.

On January 10, 1880, Jim Chisum and three hands, herding a small bunch of cows, camped near Fort Sumner. The stock, rounded up in a canyon to the north, bore crudely altered Chisum brands and so represented recovered stolen property. With two companions, Billy Bonney rode out to the camp and asked to inspect the brands. Chisum, who suspected Billy himself of the brand artistry, agreed.

Afterward, Billy said to Chisum, "Bring your boys down to the fort, it's my treat."

At Bob Hargrove's saloon in Fort Sumner, a Texas braggart and bully named Joe Grant was already obnoxiously drunk. Earlier he had accosted Billy Bonney with the challenge, "I'll bet $25 that I kill a man today before you do." Now he staggered over to Jack Finan, one of the Chisum hands, admired the ivory-handled revolver in Finan's holster, pulled it out, and replaced it with his own. Rather than antagonize the drunk, Jack said nothing.

Billy drifted over to Grant, looked at Finan's pistol, and observed, "That's a mighty nice looking six-shooter you got." Casually lifting it out of Grant's holster, Billy examined it admiringly and deftly spun the cylinder. Earlier, Finan had fired several shots at a mark, leaving three of the chambers loaded with empty shell cases. When Billy handed the pistol back to Grant, the cylinder was positioned so that the hammer would fall on one of these cases rather than a loaded round.

Grant grew louder and more menacing, smashing bottles on the back bar and vowing to shoot someone. Eyeing Jim Chisum, he proclaimed his intention of killing John Chisum.

"Hold on," said Billy, "you got the wrong sow by the ear." This was John's brother Jim, he pointed out.

"That's a lie," shouted Grant.

Billy turned and walked toward the door. As Jim's son Will described it, "Grant squared off at Billy, who when he heard the click whirled around and 'bang, bang, bang.' Right in the chin—could cover all of them with a half a dollar."

"Joe," observed Billy, "I've been there too often for you."

The shooting of Joe Grant earned Billy some notoriety, but like the dispatch of Windy Cahill, it had enough extenuating circumstances to prompt little concern in the Fort Sumner area. Had Billy perpetrated a cold-blooded murder, public opinion would have been aroused and the sheriff of San Miguel County moved to investigate. That the newspapers gave the event virtually no notice, and that the law never acted, stamp it as simply another saloon dispute that ended fatally.[11]

Billy's own view of the affair was summed up in a flippant remark to Postmaster Milnor Rudulph of Sunnyside, near Fort Sumner. Asked what lay behind the shooting, Billy replied, "Oh, nothing; it was a game of two and I got there first." Commented a witness, "The daring young rascal seemed to enjoy the telling as well as the killing."[12]

Another source of Billy's prominence was John Chisum. Somehow, the youth conceived the notion that Chisum owed him wages for fighting McSween's battles in the Lincoln County War. If Billy truly thought that, he had concocted a self-serving rationalization for his criminal activities. Chisum lent no more than his name and sympathy to the McSween cause and in fact had been absent from the territory during much of the war. Certainly he never intimated that he would bankroll any of the McSween warriors.

Nonetheless, Billy indignantly voiced his claim whenever he had the chance. Once, indeed, in the spring of 1880, he accosted Chisum personally at Fort Sumner.

As Will Chisum heard it from his father, Old John replied, "Billy, you know as well as I do that I never hired you to fight in the Lincoln County War. I always pay my honest debts. I don't owe you anything, and you can kill me but you won't knock me out of many years. I'm an old man now."

Billy hesitated a moment, then replied, "Aw, you ain't worth killing."[13]

According to popular belief, Billy vowed to get his due by plundering the Chisum herds. If so, like Joe Grant, Billy had "the wrong sow by the ear." By 1880 the only Chisum cows in the Pecos Valley belonged to Jim and Pitzer Chisum. Billy made one known foray against their stock, according to charges they filed in district court in Las Vegas. On March 10, 1880, he made off with ten steers, ten bullocks, and two cows with a total value of $220—scarcely a crippling loss.[14]

Yet even at the time, both Billy and Chisum perpetuated the notion of a deadly feud, and it gradually became part of the public perception. For at least some of his rising fame, therefore, the Kid could credit John Chisum himself.

As a third basis of growing distinction, Billy found himself singled out as a supplier of stolen beef to Pat Coghlan. In May 1880, with Charley Bowdre and Tom O'Folliard, Billy assembled nearly sixty head of Panhandle beef at Los Portales, then drove them west to the neighborhood of White Oaks and sold them to Tom Cooper, a middleman acting for Pat Coghlan. This yielded Billy and his comrades a little more than seven hundred dollars for their labors, hardly a big take, and returned Coghlan one hundred percent on his investment.[15]

At this same time, plagued by rustlers, the Texas victims banded together and formed the Panhandle Stock Association. In autumn the association hired a detective, Frank Stewart, and sent him with four cowboys on a scout into New Mexico. At White Oaks, draped over a corral fence, Stewart's group found hides with the LIT brand, and from residents they picked up accusations that threw the blame on Billy Bonney. Acting on Stewart's report, the Texas ranchers decided to send an expedition to New Mexico to recover their cattle and, if possible, put an end to the rustling career of the Kid.[16]

Not only the Panhandle stockmen had Billy in their sights. Early in September 1880 complaints reached the U.S. Treasury Department that counterfeit bank notes were being passed in Lincoln and White Oaks. Suspicion fell on two of Billy's sometime confederates, Tom Cooper and Billy Wilson. The U.S. Secret Service sent a "special operative," Azariah F. Wild, to investigate. Basing himself in Lincoln early in October, Wild launched a probe that linked the counterfeiters to the Fort Sumner rustlers and that shed occasional light on the doings of Billy Bonney.[17]

Wild's inquiries seemed to point to the livery stable of W. H. West and Sam Diedrick in White Oaks as a center of dealings in both illicit money and illicit beef. Another gathering place for the malefactors was Beaver Smith's saloon in Fort Sumner. Still another was the ranch of Sam Diedrick's brother Dan at Bosque Grande, Chisum's old headquarters on the Pecos twenty-eight miles north of Roswell. Wild thought not only Wilson and Cooper guilty of passing the bogus money, but other rustlers as well, including the Kid.

The state of justice in Lincoln County, and indeed in all New Mexico, appalled Operative Wild. In Lincoln the citizens stood in such dread of the outlaws that they would not testify in the courts, even though they knew the guilty parties and what they had done. Only a few would help Wild, and then only in the deepest secrecy.

He could not trust Sheriff George Kimball, who was friendly with the culprits and often played cards with "Billy Kid." Nor could Wild get the cooperation he thought his due from the U.S. marshal for New Mexico, John Sherman, and the U.S. attorney, Sidney M. Barnes. Because of their lack of energy, he concluded, men such as the Kid, although wanted on federal charges, could range with impunity from Fort Sumner to Lincoln, committing fresh crimes and terrorizing the citizens.

Impatient with the lethargy of the federal authorities in Santa Fe, Wild decided to mount his own offensive against the outlaws. He found two men he thought he could trust, John Hurley and Robert Olinger, both members of the Dolan faction in the Lincoln County War and veterans of Peppin's posse in the Five-Day Battle. After much delay, Wild got Marshal Sherman to issue commissions naming them deputy U.S. marshals. On the basis of their arresting authority, Wild then succeeded in lining up as many as thirty or forty of the county's substantial citizens in a "posse comitatus" committed to wiping out the infestation that plagued them. As federal possemen, their ostensible mission was running down counterfeiters, but their true interest lay in attacking the larger affliction of stock theft.

Two pillars of the Roswell establishment who thought Wild offered a rare opportunity to clean up Lincoln County were John Chisum and Joseph C. Lea. Even before throwing in with Wild, they had taken steps that would complement his plan. Casting about for someone to replace George Kimball as sheriff of Lincoln County, they had fixed on Patrick F. Garrett.

Pat Garrett had come to Fort Sumner in the autumn of 1878, fresh from the buffalo plains and several seasons as a hide hunter. His gangly frame, soaring to six and a half feet in his boots and hat, gave him instant recognition among residents. "Juan Largo," the Hispanics dubbed him, and at their *bailes* he cut as fine a figure as Billy Bonney. Pat acquired a Hispanic wife and, after her untimely death, another. For a time he worked the range, then tended bar in Beaver Smith's saloon, where he became even better known to the valley dwellers.

Garrett, thirty in 1880, quickly gained a reputation as a tough, resolute fellow, quiet and soft-spoken but not to be trifled with. "Coolness, courage, and determination were written on his face," noted one who knew him.[18] John Chisum admired his marksmanship, horsemanship, and cool bravery. As early as April 1879, Chisum recommended him to Governor Wallace as an ideal man to help bring order to the Pecos. As the election of 1880 approached, Chisum and Lea persuaded Garrett to move to Roswell and run for sheriff of Lincoln County.[19]

Billy naturally favored Garrett's opponent, Kimball. Billy had nothing against Pat; they had known each other at Fort Sumner in the autumn of 1878, although probably not in close friendship. But Kimball had treated Billy fairly and with understanding during the three months of "imprisonment" following his pact with Governor Wallace, and that had planted a lasting gratitude. Now Kimball winked at Billy's illicit activities when he operated in the neighborhood of White Oaks and, as Wild noted, played cards with him when he came to Lincoln. As the election neared, Billy's visits to White Oaks increasingly featured politicking in behalf of Kimball, especially among Hispanic voters.[20]

Garrett's law-and-order platform, however, proved enticing to the people of Lincoln County. On November 2, 1880, they went to the polls to award him the sheriff's badge, 320 votes to 179 for Kimball.[21] Acknowledging the electorate's decision, Kimball promptly appointed Garrett a deputy sheriff for the two months remaining until he formally took office on January 1. With Kimball therefore a lame duck, throughout November and December 1880 Garrett functioned as sheriff in all but name.

More important for Azariah Wild's purposes, Garrett also served as a deputy U.S. marshal. Through some clerical error, Marshal Sherman had mailed two commissions for John Hurley. On one, Wild simply crossed out Hurley's name and substituted Garrett's.[22] Thus did Pat Garrett become a key figure in Wild's strategy.

By November 1880, Billy Bonney had achieved a reputation that made him a major target of two separate manhunts. The Panhandle stockmen had been persuaded that he was the worst of the thieves preying on their herds, and their expedition to New Mexico aimed at eliminating him. Likewise, Operative Wild's wanted list, doubtless heavily influenced by John Chisum, featured Billy along with Cooper, Wilson, and others.

Billy only partly deserved his new reputation. Until the fall of 1880, consistent with his continuing ambivalence about a life of crime, he had engaged in the narrowest possible range of criminal activity. So far as is known, he never held up a bank or a stagecoach, never burglarized a store or waylaid a traveler. He confined himself to stock theft, the offense least condemned by frontier citizens. As his friend Dr. Hoyt observed, "his only peculations had been rounding up cattle and horses carrying someone else's brand, a diversion more or less popular among many old-time cattlemen, and at that period not considered a crime—if one could get away with it." Of Billy and his friends a newspaper commented, "They neither murder men, except in self-defense, nor outrage women. The cow and the horse are their objective and offensive pursuit."[23]

As Billy spent more and more time at White Oaks, however, he turned to other kinds of crime as well. When in town he frequented the West and Diedrick stables and consorted with men such as Wilson and Cooper, whom Wild knew to be "shovers of the green." It would be surprising indeed if Billy did not also shove the green.

The people of the mining camp, moreover, singled Billy out as a particularly undesirable visitor. They feared and resented his presence. As newcomers to the territory, prospectors drawn by a mineral bonanza, they knew nothing of the qualities that endeared him to so many residents of Lincoln and Fort Sumner. They knew only that he used White Oaks as a dumping ground for stolen cattle and as a source of stolen horses to be dumped elsewhere. Moreover, few Hispanics had gravitated to White Oaks, which deprived Billy of his usual reservoir of ardent defenders.

Finally, Wild assembled convincing evidence that Billy had perpetrated another federal crime—robbing the U.S. mail. On October 16 bandits stopped the mail buckboard near Fort Sumner and relieved the driver of his pouches. The soldiers at Fort Stanton had just been paid, and many had mailed cash to banks or to family elsewhere. Witnesses named Billy Bonney and Billy Wilson as prominent among the robbers.[24]

From small-time rustler, therefore, Billy had progressed to big-time rustler of both cattle and horses, and he had branched out to other forms of crime as well. By the autumn of 1880, he had become far more unambiguously the criminal than when he had "skinned out" from Lincoln a year earlier, far less deserving of the clemency Governor Wallace had promised in exchange for his testimony.

November 1880 was to bring even more notoriety. As a result, for the Panhandle stockmen, for the possemen gathering under Wild's federal auspices, and for the new sheriff with a mandate to clean up Lincoln County, Billy Bonney would suddenly become *the* man to get.

The Celebrity

Despite growing visibility as an outlaw, the Kid still sought release from the legal troubles that continued to plague him. Nor had his case been entirely forgotten.

As with his other involvements growing out of the Lincoln County War, Governor Wallace had entrusted Billy's case to Ira E. Leonard, the Las Vegas lawyer who had stood in for the governor at the spring 1879 term of territorial court in Lincoln and later at the Dudley court of inquiry. A Missouri judge before migrating to New Mexico for his asthma, Leonard badly wanted to replace Warren Bristol on the bench of the Third Judicial District Court. In urging the appointment on the president, Wallace created an obligation that Leonard, who had moved his practice to Lincoln, satisfied in part by following up on the governor's promises to Billy Bonney.

Since Leonard had penned one of the letters to the Secretary of the Treasury that brought Azariah Wild to Lincoln, the Secret Service operative promptly linked up with the attorney. On October 6, 1880, less than a week after Wild arrived in Lincoln, Leonard began to unfold a plan that could benefit both his purposes and Wild's.

Wallace, Leonard revealed, had been pressing him to do something for Billy Bonney. For his part, however, the governor "had failed to put it in shape that satisfied Judge Leonard." At the same time, Leonard had received a letter from Billy saying that he was tired of dodging the law and wanted the issue resolved. Wild concluded, as Leonard surely intended him to conclude, "that we can

139

use Antrom [*sic*] in these [counterfeiting] cases provided Gov Wallace will make good his written promises and the U.S. Attorney will allow the case pending in the U.S. Court to slumber and give him (Antrom) one more chance to reform."

What Leonard had in mind, with Wild's connivance, was the same kind of deal with Billy in the federal court that Wallace had promised him in the territorial court. Billy would provide evidence leading to the arrest and conviction of the counterfeiters, and in return the U.S. attorney for New Mexico would be induced to let the federal charges against him "slumber." Leonard posted a letter to Billy asking him to come at once for consultation. Wild looked forward to meeting the young outlaw within a week.[1]

Billy came, but in six weeks rather than one, and then on other business as well. By that time, Wild and Leonard had fallen out—over Leonard's insistence on dictating strategy, according to Wild.[2] Billy's other business, moreover, not only prevented him from meeting with Leonard but also gave him new public visibility as a criminal. His last chance at clearing away his legal troubles fell casualty to the rupture between Leonard and Wild and to his own misbehavior.

★

"Padre Polaco," people called the jovial old storekeeper at Puerto de Luna, forty miles up the Pecos from Fort Sumner. The appellation recorded his Polish birth and his former status as a priest, but also it was much easier to pronounce than his proper name, Alexander Grzelachowski (Gre-ze-la-hóf-ski). Padre Polaco's mercantile business prospered, and he ran some stock on the grassy plains east of Fort Sumner. The Kid stopped often at the Grzelachowski store in Puerto de Luna and bantered with the friendly proprietor.[3]

Cordial relations did not always restrain Billy from stealing from people he looked on as friends. As Will Chisum remarked, "When he wanted something, he would just take it." About November 15, 1880, with O'Folliard, Bowdre, Wilson, Pickett, Buck Edwards, and Sam Cook, Billy rode up to Barney Mason, herding some of Pete Maxwell's cattle east of Sumner. According to Mason, "they asked me where A. Grzelachowski's horses were. I told them. Wilson told me to give him Pete Maxwell's rifle and I did so. Another one asked me for the loan of a saddle and they told me that they had come to steal the Padre Polaco's horses." They did: four stallions, four geldings, four mares, and four fillies, valued in all at sixteen hundred dollars.[4]

Mason readily complied with the demands on him because, he later explained, he feared for his life. These rustlers were suspected of robbing the mail, and he thought they might have read his exchange of correspondence with Pat Garrett. The newly elected sheriff counted Mason a trusted friend, although he had a checkered past and as recently as October had been caught altering the brands of cattle that did not belong to him.[5] A Texan of Irish heritage, twenty-six, short, stocky, red-faced, red-haired, and hot-tempered, Mason had in fact been summoned by Garrett to a mission menacing to Billy and his friends. Within less than a week, it would take Mason to White Oaks as an "informer" on the payroll of Azariah F. Wild.[6]

Billy too headed for White Oaks, intent on disposing of Padre Polaco's horses. With him went Wilson, Cook, Edwards, and Rudabaugh. Forty miles short of their destination, the party reined up at the Greathouse and Kuch ranch, a way station on the road linking Las Vegas and White Oaks.

For the Kid, this was a favored place for holding and disposing of stolen stock. One of the proprietors, Fred Kuch, had boasted to Operative Wild of his extensive smuggling operations in Mexico. The other, "Whiskey Jim" Greathouse, had a long record of selling whiskey to Indians and otherwise operating on the dark side of the law. "Greathouse was a rather tall man, with a heartless, staring countenance, and always wore a white hat, clown fashion," recalled one who knew him. He was said to have introduced Billy to Dave Rudabaugh, and since Billy's advent in the White Oaks neighborhood he and Whiskey Jim had been sometime partners in crime.[7]

Billy sold four of the horses to Greathouse and headed for White Oaks to sell the rest. There, on the night of November 20, the horse thieves stocked up on provisions—blankets, overcoats, rifles, and other merchandise. The angry excitement in White Oaks over the presence of the outlaws suggests that they failed to pay for these goods. They left the newly acquired property at the West and Diedrick livery to be hauled out to their camp.[8]

The next day the party again showed up in White Oaks, and coincidentally that very night Barney Mason, now working for Garrett and Wild, wandered into the West and Diedrick corral and came face-to-face with the two Billies and Dave Rudabaugh. Nervously, Barney beat a hasty retreat and alerted the law to the whereabouts of the outlaws. By the time a posse reached the scene, however, they had disappeared.[9]

Early on November 22, tipped off that the outlaws were camped at a sawmill near town, Deputy Sheriff William H. Hudgens and a posse of eight set forth to investigate. They found the camp abandoned but spotted a fresh trail and followed it. A few miles out, they met a wagon bearing Mose Diedrick, Dan and Sam's brother, and another man. Correctly surmising them to be on the way back from delivering provisions to the quarry, the deputy placed them in arrest, then continued rapidly on the trail.

Camped at Coyote Springs, Billy and his friends had little warning of their peril. They managed to mount before firing broke out, but both Bonney and Wilson had their horses shot from beneath them and had to flee on foot. Rudabaugh, Cook, and Edwards escaped in other directions. In the outlaw camp, the posse appropriated the provisions brought out by Mose Diedrick together with other possessions abandoned in the haste of flight. Bonney and Wilson, joined by Rudabaugh, made their way back to the Greathouse ranch.[10]

That the Kid and his comrades had stirred up the people of White Oaks became apparent at dawn on November 27, when they awoke to find the Greathouse ranch closely surrounded by Hudgens and a posse of thirteen men. Joe Steck, a Greathouse employee, went outside that morning, encountered an array of Winchesters, and returned with a note calling on the men inside to give up. "I took the note in and delivered it to the one I knew to be Billy the Kid," recalled Steck. "He read the paper to his compadres, who all laughed at the idea of surrender." Accompanied by Greathouse, Steck returned with the outlaws' refusal.[11]

Efforts now focused on Billy Wilson, who faced less serious charges than Bonney and Rudabaugh. He balked at coming out to talk but asked to have Jimmy Carlyle, a popular White Oaks blacksmith, come in and discuss terms of surrender. Hudgens agreed only after Greathouse offered himself as hostage for Carlyle's safety.

Unarmed, Carlyle entered the house and promptly found himself a prisoner. The men inside, presumably excepting the Kid, were drinking heavily at Whiskey Jim's bar. Billy made Carlyle drink too, so much so that by noon, according to Steck, he was "getting under the influence of liquor and insisting on going out." Billy refused to release him, at the same time keeping up an intimidating banter that, combined with the liquor, worked Carlyle into a panic. Hour after hour the standoff continued, as both sides grew increasingly nervous and as Carlyle came more and more to fear for his life.

The crisis occurred at about 2:00 in the afternoon, when the anxious possemen sent in an ultimatum threatening to kill Greathouse if Carlyle were not released within five minutes. Shortly, one of the posse fired a shot, probably accidentally. Steck, just emerging from the house once again, described what happened next: "I stopped and turned when, crash, a man came through a window, bang, bang, the man's dying yell, and poor Carlyle tumbled to the ground with three bullets in him."

Gunfire rattled from the barricades on all sides of the house, with "bullets flying from all directions," remembered Steck, and then the battleground fell silent. Carlyle lay lifeless where he had fallen, ten feet from the shattered window.

Cold, hungry, thirsty, and dismayed by the slaying of Carlyle, the posse lost heart. Couriers had already been sent for reinforcements and provisions, but the possemen decided to pull out and ride to meet them. That night, discovering the siege lifted, the Kid and his friends slipped out and made their way toward the Pecos.

When the lawmen returned the next morning, they resolved that Whiskey Jim would never again harbor the likes of the Kid and his fellows, and they burned the ranch buildings to the ground.

How Carlyle came to be killed remains a matter for speculation. Billy later contended that the posse bore all the blame. "In a short time" after the dispatch of the ultimatum, he declared, "a shot was fired on the outside and Carlyle thinking Greathouse was Killed Jumped through a window, breaking the Sash as he went and was killed by his own Party they thinking it was me trying to make my Escape."[12]

Considering the tensions that had built up during seven hours of deadlock, an accidental shot could have triggered Carlyle's attempted escape. For the same reason the posse could well have believed the man crashing out of the window to be one of the fugitives trying to escape, and they may have opened fire on him. They thought that of Steck, emerging from the front door at the same time, and sent a fusillade in his direction.

Billy left unsaid whether anyone inside fired at Carlyle. Dave Rudabaugh was more candid. Later, aboard a train that took the three outlaws to jail in Santa Fe, Billy Wilson appealed to a lawman he knew to "help me out of this scrape."

"That is a hard thing to ask of me after you killed Carlyle in cold blood," was the answer.

"I didn't shoot at him and tried to keep the others from doing so," protested Wilson.

"You are a damned liar," cut in Rudabaugh. "We all three shot at him. You and I fired one shot apiece and the Kid twice."[13]

The possemen went even further, accusing Billy alone of shooting Carlyle. According to their version, given to a reporter, they "saw Carlyle leap from the window and dash down the hill toward their intrenchments. He had not gone far, however, when they saw the Kid throw half his body through the window, and, taking deliberate aim, brought down poor Carlyle, killing him instantly."[14]

Thus, who killed Carlyle remains unclear. Bonney, Wilson, and Rudabaugh almost certainly shot at him, and possemen may have targeted him also, as Billy contended. As with the Brady slaying, at least one of Billy's bullets probably found its mark, but he cannot be regarded as the sole killer of the blacksmith. At this point in his career, therefore, Billy still may be credited unequivocally with no more than two killings—Windy Cahill and Joe Grant.

Even before the shooting of Carlyle, Billy and his friends had strained the tolerance of the citizens of White Oaks. Now, Carlyle's death lifted Billy to the rank of arch-villain. As Pat Garrett (or Ash Upson) later wrote, the blacksmith's "bloody murder excited horror and indignation, and many who had viewed the career of the Kid with some degree of charity now held him in unqualified execration as the murderer of an exceptionally good man and useful citizen."[15]

At almost exactly the same moment, Billy's activities on the Pecos caught up with him. One of the proprietors of the *Las Vegas Gazette*, W. S. Koogler, returned from a journey down the Pecos full of indignation over the infestation of outlaws that prevented the territory's eastern plains from fully realizing their agricultural and stock-raising potential. He wrote a complaining letter to Governor Wallace and then, early in December 1880, ran a long article in the *Gazette* denouncing the "powerful gang of outlaws harassing the stockmen of the Pecos and Panhandle country, and terrorizing the people of Fort Sumner and vicinity." The gang consisted of "from forty to fifty men, all hard characters, the off scourings of society, fugitives from justice, and desperadoes by profession."

They spend time in enjoying themselves at Portales, keeping guards out and scouting the country for miles around before turning in for the night. Whenever there is good opportunity to make a haul they split up in gangs and scour the country, always leaving behind a detachment to guard their roost and whatever plunder they may have stored there.

This army of outlaws, concluded Koogler, "is under the leadership of 'Billy the Kid,' a desperate cuss, who is eligible for the post of captain of any crowd, no matter how mean and lawless."[16]

Other newspapers took up the refrain, spreading Billy's name and stories of his alleged exploits throughout the territory. His reputation even leaped beyond New Mexico, for on December 27,

1880, the *New York Sun*, drawing on the *Gazette*, ran a long story about the amazing outlaw chief. And no longer was he just "Kid"— the outlaw West was full of Kids. Now he was the much more personal and glamorous "Billy the Kid."

In most respects the newspaper stories were essentially accurate. Forty or fifty outlaws, or even more, had in truth imposed a reign of thievery and terror on New Mexico from Las Vegas to Seven Rivers and from the Sierra Blanca to the Staked Plains. But they did not operate as a single gang, and they did not accord allegiance to a single chief, certainly not to a youth of twenty-one. Yet within a matter of two weeks, all New Mexico came to look on "Billy the Kid" as the premier outlaw of the Southwest.

The *Gazette*'s article undermined Billy's campaign for release from the murder charges against him. In particular, it prejudiced Governor Wallace and discouraged him from extending the help he had promised in Lincoln almost two years earlier.

In a long letter to the governor, Billy denied that he captained an outlaw band. "There is no such organization in existence," he wrote. "So the gentleman must have drawn very heavily on his imagination." He conceded that "Billy, 'the Kid,' is the name by which I am known in the Country," but added that he had not followed a life of crime at the Portales. That was a tale, he said, "put out by Chisum and his tools." Instead, "I have been at Sumner since I left Lincoln making my living gambling."

Billy also told the governor about the recent shootout at the Greathouse ranch. He had gone to White Oaks at the summons of Ira Leonard, "who has my case in hand. He had written to me to come up, that he thought he could get Everything Straigtind up." But Leonard was not at White Oaks, and before Billy could follow him to Lincoln the possemen jumped him at Coyote Springs, shot his horse from under him, and then cornered him at the Greathouse ranch. He refused to surrender to them because they had no warrant for his arrest, "so I concluded that it amounted to nothing more than a mob." The posse itself, not he, shot and killed Carlyle.[17]

Whatever the mix of truth and fiction, Billy's letter shows that he wanted Wallace to believe him to be an innocent victim of a malevolent John Chisum and that he still hoped for the governor's help in avoiding the murder charges facing him. The letter, however, failed to move Governor Wallace, who gave it to the *Las Vegas Gazette* to print and ridicule.

In Santa Fe, even before receiving Billy's self-serving letter, Governor Wallace swiftly gave official sanction to the portrait etched in such bold strokes by the newspapers. Koogler had written to Wallace about conditions on the Pecos, and Wallace, casting about for some means of helping the beleaguered stockmen, settled on a reward. The *Gazette*'s article of December 3 supplied the name—Billy the Kid. Although he had only recently urged Leonard to new efforts in behalf of Billy, the governor probably reasoned that the crimes attributed to him by the newspapers dissolved any lingering obligations. On December 13, the day after Billy wrote his letter, Wallace posted a reward of five hundred dollars for the apprehension and delivery to the sheriff of Lincoln County of "Bonney alias 'the Kid.'"[18]

Although the press had laid the groundwork, only the governor could have conferred on Billy the ultimate in outlaw status—a price on his head.

Almost overnight, Billy Bonney had exploded into notoriety, not only in New Mexico but across the nation as well. The quickening tempo of his criminal activity in the autumn months of 1880 qualified him for a share of the notoriety, but only a small share. The rest of his fame was a newspaper creation. Because he was now *the* outlaw celebrity of the Southwest, and because anyone who ran him down would receive a reward of five hundred dollars, "Billy the Kid" headed the list of wanted criminals.

The Capture

CHAPTER 14

When in the neighborhood of Fort Sumner, Billy Bonney drifted from one bunking place to another. Sometimes he camped in vacant rooms of the old fort buildings, sometimes with congenial Hispanic sheepherders on the surrounding plains, sometimes with the scattering of Anglo cattlemen. In June 1880, the federal census enumerator found him living with Charley Bowdre and recorded him as "cattle worker," aged twenty-five (instead of the correct twenty). In August he put up at the dwelling of a stockman named Starke, where the attraction was a woman who had left her husband for a more exciting life.[1]

Favored stopping places were the Yerby and the Wilcox-Brazil ranches. The former, where Charley Bowdre and Tom Pickett worked, stood at the head of Arroyo Cañaditas, twenty miles northeast of Fort Sumner. As foreman, Charley lived there with Manuela, and Billy and his comrades often stayed there.

The latter ranch, a partnership between Thomas W. Wilcox and Manuel S. Brazil, stood about midway between Sumner and the Yerby headquarters, just below the forks of Taiban Creek and near a seep named Stinking Springs. Wilcox and Brazil extended their hospitality because of past friendship but also, increasingly, because they feared for their lives if they did not. Here, as elsewhere around Fort Sumner, Billy's welcome was beginning to wear thin.

Whether he sensed the rising animosity or not, Billy had commenced to think seriously of moving on, as friends like Dr. Hoyt had urged. The fiascos at Coyote Springs and the Greathouse ranch had been setbacks, and with Wilson and Rudabaugh he had endured a humiliating trek back to Sumner on foot. There he ran into further causes for despair. One was the recent "raid" on Fort Sumner engineered by Azariah Wild.

★

With Joseph Lea and Pat Garrett, Azariah Wild had begun to hatch his ambitious scheme as early as November 4. As deputy U.S. marshals, Garrett and Olinger would lead a "posse comitatus" of fifty men north from Roswell. At Fort Sumner they would combine with Frank Stewart and the Panhandle cowboys in a sweep of the outlaw haunts. Barney Mason would report on where the fugitives were most likely to be found.[2]

Originally set for November 21, the operation encountered its first delay when Barney Mason, en route from Fort Sumner to Roswell, paused at the Diedrick ranch at Bosque Grande. There Dan Diedrick invited him to undertake a mission in behalf of the counterfeiters—a trip to Mexico to dispose of thirty thousand fake dollars in exchange for cattle. When informed of this, Wild could not resist the temptation to use Mason as a double agent, and he sent him to White Oaks to develop the invitation further with West and Sam Diedrick. There, as already recounted, Mason chanced on the Kid and his friends in the West and Diedrick corral, and he also discovered that the tumult stirred by their activities had spooked the counterfeiters and had caused them to put Mason's assignment on hold.

Other delays followed. For one, snowstorms swept the mountains and plains, making travel difficult. For another, a distemper epidemic immobilized large numbers of horses. At last, however, an expedition numbering thirteen men pushed off from Roswell on the night of November 29. Garrett and Olinger led, Mason accompanying.

On the edge of Roswell the posse chanced to meet Sam Cook, one of Billy's partners in the theft of Padre Polaco's horses and the fight at Coyote Springs, where Cook had become separated from his cohorts. Locking Cook up in Roswell, the party proceeded up the

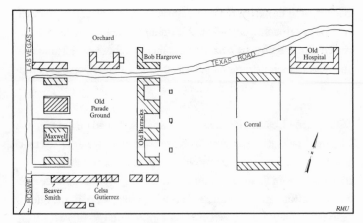

Fort Sumner, New Mexico, 1880–81

Pecos to the Diedrick ranch at Bosque Grande. Here they hoped to find men for whom they had warrants. Instead they scooped up two other wanted men, John J. Webb, Rudabaugh's old friend from Las Vegas, and George Davis, a horse thief. Both had just broken out of the Las Vegas jail. Here too Garrett received a message from Lea, in Roswell, telling of the Kid's fight on the twenty-seventh at the Greathouse ranch.[3]

The Fort Sumner raid fell far short of Wild's expectations. Garrett learned from Beaver Smith that the Kid, Wilson, and Rudabaugh had not yet returned from White Oaks but that Bowdre and O'Folliard were at the Yerby ranch. Riding up the Cañaditas, the posse jumped Tom O'Folliard and chased him in a running gun battle from which he escaped only because he rode a fresher mount than did his pursuers. At the Yerby ranch they seized two mules and four horses, stolen property Billy claimed as his. They then rode all the way over to the "outlaw stronghold" at Los Portales, but found no purloined stock.

Returning from Los Portales, Garrett learned that Charley Bowdre wanted to square himself with the law. On December 5, in a truce parley arranged by Tom Wilcox, Charley met with Garrett on the road just outside Sumner and talked over the possibility of surrendering and facing trial for the murder of Buckshot Roberts.

150

Garrett told him that Joseph Lea and fellow Roswell stalwarts would help him if he would cut his ties with the Kid and other outlaws. Charley said he would try, although he could not help but feed them when they came to the Yerby ranch. Garrett warned that he better act quickly, before the posse ran him down and killed or captured him.[4]

The grand sweep envisioned by Wild had fizzled. Garrett's expedition netted two fugitives, but not the ones sought. Despite a courier sent from Roswell, Stewart's Texans remained on the Pecos. A third initiative, by the "White Oaks Rangers" who had cornered Billy at the Greathouse ranch, also petered out when the pursuers gave up the chase. On December 6 Garrett and Mason, with prisoners Webb and Davis in tow, set forth from Fort Sumner for Las Vegas. Olinger led the rest of the posse back to Roswell.

★

Within a day or two after Garrett's departure, the Kid, with Wilson and Rudabaugh, limped into Fort Sumner. Here Billy learned that the *Las Vegas Gazette* had named him New Mexico's star outlaw and called for his apprehension, that Garrett's posse had seized his stock and almost caught Tom O'Folliard, and that Charley Bowdre was on the point of defecting. As a result of his parley with Garrett, Charley had abandoned his dwelling at the Yerby ranch, moved Manuela into Fort Sumner, and now camped at various places on the range.

Uniting with O'Folliard and Tom Pickett, the Kid, Wilson, and Rudabaugh remounted themselves and divided their time among the Yerby ranch, the Wilcox-Brazil ranch, and Fort Sumner.[5] When in town they bunked in one of the vacant rooms of the old military hospital building on the east edge of the compound. Manuela Bowdre and her mother occupied other rooms of this building, and Charley stayed there when he was in town. On most nights the men were to be found in Beaver Smith's saloon, drinking and gambling.

They also planned their departure from Fort Sumner, for they had decided that the time had come to pull up stakes and leave the area altogether. During this period, on December 12, Billy wrote his disingenuous letter to Governor Wallace proclaiming his innocence of all wrongdoing.

Three days later, on December 15, Bowdre also took pen in hand to enlist the good offices of Joseph Lea. Charley told of vacating the Yerby ranch and taking to the open range. "I thought this a duty due Mr. Yerby," he wrote, "for if there is nothing to eat at the ranch no one will go there & there will be no chance of a fight coming off there." He thought the law should quit hounding him, he told Lea. Only the misfortune of an indictment distinguished his case from that of dozens of other participants in the Lincoln County War and prevented him from pleading the governor's amnesty and going free. If Lea could intercede with Governor Wallace and get the charges dropped, Bowdre wanted to settle down and lead an honest life.

As for Billy Bonney and Billy Wilson, Bowdre informed Lea that they would probably move elsewhere and start life anew. "I saw the two Billies the other day," he wrote, "& they say they are going to leave this country. That was my advice to them for I believe it is the best thing they can do." According to Garrett, Bonney also wrote to Lea announcing his intention to "leave the country for good."[6]

As Garrett had informed Bowdre, however, he and his men "were after the gang and would sleep on their trail until we took them in, dead or alive." Still bearing the deputy U.S. marshal's commission that empowered him to operate beyond Lincoln County, Garrett had been far from idle. In Las Vegas he met up with Frank Stewart, the Panhandle stockmen's detective, and learned that they had dispatched two parties of cowboys to search for their stolen cattle in New Mexico. Numbering a dozen or more men, with two chuck wagons, this expedition was on the Pecos below Anton Chico, bound for White Oaks. With Mason and Stewart, Garrett set forth to overtake the Texans.[7]

The three men reached the camp of the cowboys early on December 15. The ranch owners had not told the hands the whole truth about their mission, only that they were to recover stolen cattle. In seeking volunteers for a quick dash on Fort Sumner, therefore, Stewart and Garrett spoke guardedly. Most of the men guessed the purpose, and not all wanted to tangle with the Kid and his friends. Six men volunteered, while the rest elected to continue on the road to White Oaks.[8]

The party laid over for a night and a day in Puerto de Luna, where they rested their horses, warmed themselves in Grzelachowski's store, and tried to recruit more fighters. Emboldened by free-flowing whiskey, the townsmen signed up in force only to vanish when the departure time came the next day, December 17. "Without shame they had sneaked off into the night," commented Charles Rudulph, who with George Wilson and the brothers Juan and José Roybal represented Puerto de Luna and rounded out the posse at thirteen men.[9]

Already on the seventeenth, Garrett had commissioned José Roybal as a spy. Padre Polaco had recommended the young Hispanic as exceptionally reliable, and that afternoon he proved it. Nosing around Fort Sumner, he discovered the presence of all the fugitives—Bonney, Rudabaugh, Wilson, Bowdre, Pickett, and O'Folliard. In the evening, under graying skies, Roybal crossed the Pecos and headed up the road toward Puerto de Luna. Suspicious, Pickett and O'Folliard followed, halted the boy, and grilled him at length. With an air of innocence, José explained that he was but a simple sheepherder searching for stray sheep. Convinced, O'Folliard and Pickett returned to town.[10]

Near midnight, at a ranch about twenty-five miles up the Pecos, Roybal linked up with Garrett and his men and relayed his observations in Sumner. After a hasty meal of "pickled tripe, roast beef, and plenty of horse feed," according to Lou Bousman, the riders resumed their journey, flurries of wind-driven snow stinging their faces.

Billy and his friends, meantime, were alert to an approaching danger, as the action of O'Folliard and Pickett in following Roybal suggests. The mail carrier from Las Vegas had told them that Pat Garrett and Barney Mason were on their way back to Sumner, but he had known nothing of the eleven other men who now rode with them. On the night of the seventeenth, after Roybal had left town,

Billy and his comrades rode out too, putting up for the night at the Wilcox-Brazil ranch. They intended to return on the nineteenth with a load of beef, stock up on provisions, and carry out their intention to seek new fields of endeavor. According to Rudabaugh, their destination was Mexico.[11]

Amid densely falling snow, Garrett and his posse reached Sumner before daybreak on December 18, only to discover that the quarry had skipped town the night before, after Roybal's departure. Carefully, skillfully, Garrett set about baiting a trap to lure them back. Hiding his men in the old military hospital on the east edge of the compound, Garrett himself went visibly around the community. He talked with one Yginio García, suspected of being a compadre of the Kid's, who was about to leave for his place south of town. Garrett refused to let him go, but then gave in to his pleas that his children needed milk.

As Garrett doubtless foresaw, word of his presence in Fort Sumner swiftly reached the Kid and his friends. On the road south of Sumner, two of Billy's occasional accomplices, Bob Campbell and José Valdez, met Yginio García. He told them that he had just seen Pat Garrett in Fort Sumner. While Valdez hurried to Sumner to learn more, Campbell scrawled a message to Billy and sought out a boy to speed it to the Wilcox-Brazil ranch. Alarmed by Campbell's note, Billy called off his trip into town; the snowstorm made travel difficult anyway. The next morning, however, he instructed Juan (or Johnny) Gallegos, Wilcox's young stepson, to ride into Sumner and scout the situation.

In Fort Sumner, meanwhile, Garrett had talked with José Valdez and suspected his purpose. On the morning of the nineteenth he spotted Juan Gallegos and guessed his assignment also. Both Wilcox and Brazil hosted the Kid and his friends through fear rather than friendship, Garrett knew, and he hoped that they might be enlisted in his mission. Approaching Juan, Garrett persuaded him to aid in tricking Billy. Next the lawman hunted up José Valdez and forced him to write a note to Billy stating that Garrett and a posse had been in Fort Sumner but had pulled out and were headed for Roswell. Finally, Garrett himself penned a message to Tom Wilcox divulging his plans and asking his aid in trapping Billy. Bearing both notes, with a warning not to get them mixed up, Juan returned to the ranch.

The note delivered to Billy by Juan Gallegos produced the intended effect. Shouting scorn for the timid lawmen, the Kid and his companions at once readied their horses for the ride into Sumner. The storm had abated, snow lay deep on the plains, and banks of fog reflected a bright moon.

In the old hospital building, that night of December 19, the posse settled in to wait. Garrett felt certain the fugitives would come and would stop at Manuela Bowdre's rooms before going elsewhere. He posted Lon Chambers outside to keep watch while he, Barney Mason, Tom Emory, and Bob Williams spread a blanket on the floor next to the blazing fireplace and launched into a game of poker. Jim East wrapped himself in a blanket and curled up in a corner to get some sleep. About 8:00 P.M. Chambers opened the door and announced horsemen approaching on the road from the east.

"Get your guns, boys," said Garrett. "None but the men we want are riding this time of night."

The lawmen slipped out the door. With Chambers and one of the Roybal brothers, Garrett took a station in the shadows at the east end of the porch, where harness hung on the wall to provide added concealment. Mason and the others went around the building in the opposite direction to intercept the outlaws if they continued toward the town's plaza (the old parade ground).

O'Folliard and Pickett rode in the front, the others lagging behind. The two spurred their horses up to the building, and O'Folliard's horse nuzzled his head under the portal roof.

"Halt," shouted Garrett.

Startled, Tom went for his pistol, and both Garrett and Chambers fired their Winchesters at the same time. The horse reared and dashed off, Tom crying in pain. The two then fired at Pickett, who also yelled as if hit and galloped away.

The rest of Garrett's men appeared at the other end of the building and opened a random fire, ineffective in the thickening fog. The Kid and his remaining companions swiftly reined about and, with their horses kicking up clods of snow, galloped off on the road to the east.

Tom O'Folliard's horse trotted away for about 150 yards, then wheeled and drifted slowly back to the building, Tom slumping in the saddle.

"Don't shoot, Garrett," he stammered. "I'm killed." Garrett's bullet had caught Tom in the left chest, just below the heart.[12]

The possemen helped Tom off his horse, carried him inside, and laid him on Jim East's blanket near the fire. The poker group resumed their game, and East sat down by the fire.

"God damn you Garrett," exclaimed Tom. "I hope to meet you in hell."

"I would not talk that way, Tom," replied Garrett. "You are going to die in a few minutes."

"Aw, go to hell, you long-legged son-of-a-bitch," said Tom.

"The game went on," East related, "and the blood began running inside Tom. He began groaning and asked me to get him a drink of water. I did. He drank a little, lay back, shuddered, and was dead."[13]

The other outlaws fled back to the Wilcox-Brazil ranch. Rudabaugh's horse had been hit and died along the way. Dave climbed up behind Billy Wilson for the rest of the ride. According to Garrett, Tom Pickett bolted off to the north. Although unhit, he was "nearly scared to death. He went howling over the prairie, yelling bloody murder." After a run of twenty-five miles, the horse collapsed, and he had to make his way on foot to the Wilcox-Brazil ranch.[14]

"Depressed and disheartened," in Garrett's words, Billy and his partners paused only briefly at the ranch. Fearful of a swift pursuit by the posse, they pulled off into the hills. Throughout the next day, December 20, as another snowstorm swept the plains, they remained in hiding, keeping their field glasses trained on the ranch to see whether Garrett and his men appeared. After dark, the four crept back to the sheltering buildings, reunited with Tom Pickett, took supper, and plotted the next move. Although suspicious that Wilcox and Brazil had somehow contributed to their surprise in

Fort Sumner, they decided nonetheless to send Brazil into town on a scouting mission.

Garrett and his men stuck close to their fireplace on December 20, either likewise plotting strategy or simply uncertain of the next move. Several of the Texans went up the road to the east and found Rudabaugh's dead horse, but the new snow had erased the outlaw trail. Garrett had a coffin made. "We buried Tom Folliard rather unceremoniously," said Charles Rudulph, "with all his pursuers and a few villagers in attendance."[15]

On the morning of December 21, Manuel Brazil came into Fort Sumner on his scouting assignment for Billy and went directly to Garrett. The two arranged for Brazil to return to the ranch and tell the outlaws that Garrett was in Sumner "with only Mason and three Mexicans" and that he "was considerably scared up and wanted to go back to Roswell, but feared to leave the plaza."[16]

Brazil did not go back to the ranch until the next day, the twenty-second. There he relayed the tale that Garrett had concocted and played his dangerous double game skillfully enough to dupe Billy. The Kid wanted to ride into Sumner and fall on Garrett and his single deputy, but Charley Bowdre, probably still hoping that Lea would help him get free of the law, objected.[17] Instead, that night the five fugitives ate heartily, then set forth in the snow on the road to the east. Brazil promptly saddled up and headed toward Sumner, reaching there at midnight stiff with cold and his beard full of ice.

At once Garrett mounted his dozen men and pounded out of Fort Sumner in the frozen night. Brazil went ahead to check the ranch, then came back and met the posse with word that the out-laws had not returned but that their trail in the snow could be plainly followed by the light of a bright moon. Garrett suspected that the trail would lead to an abandoned rock house, once the shel-ter of a sheepman, that stood near Stinking Springs about three miles east of the Wilcox-Brazil ranch. About 3:00 A.M. on Decem-ber 23, the pursuers drew close to their objective.

All five outlaws—Bonney, Rudabaugh, Bowdre, Wilson, and Pickett—lay wrapped in their blankets on the floor of the rock house, their snores plainly audible to the lawmen creeping into positions outside. Pressed by Garrett, discomfited by the loss of O'Folliard, they meant to leave the Fort Sumner country altogether. Regarding the Wilcox-Brazil ranch as unsafe, they had ridden over to the rock house to spend the night before pulling out. It was a one-room structure, with openings that had once been a door and a window. The men had led two of their horses inside and had tied the other three outside to projections of the vigas that supported the flat roof.

Leaving Juan Roybal to tend the horses, Garrett divided his force and worked into positions on two sides of the house. He himself led one party up an arroyo that provided cover within easy firing distance of the door and window while Stewart circled with the remaining men to the rear of the house. Garrett wanted to rush into the house at once, but Stewart demurred. The lawmen therefore picked firing positions and settled into the snow to await daybreak.[18]

As the frigid white landscape brightened with first light, Garrett's men saw a single figure, carrying a nose bag full of grain for the horses, emerge from the house. Convinced that the Kid would not allow himself to be taken without a fight, Garrett had resolved not to try but to shoot at once when he had the fugitive in his sights. The others, he felt sure, would then surrender. A "Mexican" hat with a wide brim, together with other distinctive clothing, satisfied Garrett that here was his man. At Garrett's signal, his companions took careful aim with their Winchesters and fired as one. Reeling from the impact of the bullets, the man fell back into the doorway and vanished inside.[19]

The fusillade had not struck the Kid but his friend and comrade of the Lincoln County War, Charley Bowdre. Billy Wilson shouted to Garrett that he had hit Bowdre, who wanted to surrender. Garrett assented, if Bowdre would come out with his hands up.

"They have murdered you, Charley," Garrett heard the Kid say, "but you can get revenge. Kill some of the sons-of-bitches before you die." Pulling Charley's belt around so that the holstered pistol hung in front of his body, the Kid shoved his friend out the door.

His hands in the air, Bowdre staggered slowly to where Garrett waited, whispered "I wish, I wish, I wish—I'm dying," and collapsed.

"I took hold of him," said Garrett, "laid him gently on my blankets and he died almost immediately." [20]

Shortly afterward, Garrett noted movement in the rope that bound one of the outlaw horses. Obviously, the fugitives were pulling their mounts inside prior to making a break. Just as they were about to get one through the door, Garrett fired, dropping the horse in the doorway. To put a stop to this tactic, Garrett took careful aim and cut the ropes tying the other two animals, which sprang away from the house and trotted off. [21]

The desperate predicament of the outlaws did not dampen Billy's good humor. For a time he and Garrett bantered back and forth, the Kid inviting Garrett in for coffee, Garrett inviting the Kid out to surrender. "The Kid told him to go to hell," recalled East.

"We heard them picking on the other side of the house," according to East, evidently in an attempt to break through or at least fashion firing ports. "Garrett sent Tom Emory and me around to stop that," East continued. "We fired a shot or two at the place and they stopped."

Billy was trapped and he knew it. Garrett's quick thinking and accurate aim had thwarted the escape plot, as Billy later admitted. "If it hadn't been for the dead horse in the doorway I wouldn't be here," he told a Las Vegas reporter several days later. "I would have ridden out on my bay mare and taken my chances of escaping. But I couldn't ride out over that, for she would have jumped back, and I would have got it in the head. We could have stayed in the house but there wouldn't have been anything gained by that for they would have starved us out. I thought it was better to come out and get a good square meal." [22]

Garrett, meantime, had the needs of his own men in mind. He took half of them to the Wilcox-Brazil ranch and fed them breakfast, then sent the other half. Late in the afternoon, in preparation for a long siege, Brazil drove up in a wagon loaded with firewood, horse feed, bacon, and other "grub." The aroma of roasting meat wafted into the rock house and evoked Billy's vision of "a good square meal." Almost at once, at about 4:00 P.M., a dirty white rag tied to a stick fluttered from the window. Rudabaugh shouted that they wanted to surrender. Garrett replied that they could come out with their hands up.

Rudabaugh emerged alone. He said that all would give up if Garrett could guarantee their protection from violence—a pressing concern to Rudabaugh because of the sentiment against him in Las Vegas. He wanted to make certain they would be taken to Santa Fe and arraigned on federal charges rather than turned over to Las Vegas authorities. Garrett acceded. Rudabaugh went back into the house. Shortly, all four came out with their hands up.

As they approached, Barney Mason leveled his rifle at the Kid and exclaimed, "Kill the son of a bitch, he is slippery and may get away."

Mason, as East observed, was "a damned old no-good troublemaker." East and Lee Hall "threw our guns down on him and said: 'If you fire a shot we will kill you.'" Barney backed off.[23]

From the Wilcox-Brazil ranch Garrett sent three men with a wagon back to the rock house for the body of Bowdre. Mrs. Wilcox fed the entire bunch, and they spent the night at the ranch, the prisoners closely watched and their guards instructed to shoot them on the slightest provocation. Of the captives, Rudulph recalled: "There was Billy, cheerful and chattering, excitement lighting up his face; Rudabaugh, also joyful and talkative; Tom Pickett, scared half to death, pondering his fate; and Billy Wilson, probably the least to blame, ashamed and uncommunicative."[24]

Shortly before noon on December 24, the lawmen and their catch reached Fort Sumner, where they paused long enough to iron the prisoners and eat a hearty meal. While there, Billy presented Jim East with his Winchester rifle. But, as East remembered, "old Beaver Smith made such a roar about an account he said Billy owed him, that at the request of Billy, I gave old Beaver the gun."[25]

After the men had eaten, a Navajo woman appeared. She was Deluvina Maxwell, a captive of the Ute Indians liberated by Lucien

Maxwell in her youth and now, at twenty-two, a voluntary "slave" of the Maxwells. She said that Mrs. Maxwell, the widow of Lucien, asked if Garrett would let Billy come for a last farewell with her daughter Paulita. Consenting, Garrett assigned Jim East and Lee Hall to serve as guards. Dave Rudabaugh had to go too, since he and Billy were shackled together.

At the Maxwell house, the men found "Mother" Maxwell, Deluvina, and Paulita. Mrs. Maxwell asked if Billy could be freed long enough to go into the next room with Paulita and "talk awhile." Although the two probably had things other than escape in mind, East and Hall believed "it was only a stall of Billy's: to make a run for liberty." They refused, and as East told it, "The lovers embraced, and she gave Billy one of those soul kisses the novelists tell us about, till it being time to hit the trail for Vegas, we had to pull them apart, much against our wishes, for you know all the world loves a lover." [26]

Another, less romantic scene also unfolded at Fort Sumner. As the procession drew up at the old hospital, recalled Charles Rudulph, "we were met by a deranged, lamenting Manuela Bowdre. She kicked and pummelled Pat Garrett until she had to be pulled away." Garrett asked Jim East and Lou Bousman to carry the corpse into Manuela's rooms. "As we started in with him," said East, "she struck me over the head with a branding iron, and I had to drop Charlie at her feet. The poor woman was crazy with grief." Garrett told Manuela to buy Charley a new suit for his burial and have it charged to him. He also paid someone to dig a grave. [27]

In the early afternoon, Pat Garrett led his horsemen out of Fort Sumner on the road up the Pecos.

On this same day, Joseph C. Lea sat at his desk in Roswell and wrote a letter to Governor Lew Wallace. In it he told of Charley Bowdre's dilemma and his desire to free himself from his fellow outlaws and lead an honest life. Bowdre, wrote Lea, was "a man far above ordinary in point of intelligence." All who knew him "say you can depend on his word & I have no doubt of it." At present he was "a man between two fires." But if the governor would talk with the district attorney and get the charges against Bowdre dropped, Lea and his friends thought it "decidedly best for the country and all concerned." "We had better try to make a good man of him," he concluded, "& we have many reasons for believing that we can."[28]

It was Christmas Eve of 1880. Lea folded his own letter with Charley Bowdre's letter to him of December 15 and sealed them in an envelope addressed to Governor Wallace in Santa Fe. To the north, Pat Garrett stowed his prisoners in Brazil's wagon and set out from Fort Sumner for the long cold ride to Las Vegas. And in the abandoned hospital building at Fort Sumner, the grieving Manuela Bowdre dressed her dead husband in a new suit paid for by Pat Garrett, laid out his body, and encircled it with glowing candles.[29]

The Sentence

Late in the afternoon the day after Christmas 1880, Sunday, a rider galloped into the Las Vegas plaza with word that Pat Garrett and Frank Stewart were approaching town with Billy the Kid and three of his gang. "People stood on the muddy street corners and in hotel offices and saloons talking of the great event," reported the *Gazette*. As the procession rolled into the plaza, thronged with excited citizens, "astonishment gave way to joy." Manuel Brazil drove the wagon containing the four outlaws while Garrett, Stewart, Barney Mason, Jim East, and Tom Emory rode guard on all sides.[1]

From the veranda of the Grand View Hotel, one of the spectators noted that Billy the Kid was chained to Dave Rudabaugh, "a fierce looking, dark-bearded man, who kept his slouch hat pulled well down over his eyes, and who looked neither to the right nor to the left." Billy, in contrast, "was in a joyous mood. . . . He wore a hat pushed far back, and jocularly greeted the crowd. Recognizing Dr. Sutfin [the hotel proprietor], he called, 'Hello, doc! Thought I jes drop in and see how you fellers in Vegas air behavin' yerselves.'"[2]

The grand entry into Las Vegas highlighted a trait that had been gaining strength in Billy Bonney for nearly a year, as his name took on increasing prominence. At Fort Sumner and White Oaks, at the Greathouse ranch, during the siege and surrender at Stinking Springs, and now in daunting circumstances at Las Vegas, his behavior stamped him as irrepressibly cocky. He reveled in his new notoriety, and he poured out his conceit in bursts of lighthearted banter that harmonized well with his extroverted personality. The Las Vegas crowds greeted Rudabaugh with loathing, but they looked on the Kid with the curiosity and wonder due a celebrity.

Throughout his brief stay in Las Vegas, Billy played to the crowd. The next morning, December 27, Sheriff Desiderio Romero admitted a *Gazette* reporter into the jail to talk with the outlaws while they were being made presentable for the railway journey to Santa Fe. Their shackles had to be removed for them to don the new clothes Garrett had sent for. During this process, a "glum and sober" Billy Wilson "scarcely raised his eyes and spoke but once or twice to his compadre," observed the reporter. "Bonney, on the other hand, was light and chipper and was very communicative, laughing, joking and chatting with bystanders."[3]

"You appear to take it easy," remarked the newsman.

"Yes," replied the Kid. "What's the use of looking on the gloomy side of everything. The laugh's on me this time." Then, glancing around, he asked, "Is the jail at Santa Fe any better than this? This is a terrible place to put a fellow in."

"There was a big crowd gazing at me wasn't there," said Billy, clearly pleased with his notoriety. "Well, perhaps some of them will think me half man now; everyone seems to think I was some kind of animal."

The reporter agreed that Billy did not look like an animal:

He did look human, indeed, but there was nothing very mannish about him in appearance, for he looked and acted a mere boy. He is about five feet eight or nine inches tall, slightly built and lithe, weighing about 140; a frank open countenance, looking like a school boy, with the traditional silky fuzz on his upper lip; clear blue eyes, with a rougish snap about them; light hair and complexion. He is, in all, quite a handsome looking fellow, the only imperfection being two prominent front teeth slightly protruding like squirrel's teeth, and he has agreeable and winning ways.

As the shackles were riveted back in position over the new clothing, Billy observed, "I don't suppose you fellows would believe it but this is the first time I ever had bracelets on." In this boast he stretched the truth slightly: bracelets had encumbered him briefly in Arizona.

The captives had scarcely been lodged in the Las Vegas jail when the temper of the town turned ugly. Hostility focused on Ruda-baugh, whose abortive attempt to break John Webb out of jail had cost the life of a jailer. Fearing a lynch mob, Garrett and his men stood guard at the jail throughout the night of December 26, then prepared to hurry the prisoners out of town the next day.

Sheriff Romero demanded the surrender of Rudabaugh. Garrett refused. He held three of the prisoners on federal charges—Bonney for the murder of Buckshot Roberts on a federal reservation, Wilson for counterfeiting, and Rudabaugh for robbing the U.S. mail. As a deputy U.S. marshal, Garrett intended to take the federal fugitives to Santa Fe and turn them over to the chief U.S. marshal. Romero could have Tom Pickett, but Garrett made it clear, as he had promised Rudabaugh at Stinking Springs, that the others would remain in federal custody.[4]

Shortly after noon on the twenty-seventh, Garrett loaded Bonney, Wilson, and Rudabaugh into public hacks and hauled them from Old Town, the site of the jail, to New Town, where the railway depot stood. Stewart, Mason, East, and Emory went along as guards, together with another deputy U.S. marshal, James W. Bell.[5] The train to Santa Fe rested on a sidetrack, delayed until a northbound train could pass. The deputies and their prisoners boarded the smoking car and settled in their seats to wait.

Spurred by angry citizens, Sheriff Romero had not given up. He had telegraphed Governor Wallace for an order barring the removal of Rudabaugh. Receiving no answer as the train's departure time approached, Romero formed a posse of thirty-five men and descended on the depot.

Garrett stood on the platform at one end of the smoking car as a group of five men, headed by the sheriff's brother, approached.

"Let's go right in and take him out of there," said one, and they pushed up the steps to the platform.

"I merely requested them, in my mildest tones, to get down," said Garrett, "and they slid to the ground like a covey of hardback turtles off the banks of the Pecos."[6]

Determined to prevent the train from leaving, Romero sent a force to seize the switch to the main line and another to neutralize the engineer and the fireman. The rest of the men, backed by a gathering mob, crowded around the coach containing the prisoners.

Undaunted, Billy chose this moment to have another interview with the *Gazette*'s reporter. Leaning from the window, he exclaimed, "If I only had my Winchester, I'd lick the whole crowd." "The prospects of a fight exhilarated him," commented the newsman.

Billy then launched into a protestation of innocence such as he had already inflicted on Governor Wallace:

I wasn't the leader of any gang—I was for Billy all the time. About that Portales business, I owned the ranche with Charlie Bowdre. I took it up and was holding it because I knew that sometime a stage line would run by there and I wanted to keep it for a station. But, I found that there were certain men who wouldn't let me live in the country and so I was going to leave. We had all our grub in the house when they took us in, and we were going to a place about six miles away in the morning to cook it and then light out. I haven't stolen any stock. I made my living by gambling but that was the only way I could live. They wouldn't let me settle down; if they had I wouldn't be here today. Chisum got me into all this trouble and then wouldn't help me out.[7]

The temper of the growing mob, meantime, had turned ominous. Men brandishing Winchesters surged against the smoking car.

Garrett shouted, "If you wanted the men so badly why didn't you go out and take them?"

"We'll take them now," cried several.

Stewart answered, "As soon as the first shot is fired we will free every man and arm him."[8]

"We shoved up the windows," remembered Jim East, "and Tom

Emory took one and I another. . . . We made all the prisoners get down on the floor of the coach so they could not shoot them through the windows."[9]

For a time bloodshed seemed inevitable. Garrett and his deputies clearly meant business. But voices of moderation gradually made themselves heard in the crowd, and the combative urge subsided. As a face-saving gesture, Garrett agreed to take two representatives of the sheriff with him to Santa Fe to certify that the prisoners had been safely locked in the jail there.

At the head of the train, although the main line was now clear and the switch thrown, the possemen held the engineer and the fireman at bay with rifles. The trainmen blustered about obstruction of the U.S. mail, but that failed to deter the irate townsmen. Finally J. F. Morley, a former railway engineer now serving as a postal inspector, jumped into the cab and hit the throttle. "He was a little excited, I guess," observed Jim East, "jerked it wide open, and the wheels spun around a few times but took hold and by the time we got to the end of the siding it seemed like we were going a mile a minute, and the Mexicans stood there with their mouths open. The engineer and fireman caught the train as it pulled out."[10]

That evening, at the railway depot in Santa Fe, Pat Garrett turned over his captives to federal authorities, who promptly clapped them in the county jail on Water Street. Townspeople poured out their thanks to the lawmen for ridding the territory of its most notorious desperadoes. "The arrival here of the prisoners created a good deal of excitement," reported the *New Mexican* the next day, "and Sheriff Garrett is the hero of the hour."[11]

Garrett basked in the accolade but had more tangible evidence of public gratitude in mind—the five-hundred-dollar reward the governor had posted for Billy the Kid two weeks earlier. But Wallace had left for the East on December 28, and the acting governor, territorial secretary William G. Ritch, seized on a technicality to withhold payment. Indignant citizens took up a purse and advanced Garrett the amount of the reward.[12]

With Garrett and his "posse of brave men" the heroes of the hour, the Kid suffered an abrupt eclipse. For nearly three months, while awaiting trial, he endured an unaccustomed immobility. Even so, his busy mind never stopped seeking some way out.

His first thoughts turned to Governor Wallace, whose bargain nearly two years earlier remained firmly fixed in his memory. On January 1, 1881, Billy scrawled a short note to the dignitary whose office now stood scarcely two blocks from his cell: "I would like to see you for a few moments if you can spare the time."[13] But, as the Kid soon learned, Wallace was not in his office but on a train speeding toward Washington, D.C.

Billy next tried to find legal help. Ira Leonard, also en route for the East, visited him sometime in January and promised to stop on the way back. When he failed to appear, Billy turned to Dave Rudabaugh's attorney, Edgar Caypless, who not surprisingly wanted a retainer. To raise the money, Billy sold Caypless the beautiful bay mare, judged by many to be the fleetest in New Mexico, that had borne him in many an adventure and that, but for a blocked doorway, might have extricated him from the rock house at Stinking Springs. But Billy's title to the mare turned out to be clouded. After Stinking Springs, he had given her to Frank Stewart—or so Stewart claimed—and Stewart in turn had presented her to the wife of the proprietor of the hotel at the Las Vegas Hot Springs, W. Scott Moore. Caypless brought suit against Moore for possession of the animal, but pending the outcome of the case Billy languished in jail without any help from the lawyer.[14]

Billy now tried more direct measures. In February, with Rudabaugh and Wilson, he began the slow and tedious task of digging beneath the cell wall toward the street, hiding the dirt and stones in the bedticking and in turn using it to cover the excavation. Fearing just such an attempt, Sheriff Romulo Martínez planted an informer in the jail and, virtually on the eve of success, learned of the scheme. On the last day of February, Martínez and Marshal Sherman's chief deputy, Tony Neis, barged into the cell, uncovered the hole, and aborted the plot. Billy and his friends wound up heavily ironed and constantly guarded.[15]

Thwarted, the Kid turned once more to Governor Wallace, now back from his eastern travels. On March 2, only two days after the collapse of the escape stratagem, he again wrote to Wallace, this time throwing in a hint of blackmail:

I wish you would come down to the jail to see me. It will be to your interest to come and see me. I have some letters which date back two years and there are Parties who are very anxious to get them but I shall not dispose of them until I see you. that is if you will come immediately.[16]

Billy had in mind the letters Wallace had written him in March 1879, offering amnesty in the Brady killing in exchange for testimony in the Chapman killing. Publication of the letters could not have caused much political harm, especially since a new president had been elected and Wallace hoped for an appointment that would post him to a more appealing place than New Mexico. Doubtless also irritated by the crude threat, he ignored the missive. Two days later, March 4, Billy wrote again:

I wrote you a little note the day before yesterday, but have received no answer I Expect you have forgotten what you promised me this month two years ago, but I have not, and I think you had ought to have come and seen me as I requested you to. I have done everything that I promised you I would, and you have done nothing that you promised me. I think when you think the matter over, you will come down and see me, and I can then explain everything to you.

Judge Leonard Passed through here on his way east in January and promised to come and see me on his way back, but he did not fulfill his Promise. it looks to me like I am getting left in the cold. I am not treated right by Sherman. he lets every Stranger that comes to see me through curiosity in to see me, but will not let a single one of my friends in, not even an attorney. I guess they mean to send me up without giving me any show, but they will have a nice time doing it. I am not entirely without friends. I shall expect to see you some time today

Governor Wallace read the letter, filed it with Billy's earlier messages, and made no response. Possibly he felt a twinge of guilt, though probably not. He could rationalize his behavior as well as could Billy, and the boy's effrontery surely roused indignation in the stately occupant of the Palace of the Governors.

So far as it went, the letter expressed the truth. Billy had done everything he promised, and Wallace had done nothing, at least nothing that had produced any benefit. The tone of reproach and injured innocence would have been justified in the summer of 1879. In the spring of 1881 it no longer reflected reality. However much the press had magnified his stature as a criminal, Billy had incontestably turned more and more to crime in 1880. He had thus forfeited whatever claim he had once had on executive clemency. Whether or not Billy truly believed that he still deserved the governor's aid, he perceived his prospects with clarity: he had become New Mexico's No. 1 outlaw, and "they" did indeed intend to send him up, with or without "any show."

Time had run out. Billy was to be tried in Judge Bristol's court in Mesilla, and as the spring term approached, so did the end of the Kid's sojourn in the Santa Fe jail. On March 27 he made one final attempt to catch the governor's attention: "for the *last time* I ask, Will you Keep your promise. I start below tomorrow Send answer by bearer."

Although no bearer arrived with an answer, Ira Leonard appeared to accompany Billy to Mesilla as his defense attorney, a development that may have reflected Wallace's intent that the youth have at least some "show" in Judge Bristol's hostile courtroom. Dave Rudabaugh had already been returned to Las Vegas to stand trial, but Billy Wilson accompanied the Kid to face counterfeiting charges in Mesilla. On March 28, with a studied absence of publicity, Tony Neis and another deputy marshal ushered the two Billies aboard a railway coach for the trip down the Rio Grande.[17]

Word of the move spread quickly in advance. At Rincon, where the main line of the Santa Fe turned west, the party had to switch to another train for the short run into Las Cruces. A menacing mob had gathered, but the deputies faced it down. In Las Cruces another mob threatened the prisoners, but Billy himself, with his customary good humor, defused the tension. When someone asked which was Billy the Kid, he placed his hand on Leonard's shoulder and quipped, "this is the man."[18]

Locked in the squalid Mesilla jail, Billy confronted nearly impossible odds. Both federal and territorial indictments hung over him, and prosecutors had only to work their way from one indictment to the next until one ended in conviction. New Mexico's court system worked against him, for federal and territorial courts were virtually the same. Prosecutors differed, and records remained separate, but Judge Bristol presided over both courts from the same bench in the same courtroom.

The federal charge took precedence. Ironically, it had originated as a cynical ploy of the Dolan forces in the Lincoln County War. The shooting of Buckshot Roberts at Blazer's Mills had occurred on an Indian reservation and thus afforded a pretext for mobilizing federal officers on Dolan's side. This indictment, wrung from a federal grand jury in Mesilla in June 1878, had named all the Regulators who had taken part in the fight and had thus made them all federal fugitives. As nearly everyone knew, Charley Bowdre had shot Buckshot Roberts, and it was his indictment for this deed in the territorial court that had prevented him from claiming Governor Wallace's amnesty and thus had led him ultimately to the rock house at Stinking Springs. Billy's name on the federal indictment, however, had provided rationale for his pursuit and apprehension by Pat Garrett in his capacity as a deputy U.S. marshal. Both as a question of guilt and as a question of federal jurisdiction, the case against Billy could hardly have been thinner, but it had sufficed to ensnare him. Not entirely without reason did he believe that "they" meant to get him, show or no show.

On March 30, 1881, Judge Bristol convened the U.S. district court in a rundown adobe building fronting the Mesilla plaza. His gavel fell on a scarred wooden table resting on a raised platform. An open space, for the presentations of the attorneys, separated him from the rough wooden benches filled with spectators. Similar makeshift furniture accommodated the jurors.[19]

When the clerk of the court called the Roberts case, Billy stood to say that he had no attorney and no money to engage one. Judge Bristol then appointed Ira Leonard to conduct the defense. This charade was probably contrived to enable Leonard to draw a modest fee from the court for serving as a public defender. U.S. Attorney Sydney M. Barnes then read the indictment, and the formal plea was set for the next day.[20]

The case against Billy occupied little of the court's time. The next day, March 31, he entered a plea of not guilty. But when the case came up for argument on April 5, Leonard withdrew the plea and substituted another, alleging lack of federal jurisdiction. Blazer's Mills, he contended, was private property and not part of the reservation. In fact, Dr. Blazer had settled at South Fork before the establishment of the reservation, and the question of title (and thus jurisdiction) continued to be caught up in a long-running dispute between him and the Indian Bureau. Barnes advanced some lame arguments, but Judge Bristol needed only a day to find Leonard's position tenable. On April 6 he dismissed the case but directed that the defendant be handed over to territorial authorities for trial in the Brady killing.[21]

Two days later, April 8, Judge Bristol doffed his federal robes and donned his territorial robes. Billy's implacable persecutor, William L. Rynerson, was no longer district attorney. His successor, Simon B. Newcomb, rose to call Billy to the docket once again. For unknown reasons, Leonard bowed out of the defense. Judge Bristol appointed the local partnership of Bail and Fountain as counsel.

Both John D. Bail and Albert J. Fountain were men of ability and integrity. Fountain was already well on the way to becoming one of New Mexico's most notable public men. As editor of the *Mesilla Independent*, he had crusaded against Jesse Evans and his fellow "banditti" in 1877–78, but he had dropped newspapering after outlaw retaliation almost cost the lives of his sons. As attorney, militia officer, and flamboyant political partisan, Fountain was one of southern New Mexico's most prominent figures.[22]

What defense Bail and Fountain offered is lost to history, as indeed is the thrust of the prosecution. That a trial of such public interest then and since should have left so little record is baffling and disappointing. Neither in surviving court records nor in surviving newspapers is there more than a skeleton account of the testimony and arguments. The witnesses for the prosecution are known, as are the names of the jurors, all Hispanic. The trial lasted only two days,

April 8 and 9. Whether Bail and Fountain put the Kid on the stand in his own defense is unknown.[23]

Testifying for the prosecution, Isaac Ellis, Bonifacio Baca, and J. B. Mathews took the stand. As one of Sheriff Brady's companions on the morning of the killing, and as the man who had put a bullet through the Kid's thigh, Mathews surely offered direct and compelling evidence. Ike Ellis, usually viewed as friendly to the Kid and the other Regulators, operated the store at the east edge of Lincoln. His contribution to the trial can scarcely be guessed; if he saw the shooting, the fact is unrecorded. Bonnie Baca, Saturnino Baca's young son and supposedly the Kid's friend, may well have watched all or part of the event, for the Bacas lived nearby. Billy felt especially grieved that Bonnie appeared against him.

The defense attorneys seem to have directed most of their efforts toward influencing Judge Bristol's charge to the jury, although it is difficult to understand how their view of the case favored their client. They wanted the jury to find the defendant either not guilty or guilty of murder in the first degree—that is, premeditated murder. A guilty finding, in their view, required no reasonable doubt that Billy had fired the fatal shot, or had assisted in firing it, or had counseled or commanded its firing.

In substance, Judge Bristol incorporated Bail and Fountain's position into his instructions to the jury, but he went much further. In force and content his directions virtually dictated a guilty finding. Dwelling at length on the meaning of "premeditation" and "reasonable doubt," he all but defined those critical concepts out of existence.

In fact, on the strength of Mathews's testimony alone, there could be little reasonable doubt, however defined, that Billy met at least the third test of premeditated murder as his own counsels viewed it. If he did not fire the fatal shot or share in firing it, he surely counseled or commanded others to fire it. The jury needed hardly any time to come up with the required verdict.

For first-degree murder, New Mexico law left no discretion in sentence to judge or jury. In returning its verdict of Billy's guilt, therefore, the jury did "assess his punishment at death." At 5:15

P.M. on April 13, 1881, Billy and his attorneys faced Judge Bristol for the formality of sentencing. Asked if he had anything to say, the defendant, the record noted, "says nothing." Thereupon, the judge directed that the prisoner be turned over to the sheriff of Lincoln County to be confined in jail in Lincoln until May 13 and that on that day, between the hours of nine and three, "the said William Bonney, alias Kid, alias William Antrim be hanged by the neck until his body be dead."

Billy voiced his feelings two days later, on April 15. Asked by a reporter if he expected a pardon, he replied:

> *Considering the active part Governor Wallace took on our side and the friendly relations that existed between him and me, and the promise he made me, I think he ought to pardon me. Don't know that he will do it. When I was arrested for that murder [Brady's] he let me out and gave me the freedom of the town, and let me go about with my arms. When I got ready to go [from Lincoln, in June 1879] I left. Think it hard I should be the only one to suffer the extreme penalty of the law.*[24]

A little more than a week later, the governor commented on this statement. Of the Kid, a Las Vegas reporter observed to Wallace, "He appears to look to you to save his neck."

"Yes," was the reply, "but I can't see how a fellow like him should expect any clemency from me."

"Although not committing himself," added the reporter, "the general tenor of the governor's remarks indicated that he would resolutely refuse to grant 'the Kid' a pardon. It would seem as though 'the Kid' had undertaken to bulldoze the governor, which has not helped his chances in the slightest."[25]

In his self-deception, Billy failed to appreciate his own role in shaping the governor's attitude. By turning more and more openly to crime in 1880, he denied Wallace maneuvering room to work out some acceptable form of executive clemency. Even so, as late as October 1880, the governor was pressing Ira Leonard to do something for the Kid. With the young outlaw's leap to fame in December 1880, however, Wallace lost all chance to help without incurring serious political consequences. And as the reporter noted, Billy did not improve his prospects by trying to bulldoze the governor.

Still, Billy had reason to believe that he had been unjustly treated. He had lived up to his part of the bargain, and others by the dozen were as guilty of crime as he. Among fifty or more men indicted for offenses in the Lincoln County War, only he was convicted of any crime—and that conviction, as he noted, carried "the extreme penalty of the law."

Another truth must also enter into the judgment of Billy's fate. However many other offenders deserved punishment, including those who shared in the crime for which he alone was tried, there is virtually no chance that at least one of the bullets that killed Sheriff Brady was not fired by the Kid. Only he stood convicted, but there can be no reasonable doubt of his guilt.

The Escape

At 10:00 P.M. on April 16, 1881, deputies quietly loaded Billy the Kid into a wagon in front of the Mesilla jail and made ready to take the road to the east. As a precaution against either an attempted lynching or an attempted rescue, authorities had spread word that he would be sent to Lincoln County in the middle of the following week. Instead, on Saturday night they slipped him out of town under cover of darkness. Seven men rode guard—a deputy U.S. marshal, a deputy sheriff of Doña Ana County, and five men specially deputized for the mission.

Three of the guards could hardly be viewed as unbiased toward the prisoner. All three had fought for Jimmy Dolan in the Lincoln County War, and all three had participated in the fatal battle at the McSween house on July 19, 1878. Billy Mathews had headed the posse that killed Tunstall, had drilled Billy in the thigh at the time of the Brady killing, and had testified against him in Judge Bristol's court. A second deputy was John Kinney, still the rustler king of southern New Mexico but, as in the final frays of the Lincoln County War, still not averse at times to playing lawman. The third was Charles Robert Olinger.

One of two brothers who had attached themselves to Hugh Beckwith's clan at Seven Rivers, Bob Olinger had served as a deputy U.S. marshal for more than a year. He had ridden with Pat Garrett in the failed raid on Fort Sumner in November 1880, and he claimed Marshal Sherman's chief deputy, Tony Neis, as a close friend. "Pecos Bob," he styled himself, and his appearance fortified the label. A fellow officer described him as

two hundred pounds of bones and muscle, six feet tall, round as a huge tree trunk, with a regular gorilla-like chest that bulged out so far his chin seemed to be set back in his chest. He had a heavy bull neck, low-browed head, short and wide, topped with shaggy hair, bushy eyebrows, and a hat-rack mustache. His arms were long and muscular, with fists like hams. Despite his build and size he was quick as a cat, and always got the best of the deal in any encounter he figured in. He could take punishment as well as hand it out. He loved to show off, and it was one of his tricks to throw his .45's and keep a string of fire from both muzzles as long as the bullets lasted.[1]

Olinger stirred contradictory emotions among those who knew him. "Bob Olinger was a damned rascal and deserved killing," declared Gus Gildea. "Bob was a murderer," said Jake Owens, who watched him extend a hand in friendship to a victim and coolly shoot him in the belly with the other. "Bob Olinger was considerate and generous," recalled Lily Casey Klasner, who probably was in love with him. "Noble fellow . . . brave, generous, and true as steel," pronounced the Santa Fe *New Mexican*.[2]

Whichever—and the weight of opinion brands him a callous bully—Olinger and Billy the Kid despised each other. Olinger held Billy responsible for the death of his friend Bob Beckwith in Mc-Sween's backyard on the night of the final shootout. According to an acquaintance, Olinger declared that the Kid "was a cur and that every man he had killed had been murdered in cold blood and without the slightest chance of defending himself." "There was a reciprocal hatred between these two," observed Pat Garrett, "and neither attempted to disguise or conceal his antipathy for the other."[3]

With a perverse satisfaction that he made no effort to hide, Olinger settled in the wagon on the seat facing Billy, who was handcuffed and shackled with leg-irons to the back seat. Kinney climbed in beside Billy, and Mathews hoisted himself into the seat next to

Olinger. Deputy Sheriff Dave Woods drove the wagon, and Tom Williams, D. M. Reade, and W. A. Lockhart rode flank and rear.

In Las Cruces, the party paused in front of the newspaper office of Harry Newman. The Kid, reported Newman, "appeared quite cheerful and remarked that he wanted to stay with the boys until their whiskey gave out, anyway. Said he was sure his guard would not hurt him unless a rescue should be attempted and he was certain that would not be done unless perhaps 'those fellows over at White Oaks come out to take me,' meaning to kill him." He made some unflattering comments about the Mesilla jail and John Chisum, and off the cavalcade clattered.[4]

The officers and their charge took almost five days to reach Fort Stanton. On April 20 they spent the night at Blazer's Mills, where the loquacious Billy reenacted in pantomime the shootout of April 4, 1878, and the killing of Buckshot Roberts. The next day, at Fort Stanton, Lincoln County Sheriff Pat Garrett formally took responsibility for the Kid, and the party rode on into Lincoln.[5]

Lincoln had never had a jail, observed Garrett, "that would hold a cripple."[6] Billy was hardly a cripple, and the sheriff, keenly aware of his prisoner's daring and cunning, decided not to drop him into the old cellar jail. Instead, he would be confined under constant guard in a room next to the sheriff's office in the newly acquired county courthouse. This was the old Murphy-Dolan store on the west end of town that had played so conspicuous a part in the Lincoln County War. Billy was lodged in the northeast corner room on the second floor. The task of guarding him was assigned to Bob Olinger and Deputy James W. Bell.

As Garrett well knew, Billy's fertile mind dwelled constantly on how to get free. Unrealistically, as he had revealed in Mesilla, he still hoped that Governor Wallace might pardon him. Also, lawyer Fountain had given the Kid reason to think further legal stratagems were worth pursuing. On April 15, while still in the Mesilla jail, Billy had written to attorney Edgar Caypless in Santa Fe urging him to press the suit to recover the contested mare, sell her, and turn over the money to Fountain.[7] And finally, of course, he schemed endlessly to contrive a plan of escape—a vaulting aim considering handcuffs, leg-irons, and two watchful guards.

Olinger's persistent taunting spurred the determination to get free. "Olinger was mean to him," testified the Kid's friend John Meadows. "In talking about it to me Kid said, 'He used to work me up until I could hardly contain myself.'"[8]

By contrast, Bell treated Billy well. As a close friend of Jimmy Carlyle's, whose death at the Greathouse ranch everyone held Billy responsible for, Bell had good reason to despise his charge. But he was kindly, generous, and widely liked, and he did not take out his spite on the helpless prisoner. "Never, by word or action, did he betray his prejudice, if it existed," said Garrett of Bell. In return, Billy had confidence in Bell and "appeared to have taken a liking to him."[9]

Garrett also treated Billy considerately. They discussed the boy's various exploits and impending fate. As always, Billy was adept at self-justification. "He appeared to have a plausible excuse for each and every crime charged against him," said Garrett, "except, perhaps, the killing of Carlyle." At times he seemed to Garrett on the point of talking openly, but always he would draw back and intimate that no one would believe any explanation he made. "He expressed no enmity towards me," related Garrett, "but evinced respect and confidence in me . . . acknowledging that I had only done my duty, without malice, and had treated him with marked leniency and kindness."[10]

"I knew the desperate character of the man," said Garrett later, "that he was daring and unscrupulous, and that he would sacrifice the lives of a hundred men who stood between him and liberty."[11] Repeatedly cautioning Olinger and Bell never to relax their vigilance, the sheriff laid down procedures to ensure that Billy had no chance to make a break.

A friend gave Olinger a similar warning. "You think yourself an old hand in the business," he warned. "But I tell you, as good a man as you are, that if that man is shown the slightest chance on earth, if he is allowed the use of one hand, or if he is not watched every moment from now until the moment he is executed, he will effect some plan by which he will murder the whole lot of you before you have time to even suspect that he has any such intention."

Olinger just smiled and replied that the Kid had no more chance of escaping than of going to heaven.[12]

On April 28, with Garrett in White Oaks collecting taxes, Billy made his move. Whether he planned it in advance or acted on impulse is not known. His mind may have been set in motion that morning by more of Olinger's abuse. Ostentatiously, the deputy loaded his double-barreled shotgun with eighteen buckshot in each barrel. Looking meaningfully at the Kid, he remarked, "The man that gets one of those loads will feel it."

"I expect he will," Billy replied, "but be careful, Bob, or you might shoot yourself accidentally."[13]

Bell and Olinger were responsible for five other prisoners as well, held in another room of the courthouse. They had been arrested a week earlier at South Fork after a dispute over water rights erupted in gunfire, taking the lives of four Tularosa residents. Now the accused murderers awaited grand jury action. About 6:00 P.M. on Thursday evening April 28, Olinger escorted these men across the street to the Wortley Hotel for dinner.[14]

The Kid asked Bell to take him to the privy behind the courthouse. Returning, Bell carelessly lagged behind. An interior staircase connected a back door with the upstairs center hall. Although burdened with leg-irons and chains, Billy reached the top of the stairs before his guard and turned into the hall out of view. Handcuffs did not pose a problem for Billy because his hands were smaller than his wrists. Quickly he slipped the cuffs off one wrist. When Bell appeared at the head of the stairs, Billy swung the loose cuff in vicious blows that laid open two gashes on the guard's scalp. Bell went down, Billy jumped on him, and the two scuffled for Bell's holstered revolver. Billy later explained that he wanted to get the drop on Bell, handcuff him to Olinger, and make his escape.

In the struggle, Billy succeeded in seizing the pistol, but Bell worked loose and headed for the stairway. Billy fired, and Bell tumbled down the stairs.

"Kid told me exactly how it was done," said John Meadows. "He said he was lying on the floor on his stomach, and shot Bell as he ran down the stairs. Kid said of this killing, 'I did not want to kill Bell, but I had to do so in order to save my own life. It was a case of have to, not wanting to.'"[15]

Walking across the yard behind the courthouse, Godfrey Gauss heard the shot and the commotion. As cook for the Tunstall hands on the Feliz three years earlier, the old German knew Billy well. Now, with Sam Wortley, he shared a little dwelling and tended a garden behind the courthouse. Before his startled eyes Bell burst from the back door and lunged toward him. "He ran right into my arms," related Gauss, "expired the same moment, and I laid him down dead."[16]

Upstairs, meantime, Billy got to his feet and dragged his shackled legs into Garrett's office. There he scooped up Olinger's loaded shotgun and made his way to the northeast corner room. A window in the east wall opened onto a yard below, enclosed by a low plank fence with a gate affording entry from the street. Resting the shotgun on the windowsill, Billy waited.

Below, Gauss ran from the backyard just as Olinger and his prisoners, alerted by the gunfire, appeared in front of the Wortley Hotel. Gauss yelled for him to come quickly. Ordering the prisoners to stand firm, Olinger hurried across the street and opened the gate.

"Bob, the Kid has killed Bell," cried Gauss.

Olinger looked up and exclaimed, "Yes, and he's killed me too."

As Billy recalled it, "I stuck the gun through the window and said, 'Look up, old boy, and see what you get.' Bob looked up, and I let him have both barrels right in the face and breast." Olinger crumpled, his head and upper body shredded by the thirty-six heavy buckshot he himself had packed into the twin barrels of his shotgun.[17]

Next the Kid went to the window at the south end of the hallway overlooking the backyard and shouted at Gauss, who had made tracks for the shelter of his abode.

"Gauss, pitch me up that old pick-axe lying out there," he said, "and let me get this chain between my feet broke in two with it."

"Look out, Billy, here she comes," said Gauss, who willingly co-operated through both fear and friendship.

Billy then ordered Gauss to saddle up a horse in the corral that belonged to Billy Burt, deputy clerk of the probate court.[18]

With the pick, Billy succeeded in severing the chain connecting his leg shackles. Looping the ends over his belt, he walked to the north end of the hall and appeared on a balcony overlooking the street. A knot of men, including the other prisoners, stood in front of the Wortley Hotel while a scattering of citizens watched silently from more distant parts of the street. Two townsmen started for their Winchesters but were restrained by others. "The balance of the population," according to an observer, "whether friends or enemies of the Kid, manifested no disposition to molest him."[19]

One of the men in front of the hotel described the scene:

It was more than an hour, after he killed Olinger and Bell, before he left. He had at his command eight revolvers and six guns [rifles]. He stood on the upper porch in front of the building and talked with the people who were in Wortley's, but would not let anyone come towards him. He told the people that he did not want to kill Bell but, as he ran, he had to. He said he grabbed Bell's revolver and told him to hold up his hands and surrender; that Bell decided to run and he had to kill him. He declared he was "standing pat" against the world; and, while he did not wish to kill anybody, if anybody interfered with his attempt to escape he would kill him.[20]

Gauss had trouble saddling Burt's spirited pony but at length led him to the front of the building and tied him to the hitching rail. Before descending, Billy smashed Olinger's shotgun over the porch railing and hurled the pieces at his victim's bloody corpse.

"Here is your gun, God damn you," he shouted. "You won't follow me with it any longer."[21]

Emerging from the back door at the foot of the stairs, the Kid glanced down at the motionless form of Jim Bell.

"I'm sorry I had to kill you," he said, "but couldn't help it."

He then made his way around the building to the street, where he paused at Olinger's body.

"You are not going to round me up again," he said, nudging the corpse with the tip of his boot.[22]

Encumbered with shackles and chain as well as pistols and rifles, Billy encountered difficulty controlling the skittish pony. As he tried to swing into the saddle, the animal broke loose and trotted toward the river. He called to Alex Nunnelly, one of Olinger's prisoners standing in front of the hotel, to catch the animal and bring it back. Nunnelly hesitated, but a quick motion by Billy prompted him to do as ordered.

"Old fellow," observed the Kid, "if you hadn't gone for this horse, I would have killed you."[23]

Firmly planted in the saddle, his chains slapping his legs and thighs, Billy the Kid pointed his mount to the west and rode out of Lincoln.

"Tell Billy Burt I will send his horse back to him," he called as he vanished in the distance.[24]

He left behind a stunned town of Lincoln, whose citizens, said Garrett, "appeared to be terror-stricken." He thought the Kid could have ridden up and down the town's only street until dark without interference from a single resident. "A little sympathy might have actuated some of them, but most of the people were, doubtless, paralyzed with fear when it was whispered that the dreaded desperado, the Kid, was at liberty and had slain his guards."[25]

The news shocked the entire territory. The spectacular breakout, so clever in conception and bold in execution, validated Billy the Kid's reputation as a "dreaded desperado." Five months earlier, prompted by the *Las Vegas Gazette*, the territorial press had built him up as New Mexico's premier desperado. He had not earned such fame; his genuine deeds, however remarkable in one so young, did not qualify him for the distinction. The sensational bolt from Lincoln, however, transformed him into the territory's foremost outlaw in fact as well as in name.

In name he emerged in blacker form than ever, as newspapers drenched him in rhetorical excess. In one breathless paragraph, the *Las Vegas Optic* branded him a "young demon," a "terror and disgrace of New Mexico," a "flagrant violator of every law," a "murderer from infancy." He was "malignant and cruel," "urged by a spirit as hideous as hell," blind to "the drooping forms of widows and the tear-stained eyes of orphans." "With a heart untouched to pity by misfortune, and with a character possessing the attributes of the damned, he has reveled in brutal murder and gloried in his shame. He has broken more loving hearts and filled more untimely graves than he has lived years, and that he is again turned loose like some devouring beast on the public is cause at once for consternation and regret."[26]

While execrating his character, editors could not suppress admiration for his dramatic leap to freedom. It displayed, said the *New Mexican*, "a subtle calculation on the part of the prisoner, and a coolness and steadiness of nerve in executing his plan of escape, that the highly wrought story of Dick Turpin can hardly furnish a counterpart to."[27]

Such commentary on Billy's exploit contained little exaggeration. Traits first manifested in the Lincoln County War combined to produce a brilliant if tragically bloody feat. Crafty, utterly fearless, heedless of risk, cool under stress, instantly unflinching in taking any life that stood in his way, he surpassed both his guards in skill and intellect. Billy's sunny exterior concealed a powerfully coiled spring held in by a hair-trigger. When the spring was released, he struck like a rattlesnake, swiftly and fatally.

The guards gave Billy his opening—Olinger from arrogance and conceit, Bell from a kindly disposition lulled by Billy's relaxed good cheer. In the face of Garrett's repeated admonitions, they both underestimated their prisoner. In return, Billy killed them, Bell regretfully, Olinger jubilantly, both unhesitatingly.

Billy the Kid rode out of Lincoln on Thursday evening, April 28, 1881. In White Oaks, Pat Garrett learned of the escape the next day and promptly sent a rider overland to Socorro, on the railroad, with a message to the sheriff there: "I have just received news from Lincoln by courier that Billy the Kid escaped yesterday evening, after killing Deputy Sheriffs J. W. Bell and Bob Ollinger." Not until

Saturday night, April 30, did a one-line telegram from Socorro bring the news to Governor Lew Wallace in Santa Fe.

Only hours earlier the governor himself had written out a document that he supposed would end his troubled association with Billy the Kid. It was a death warrant, which the law required him to sign before an execution could take place. It directed that, on May 13, 1881, between the hours of 10:00 A.M. and 3:00 P.M., the sheriff of Lincoln County remove William Bonney from the county jail and "hang the said William Bonny, alias Kid, alias William Antrim, by the neck until he is dead. And make due return of your acts hereunder."[28]

As commanded, the sheriff made "due return" under the date of May 24: "I hereby certify that the within warrant was not served owing to the fact that the within named prisoner escaped before the day set for serving said warrant. Pat F. Garrett, Sheriff of Lincoln County."[29]

The Execution

As Billy Bonney trotted out of Lincoln on the evening of April 28, 1881, he could count on the help of many friends. After riding about a quarter of a mile west on the Fort Stanton road, he veered to the north and crossed the river into the Capitan foothills. He paused at the home of Ataviano Salas, whose son-in-law, Francisco Gómez, poured him a cup of coffee laced with goat's milk and listened to his story of the escape. The fugitive then rode to the home of José Cordova in Salazar Canyon. Cordova and Scipio Salazar freed him from his shackles. Next Billy headed up the canyon toward the Capitan summit, aiming for Las Tablas, on the other side of the mountains. Here lived his old compadre from the Lincoln County War, Yginio Salazar.[1]

"I talked with Kid at my house at Las Tablas the next day," recalled Salazar. "The Kid laid off there for three days. He laid out in the hills and came to my house to eat. I told him to leave this place and go to Old Mexico." While Billy slept one night near Las Tablas, his horse pulled loose from a sotol stalk and made its way back to Lincoln, to be reclaimed by its owner.[2]

Stealing a horse from a Las Tablas resident, the Kid headed east, circling the north base of the Capitans to Agua Azul, then headed south, crossing the Ruidoso above San Patricio, and making his way to the Peñasco. There he spent a night at the cabin of another old friend, John Meadows. Until late at night, the two sat on a hillside talking. Meadows suspected that the Kid had come to the Peñasco

186

to do away with Billy Mathews, who had a ranch nearby. Although Bonney denied that he would harm Mathews even if given the chance, he may well have thought to settle old scores. Somehow, the newspapers got word that he had in fact shot and killed his enemy, but the report turned out to be untrue.[3]

Like Salazar, Meadows urged the Kid to flee into Old Mexico and start life anew. Billy's southward course from Agua Azul may indicate that he was already heeding this advice. But Fort Sumner pulled at him too. It was familiar, congenial, full of friends who would help him, and home to a bevy of damsels who adored him. He thought he would go there, he told Meadows.

"Sure as you do," warned his friend, "Garrett will get you, or you will have to kill him."

"Don't you worry," replied Billy, "I've got too many friends up there. Anyhow I don't believe he will try to get me. I can stay there awhile and get enough [money] to go to Mexico on."

The next morning Billy faced his horse toward Fort Sumner. A couple of days later, at Conejos Springs, he lay asleep in his blankets when Jim Cureton and some cowboys rode nearby rounding up cattle. Startled, the Kid jumped up. The sudden movement alarmed his horse, which bolted and left him afoot. A twenty-mile hike brought him to Fort Sumner, which he reached on Saturday May 7, nine days after his escape from Lincoln.[4]

That night Billy slipped into Sumner and found a tethered horse. It belonged to Montgomery Bell, a rancher from fifty miles upriver who had come to town on business. Billy mounted and rode away bareback. Sunday morning Bell reported the theft to Barney Mason, still a deputy sheriff. Joined by Jim Cureton, Mason took the trail. About fifteen miles down the Pecos they overhauled the quarry at a sheep camp. With four Hispanic allies, Billy made ready for a fight. Mason turned tail; he knew that his part in Stinking Springs, where he had proposed to shoot Billy after he surrendered, had made him a prime target. Cureton, unarmed, rode forward and talked with the Kid, who asked him to tell Bell that he would either return the stolen horse or pay for it.[5]

Once again, even though a hunted man, Billy Bonney settled

into the comfortable life of Fort Sumner. He drifted from one sheep camp to another, bunked at times at a ranch or farm, and on occasion brazenly slipped into Sumner itself to stomp merrily at a *baile* or keep a tryst with one of his female admirers.

As the spring weeks slipped by, the public's astonishment and outrage over Bonney's spectacular breakout gave no sign of subsiding. As far away as New York and San Francisco, people waited in fascinated suspense to learn whether the fearless young killer would remain at large. Governor Wallace offered another five-hundred-dollar reward for his capture but did not stay around to gauge its effect. The new president had named him minister to the court of the Turkish sultan, a post exactly suited to his romantic temperament, and on May 30 he boarded a Pullman sleeper to put New Mexico behind him forever.

No one who read the newspapers could doubt that Bonney was living, not very secretly, around Fort Sumner. Beginning with the theft of Bell's horse, the Las Vegas press regularly reported his presence in Sumner. As the *Gazette* observed on May 19, "Billy keeps well posted on matters in the outside world as he is well thought of by many of the Mexicans who take him all the newspapers they can get hold of. He is not far from Ft. Sumner and has not left that neighborhood since he rode over from Lincoln after making his break." Added the *New Mexican* on June 16: "The people regard him with a feeling half of fear and half of admiration, submit to his depredations, and some of them even go so far as to aid him in avoiding capture."

The press even picked up a wild tale of Billy's continuing feud with John Chisum. Billy was said to have ridden up to a Chisum cow camp and shot one of three herders through the brain. To the others he said, "Now, I want you to live to take a message to old John Chisum for me. Tell him during the Lincoln county war he promised to pay me $5 a day for fighting for him. I fought for him and never got a cent. Now, I intend to kill his men wherever I meet them, giving him credit for $5 every time I drop one until the debt is squared."[6] Later exposed as entirely false, the story, besides placing Billy in the Fort Sumner area, nonetheless accurately projected the image that was taking shape in the public mind.

Garrett puzzled over what to do. On the one hand, repeated reports from Fort Sumner convinced him that Billy must be there. On the other, as he said, "it seemed incredible that he should linger in the Territory." "He was never taken for a fool, but was credited with the possession of extraordinary forethought and cool judgment, for one of his age."[7]

Simply riding up to Sumner and searching for the fugitive was hardly an answer. As Garrett later explained, the Kid returned to his familiar retreats because "he said he was safer out on the plains, and could always get something to eat among the sheep herders. So he decided to take his chances out there where he was hard to get at."[8] Short of leaving New Mexico altogether, he was right. Garrett knew that he could not count on the cooperation of the residents, who would turn away in fear or alert the quarry and hide him. Only by the wildest accident of good fortune could he hope to succeed.

In June Garrett wrote to Manuel Brazil, the Fort Sumner rancher whose help had been critical in cornering the Kid and his cohorts at Stinking Springs, and asked if he had seen any sign of Billy. Brazil replied that he had not seen Billy but was sure enough of his proximity to keep out of sight in fear of his vengeance. Garrett received the letter in Lincoln early in July.[9]

Similar word came from another source—John W. Poe. This stocky former buffalo hunter with a drooping mustache had made a name for himself as a law officer in the Texas Panhandle. Impressed with his steady competence, the ranchers hired him to replace Frank Stewart as detective for the Panhandle Stock Association. Arriving in White Oaks in March 1881, Poe took up the probe, launched by his predecessors, of the relationship between the Pecos Valley rustlers and beef entrepreneur Pat Coghlan. Poe also fell in with Sheriff Pat Garrett and agreed to be commissioned a deputy sheriff of Lincoln County.[10]

Early in July, about the time of Brazil's letter to Garrett, Poe received a tip from an old acquaintance who had fallen on alcoholic bad times and was sleeping in the loft of the West and Diedrick stable. One night he had overheard two men, probably West and Diedrick, talking below. Their conversation made it clear that Billy the Kid was hiding out in Fort Sumner and in fact had twice visited White Oaks. Although skeptical, Poe took this information to Garrett in Lincoln. Together with Brazil's letter, Poe's report prompted Garrett to mount an expedition to Fort Sumner.[11]

Under cover of darkness, the sheriff's little posse pushed off from Roswell on July 10. Besides Garrett and Poe, a third officer had been recruited. He was Thomas K. (Tip) McKinney. Traveling mostly at night on little-used trails, the trio reached the mouth of Taiban Creek, below Fort Sumner, on the night of the thirteenth. Garrett had asked Manuel Brazil to meet him here, but Brazil failed to show up. The lawmen slept until daylight.[12]

The next step was up to John Poe. Since no one in Fort Sumner knew him, the three men decided that he should ride into town and learn what he could. If that proved futile, he was to go on up the Pecos to Sunnyside and talk with Postmaster Milnor Rudulph, whom Garrett thought might be willing to tell what he knew. After dark the three were to get back together at a designated point four miles north of Sumner.

Poe carried out his mission capably. His appearance in town aroused instant suspicion. He explained that he lived in White Oaks but was returning to his home in the Panhandle for a visit. In Beaver Smith's saloon he ate and drank with townsmen, virtually all Hispanics, but failed to pry any information out of them. The most offhand reference to Billy the Kid silenced everyone and intensified the obvious distrust with which all greeted the stranger. "There was a very tense situation in Fort Sumner on that day," Poe later wrote, "as the Kid was at that very time hiding in one of the native's houses there."

In midafternoon Poe mounted and rode up the Pecos seven miles to Sunnyside. Presenting Garrett's letter of introduction, he received a friendly welcome from Milnor Rudulph. After supper Poe broached the subject of Billy the Kid. Instantly Rudulph turned nervous and evasive. He had heard that Billy was in the area, he said, but he did not believe it. Further questioning produced only more agitated equivocation. At dusk, to his host's evident relief, Poe saddled up and rode down the river to rendezvous with his comrades.

In the darkness the three pondered their next move. The reaction of the villagers to Poe's visit, the behavior of Rudulph, and the tips from Brazil and from Poe's informant all pointed to Billy's presence somewhere around Fort Sumner. Yet the foolhardiness of such a course left all three with doubts too. At length they decided to slip into Sumner under cover of darkness, keep watch for a time on a dwelling that Garrett knew housed one of Billy's paramours, and then hunt up Pete Maxwell and talk with him. He might reveal something.[13]

On the north edge of Sumner, the lawmen chanced across the camp of a traveler. Coincidentally, he turned out to be an old friend of Poe's, from Texas.[14] Unsaddling here, the trio fortified themselves with coffee and then proceeded on foot. At about 9:00 P.M. they quietly took a station among the trees of a peach orchard on the northern fringe of the community. A bright moon illumined the scene. On the east side of the old parade ground were buildings that had once served as barracks for soldiers. On the west stood a line of dwellings that had housed officers. One had been fixed up as a residence for the Maxwells. Across the parade ground from the orchard, fronting the south side, the old quartermaster storehouse had been divided into rooms. At one end, hidden by officers' row, was Beaver Smith's saloon. Billy's friend Bob Campbell lived at the other end, and next door to him lived Sabal and Celsa Gutierrez.[15]

As the lawmen crept closer to the buildings, they suddenly heard muffled voices talking in Spanish. Crouching motionless behind trees, they listened. The people were in the orchard too, not far distant, but their words could not be understood. "Soon a man arose from the ground," said Garrett, "in full view, but too far away to recognize. He wore a broad-brimmed hat, a dark vest and pants, and was in his shirt sleeves." He said something, jumped the fence, and walked into the compound.[16]

Garrett did not recognize the figure, and learned only afterward that he was Billy the Kid. Whom he had been with and where he went after entering the old fort depends on which account one wants to accept. He may have ended up with Bob Campbell, or Celsa Gutierrez, or Deluvina Maxwell, or Jesús Silva and Francisco Lobato, among others.[17] He is not likely to have gone to Paulita's, since she lived with her family in the big house on officers' row and since his companion seems to have been someone in one of the rooms of the old quartermaster building.

Here, after shucking his hat, vest, and boots, Billy decided that he wanted something to eat. A freshly butchered yearling hung from a rafter on Maxwell's north porch. With a butcher knife in his left hand and his Colt "self-cocker" in his right, he shuffled out in his stockinged feet to cut a slab of meat.[18]

By now, nearly midnight, Garrett and his companions had backed out of the orchard, circled behind the officers' line on the west, and reached the Maxwell house. It was a long adobe, shadowed by porches on three sides. A picket fence with a gate separated the east face from the old parade ground. As Garrett knew, Maxwell slept in the southeast corner room. In the July heat, the door and windows stood open. Leaving Poe and McKinney outside, Garrett entered the door, walked across the room, and sat on the edge of Maxwell's bed, next to the pillow.

Outside, the two deputies waited. McKinney squatted on the ground outside the fence. Poe sat on the edge of the porch, dangling his feet in the open gateway.

Within seconds of Garrett's disappearance into Maxwell's bedroom, Poe glanced to his right and saw a figure approaching along the inside of the fence. In the moonlight, Poe recalled, "I observed that he was only partially dressed and was both bareheaded and barefooted, or rather, had only socks on his feet, and it seemed to me that he was fastening his trousers as he came toward me at a very brisk walk." Poe thought this might be Maxwell himself or one of his guests.

The man came almost face-to-face with Poe before spotting him. Startled, he recoiled, covered Poe with his pistol, and sprang to the porch, hissing "Quien es?" As he backed away, toward the door to Maxwell's bedroom, he repeated "Quien es? Quien es?"

Poe climbed to his feet and took several steps toward the man, telling him not to be alarmed, that they would not hurt him.

"Quien es?" the man asked again as he backed into the doorway and vanished inside.[19]

In the minute or so since waking Maxwell, Garrett had asked whether Billy the Kid was at Fort Sumner. Agitated, Maxwell had replied that he was not at the fort but was nearby. At that moment, they heard voices outside and saw the man back around the door-frame.

Approaching the bed, the man asked, "Who are those fellows outside, Pete?"

Bolting up in his bed, Maxwell spat out, "That's him."

Suddenly aware of the dark shape next to Maxwell, the man sprang back, pointed his pistol, and again demanded, "Quien es? Quien es?"

Garrett was as startled as the intruder. He had not even thought to ready his pistol. Quickly he shifted his holster and at the same in-stant identified the other man. "He must have then recognized me," Garrett later conjectured, "for he went backward with a cat-like movement, and I jerked my gun and fired." The flash of exploding powder blinded Garrett, and he snapped off a second round in the direction of his target. On the verge of pulling the trigger a third time, he heard a groan and knew he had hit his mark.[20]

Pete Maxwell sprang from his bed and hit the floor in a tangle of bedclothes, then raced for the door. Garrett had already reached the porch when Maxwell tumbled out. A startled Poe and McKinney greeted them with pistols drawn. Poe almost shot Maxwell, who shouted "Don't shoot, don't shoot" just as Garrett knocked down Poe's gun hand. "Don't shoot Maxwell," he said.

Hugging the wall outside the door, Garrett gasped, "That was the Kid that came in there onto me, and I think I have got him."

"Pat," replied Poe, "the Kid would not come to this place; you have shot the wrong man."

Garrett paused in doubt, then said, "I am sure that was him, for I know his voice too well to be mistaken."[21]

An understandable caution restrained all the men from entering the darkened room to find out who had been shot and whether he was dead. As the Maxwell family and a scattering of townspeople began to gather, Maxwell walked down the porch to his mother's room and returned with a lighted candle. Placing it on the windowsill, he stepped aside and the lawmen peered in. "We saw a man lying stretched upon his back dead, in the middle of the room," said Poe, "with a six-shooter lying at his right hand and a butcher-knife at his left."[22]

Venturing inside, Garrett and his deputies examined the body that now was unmistakably revealed to be Billy the Kid. Billy bore one bullet wound, in the left breast just above the heart. Garrett's bullet had killed him almost instantly.

Maxwell was certain that Billy had fired once at Garrett, and Poe and McKinney insisted that they had heard three shots. A thorough search of the room turned up only one stray bullet, in the headboard of Maxwell's bed. Examining Billy's pistol, Garrett counted five loaded cartridges; the hammer rested on the empty sixth. The empty shell did not seem to have been fired recently, and since men usually kept an empty shell under the hammer as a safety precaution, it probably had not. The report thought to have been a third shot had been Garrett's bullet ricocheting from the wall and slamming into Maxwell's headboard, the lawmen concluded. Billy's fatal second of hesitation had left the initiative to his opponent.

By now an excited crowd thronged the porch and the old parade ground beyond the fence. As word spread that the Kid had been killed, many vented their grief and anger. A sobbing Celsa Gutierrez cursed Garrett and pounded his chest. Nasaria Yerby, Abrana García, Paulita Maxwell, and the Navajo woman Deluvina Maxwell wept, talked softly, and consoled one another. Armed young men shook their fists and shouted threats at Garrett and his deputies.[23] "We spent the remainder of the night on the Maxwell premises," said Poe, "keeping constantly on our guard, as we were expecting to be attacked by the friends of the dead man."[24]

The next morning, at Sunnyside, Milnor Rudulph and his son Charles heard the news and rode down to Fort Sumner. They found the community buzzing with confusion, anger, and controversy. Some wanted to lynch Garrett and his deputies, barricaded in a room of the Maxwell house with their guns ready for a defense. Others argued that Billy's death relieved the townspeople of a great strain and that the lawmen deserved their gratitude.

Rudulph was a sensible, widely respected, and, of particular importance at the moment, literate man. Justice of the Peace Alejandro Segura asked him to organize a coroner's jury and preside as foreman. Rudulph assented, assembled five citizens, and convened the proceedings in Pete Maxwell's bedroom, where the body still lay on the floor. Maxwell and Garrett told their stories. Rudulph then wrote out the report, and the jurors affixed their signatures or made their marks. They duly concluded that William Bonney had met death from a bullet wound in the region of the heart, inflicted by a gun in the hand of Pat F. Garrett. "And our dictum is," wrote Rudulph in Spanish, "that the act of said Garrett was justifiable homicide and we are of the opinion that the gratitude of the whole community is owed to said Garrett for his deed, and that he deserves to be rewarded." [25]

Although many residents would have vigorously dissented had they known of Rudulph's accolade, one of the jurors who laboriously scratched an X next to his name surely agreed. He was Sabal Gutierrez, husband of Celsa Gutierrez.

The women had asked for the corpse, and after the jury completed its task they had the body carried across the parade ground to the carpenter shop. There, Poe recounted, it "was laid out on a workbench, the women placing lighted candles around it according to their ideas of properly conducting a 'wake' for the dead." [26]

"Neatly and properly dressed," according to Garrett, the remains were placed in a coffin, which was borne to the old military cemetery that now served the community. There, on the afternoon of July 15, 1881, Fort Sumner paid final respects to Billy the Kid. Fittingly, he rested next to his old compadres of the Lincoln County War, Tom O'Folliard and Charley Bowdre.

For the two decades remaining to him, Pat Garrett basked in public acclaim as the officer who killed Billy the Kid. The deed took on an almost superhuman glow as the Kid's reputation blossomed into legend and as he came to be remembered as the frontier's most exalted outlaw.

Yet, able lawman that he was, Pat Garrett had got his man almost entirely by accident. He and his deputies thought that the fugitive was somewhere in the vicinity, but in trying to find him they encountered nothing but frustration. If the Kid had not blundered into the darkened bedroom at exactly the right moment, Pete Maxwell would have been one more frustration—like Rudulph, nervous but uninformative. Maxwell was their last hope; the next day, they doubtless would have saddled up and ridden back to Roswell.

By the most improbable coincidence of timing, therefore, Billy fell almost literally into Garrett's lap. To be sure, the sheriff kept his head, reacted with split-second decision, and shot accurately, although in the darkness he ran a great risk of shooting the wrong man. Even so, he triumphed less because of what he did than because of what his opponent failed to do. Billy had the same instant the lawman did in which to recognize his enemy and fire at him. He had his gun in hand, while Garrett's rested in his holster.

Why did he fail to pull the trigger? Fear of hitting Maxwell? Fear of hitting some unrecognized friend? Garrett himself provided as good an explanation as any: "I think he was surprised and thrown off his guard. Almost any man would have been. Kid was as cool under trying circumstances as any man I ever saw. But he was so surprised and startled, that for a second he could not collect himself. Some men cannot recover their faculties for some time after such a shock. I think Kid would have done so in a second more, if he had had the time."[27]

26. Although percussion weapons had become obsolete by Billy the Kid's time, many had been rechambered to fire metallic cartridges. They were reliable, inexpensive, and popular. Originally the cylinder of this 1861 Colt's Navy, a common Civil War handgun, held six paper cartridges containing powder and ball. When struck by the hammer, a separately affixed cap containing fulminate of mercury ignited the round. In this conversion, the weapon now fires six .38-caliber metallic cartridges. (Photo by Fred Ochs, Panhandle-Plains Historical Museum, Canyon, Texas)

Except as noted, photos by Ron Dillow. Technical data from Ken Pate.

27. In the late 1870s the Winchester '73 gradually overcame the prejudices of westerners against repeaters and the feelings of some, chiefly buffalo hunters, that it was underpowered. By the 1880s, accuracy, rapidity of fire, and ease of handling made the Winchester the characteristic shoulder arm of the frontier. The rifle (left) held fifteen .44-.40 center-fire cartridges in the magazine beneath the barrel, the carbine (right) held twelve. The lever beneath the stock chambered each round preparatory to firing. Billy the Kid was rarely separated from his Winchester.

28. In the favor of westerners, no handgun came close to Colt's six-shooter. Simple, sturdy, functional, easily handled and repaired, the Colt's won a large and loyal following in the West. Introduced in 1873, the single-action Colt's Army (above) gradually overshadowed all other sidearms in the U.S. military service and, as the "Peacemaker," achieved instant popularity with civilians. The 1873 model came with a 7½-inch barrel and fired a .45-caliber center-fire cartridge. Later, Colt offered a .44-caliber version and a choice of two shorter barrels, 5½ inches and 4¾ inches. Still another version, the double- action "self-cocker," found favor with many, including Billy the Kid. With the single-action, cocking the hammer rotated the cylinder and positioned a fresh round for firing. With the double-action, pulling the trigger advanced the cylinder and fired the round in one motion. The double-action came in two models, the .38-caliber "Lightning" (below) and the .41-caliber "Thunderer." The Kid carried the latter.

29. Designed for hunting, shotguns could also be used against humans, as they frequently were in the West. At close range, they did a lot of damage, and they did not have to be aimed. Escaping from confinement in Lincoln, Billy the Kid shot down Bob Olinger with his own 10-gauge Whitney. This is a Greener, available in 10- or 12-gauge, with which Wells Fargo equipped its stagecoach guards.

30. Buffalo hunters favored the durable, hard-hitting Sharps shoulder arm, which delivered maximum power at maximum range. The Sharps was single shot and, unlike the repeaters, could take cartridges of varying lengths and, thus, varying loads of powder. The Sharps Model 1874 sporting rifle (left) came in chamberings of .40, .44, .45, and .50 caliber, with charges ranging from 50 to 150 grains of black powder. Before the advent of the 1873 Springfield, the Sharps carbine (right) was a common cavalry arm. This Model 1863 percussion breechloader has been rechambered to receive a .50-.70 metallic cartridge.

31. The U.S. Model 1873 Springfield "Trapdoor" served the U.S.
Army for two decades. A hinged
"trapdoor" in front of the hammer
lifted to expose the chamber, which
received a single .45-.70- caliber
round. Infantry carried the rifle
(left), cavalry the carbine (right).

Colonel Dudley's command was
armed with these weapons when he
marched into Lincoln on July 19,
1878. Many promptly found their
way into civilian hands. Buckshot
Roberts used Dr. Blazer's Springfield rifle to kill Dick Brewer.

The Legend

CHAPTER 18

The news of Billy the Kid's death electrified the Territory of New Mexico and the sensation-loving world beyond. "The vulgar murderer and desperado known as 'Billy, the Kid' has met his just deserts at last," proclaimed the newspaper in his boyhood home of Silver City. "His death is hailed with great joy," commented the *New York Sun*, "as he had sworn that he would kill several prominent citizens, and had already slain fifteen or eighteen men." [1]

The press reports spread the Kid's name and fame throughout the nation and further inflated the image of matchless desperado that had already been planted in the public mind. In May 1881 the *Police Gazette* had described in fervent prose Billy's escape from Lincoln. [2] Now the rest of the pulp press rushed to tell his life's story.

In sixteen action-packed chapters of the *Five-Cent Wide Awake Library* for August 1881, "Don Jenardo" created the stereotype of Billy as cold-blooded killer. Sample:

"Oh! Billy, Billy," cried the terrified wretch, "for God's sake don't shoot me!"

"Hold your head still, George, so I will not disfigure your face much, and give you but very little pain."

The words were spoken in that cool, determined, blood-thirsty manner, as only the Kid could speak.

197

In quick succession, within less than a year, five "biographies" of Billy the Kid appeared in dime-novel format, including *The Cowboy's Career; or, The Daredevil Deeds of Billy the Kid, the Noted New Mexico Desperado*, by "One of the Kids"; and *Billy the "Kid" and His Girl*, one of "Morrison's Sensational Series."[3]

Such ephemera, however, was not enough to ensure Billy lasting fame. Without Marshall Ashmun Upson, he might well have vanished into oblivion.

Ash Upson was no ordinary frontier postmaster. A fragile little man with a wan complexion, a broken nose, and a face pitted by smallpox, he turned on all comers a pair of big mournful eyes that gave him a look of perpetual sadness. Yet he was convivial, droll, and benevolent. In the fifty years following his Connecticut birth, he had traveled almost everywhere in the United States. Indeed, one of his two chief characteristics was a compulsive wanderlust that kept him in almost constant motion. The other was a literary talent stemming from a classical education and several decades as a printer and journalist. Ash Upson had a gift for graphic prose, usually stimulated by the contents of a bottle, and he indulged it with flowery contributions to newspapers throughout the nation.[4]

Upson had ample opportunity to know Billy the Kid, who occasionally patronized Roswell's combination store and post office and joshed with the other customers. Although not likely intimates, the two were both open and gregarious enough to have been more than casual acquaintances. This intermittent personal connection, together with his own observations from his postmaster's vantage, made Ash an authority on Billy and his friends and the events in which they figured.

After the death of Billy the Kid, another friend called on Upson's knowledge of recent history and his endowments as a writer. Pat Garrett had been elected sheriff to put Lincoln County's outlaws out of business. After he gunned down the Kid, however, many among a people who subscribed to the code of the West muttered about the unfairness of that shot in the dark. Garrett felt the need to tell his side of the story.

Within a matter of months, Ash Upson had helped his friend tell that story.[5] Garrett took the manuscript to the publishers of the Santa Fe *New Mexican*, and the book appeared in the spring of 1882, less than a year after the demise of Billy the Kid. The title page reflected the florid style of the time: *The Authentic Life of Billy the Kid, the Noted Desperado of the Southwest, Whose Deeds of Daring and Blood have Made His Name a Terror in New Mexico, Arizona & Northern Mexico.*

Nowhere on the crowded title page did Upson's name appear. Later he claimed to have written every word.[6] Actually, the book was a collaborative effort. The first fifteen chapters bear every evidence, in both style and content, of Upson's sole authorship, and not coincidentally they cover the period before Garrett arrived on the scene. The final eight chapters, describing events in which Garrett participated, register a distinctive shift in style and radiate an authority lacking in the others.

Although not many copies of the *Authentic Life* were sold, it nevertheless had a decisive impact on the Kid's image. More than any other single influence, the Garrett-Upson book fed the legend of Billy the Kid. As the legend blossomed, writers turned to the *Authentic Life* for the authentic details. Ash Upson's fictions became implanted in the hundreds of "histories" that followed. For more than a century, only a few students thought to question the wild fantasies that flowed from Ash's imagination. In the evolution of the Kid's image, the *Authentic Life* is a book of enormous consequence. Ironically, the man most responsible for the book remains unknown except to a handful of specialists.

From Upson's inventions sprang the roots of the two dominant images of Billy the Kid—hero and antihero. Upson's portrayal of a happy, likable youth who was also a merciless killer laid a solid foundation for the rise of two towering and contradictory figures. The vicious murderer ruled for a generation, only to be challenged and overpowered by the engaging boy in the next generation. Ultimately the struggle between the two reached an uneasy equilibrium.

If the pulp writers of the early decades perpetuated the satanic Billy, Walter Noble Burns fixed the saintly Billy firmly in American popular culture. In *The Saga of Billy the Kid*, a best seller for years following its publication in 1926, this Chicago newsman created an American reincarnation of Robin Hood, who perpetrated criminal deeds in behalf of righteous causes and who was idolized by the simple Hispanic herdsmen of the Southwest, as English peasants idolized Robin Hood.

Burns fixed in legend for all time the image of Billy the Kid as "social bandit," a concept devised in the 1950s for English history and later applied to the American experience as well. The test is not whether the social bandit, like Robin Hood or Jesse James, robbed from the rich and gave to the poor, but rather whether people thought he did and thus accorded him the status of folk hero. In his own time, however undeservedly, Billy the Kid won this accolade from the Hispanic plowmen and herdsmen of New Mexico. Burns, writing in the 1920s, never heard of social bandits, but he transformed Billy into a social bandit treasured not only by a narrow Hispanic world but by the entire world.[7]

Burns appealed to popular sensibilities on two levels, the personal and the societal. Each of his characters—the Kid, Chisum, McSween, Tunstall, Murphy—personalized historical forces guiding the transformation of the wild and free frontier into settled civilization, of rural America into the industrial age. The Kid embodies youth, nobility, humanity, romance, and tragedy. He is a symbolic transition between the old and new, driven to violence by injustice, his guns blazing in protest against corruption and greed, and at last his life an essential sacrifice in the rise of the human condition.

Neither the Kid nor any other of Burns's major characters faithfully mirrored their historic counterparts. But they captured and simplified unsettling currents of history that were as pertinent in the 1920s, a period of postwar social upheaval, as they had been in the 1880s. Masquerading as history but singing with the vivid writing of a novel, Burns's *Saga* ranked a close second to the *Authentic Life* in its decisive impact on the legend of Billy the Kid.

Motion picture and television producers found the Kid irresistible. In more than forty Hollywood films, such stars as Johnny

Mack Brown, Buster Crabbe, Robert Taylor, Paul Newman, Marlon Brando, and Kris Kristofferson depicted him in a wide range of personae. Throughout the 1930s, years of depression-induced escapism, the saintly Billy prevailed. By the 1970s, years of protest and cynicism, the satanic Billy had reasserted himself. With *Young Guns* in 1988, the more sympathetic Kid began a comeback. "From western Robin Hood to tormented adolescent and from degenerate punk to a martyred symbol of freedom," writes a noted film historian, "the Billy the Kid story has been manipulated to satisfy new audiences."[8]

Similar depictions found their way into drama, verse, and music. Seeking the meaning of the Kid, poets bp Nichol and Michael Ondaatje plumbed murky philosophical depths. Balladeers celebrated both saint and satan, and in 1938 composer Aaron Copland elevated the Kid to an improbable musical pinnacle as the star of a widely acclaimed ballet. Like the principal movies of the time, the ballet was conceived in the shadow of Burns's *Saga of Billy the Kid* and thus presented the tragic and the saintly in the framework of larger historical forces.

Books and articles continued to pour off the presses. Fiction competed with history, while scholars analyzed the significance of the public's continuing fascination. They saw the shifting popular vision of Billy the Kid, like that of other giants of folklore, as symbolic of shifting popular attitudes and values. What society made of the Kid told more about society than about the Kid.[9]

Not uncharacteristically for folk figures, Billy the Kid periodically materialized in the flesh. The "Billy Rides Again" syndrome appealed to people's gullible fondness for conspiracy and cover-up as historical determinants. Garrett shot the wrong man, or faked a killing in a pact with the Kid, or conspired in some other secret maneuver that set the young man free to disappear into another life. Years later, the Kid surfaced to reclaim his true identity. Citizens of Hico, Texas, still emotionally defend their own "Brushy Bill" Roberts, who died in 1950, as the true Billy the Kid.[10]

The true Billy the Kid, of course, was not any of the personifications of legend. Yet he possessed traits that in varying measure appeared in them all. He was a killer and an outlaw, though hardly on the scale represented by legend. And he had distinctive personal qualities that are to be glimpsed in some of the Billies of legend. These qualities in fact equipped him to be much more than he was, whether killer, outlaw, or something more admirable. He might even have lived up to the legend.

Those nearest him acknowledged his talent. "He must have had good stuff in him," declared John Meadows, "for he was always an expert at whatever he tried to do." "With his poise, iron nerve, and all-round efficiency properly applied," contended Dr. Henry Hoyt, "the Kid could have made a success anywhere."[11]

"The Kid" well described Billy. Not until his final months did anyone know him as Billy the Kid. Whatever his name or alias at the moment, people always called him Kid. He was not only younger than most but also looked it. With a boyish face, medium stature, and slight build, he prompted the label as soon as he started running with men.

Yet the label could be misleading. He boasted strength and endurance, lithe and swift movement, and a suddenness of physical response that revealed an unusual quickness of mind. His intellect rested on a solid grammar-school education that made him literate though not literary, and it drew on a native intelligence that in resourcefulness, ingenuity, cunning, and mental agility and acuity lifted him above his peers.

Inextinguishable good humor marked the Kid's disposition, even in the most discouraging circumstances. He continually smiled and laughed, sang and whistled, and bantered with both friends and enemies. Gloom never seemed to dilute his cheerfulness. "Happy go-lucky all the time," commented Will Chisum. "Nothing bothered him."[12]

Consistent with his lighthearted temperament, Billy loved a good time. Unlike most frontier types, he did not need liquor to fuel his merriment. He frequented saloons and dance halls but seems to have drunk little or not at all. He excelled at poker and monte and was fond of the vigorous *bailes* of the Hispanic population.

Hispanics idolized the Kid. He spoke their language fluently, cultivated their friendship, and, unlike most Anglos, never conde-scended. At any sheep camp on the plains or in the mountains, he could be sure of food, shelter, and help. In particular, Hispanic women found the happy youth irresistible.

The bright exterior could be deceptive, for it hid a steely, cal-culating steadiness that never faltered, no matter how intense the stress. In a crisis he always kept his head. With a disarming smile, he could pursue devious or deadly aims with a fixity of purpose that one resisted at peril. "When he was rough," observed John Mead-ows, "he was as rough as men ever get to be . . . too awful rough at times, but everything in the country was rough about then." [13] Gradually many in his wide circle of admirers came to recognize the anomaly and to fear the inner Kid as much as they prized the outer Kid.

In a society that placed high value on gunmanship, the Kid ex-celled. Guns obsessed him. He practiced constantly with both Win-chester rifle or carbine and six-shooter. His dexterity with both im-pressed those who watched him perform. "He could whirl his gun about on his finger and then shoot," remembered Deluvina Max-well. "A boy from Vegas tried to act like him once and shot and killed himself." Pat Garrett thought him no better than most prac-ticed gunmen. "He shot well, though," Garrett conceded, "and he shot well under all circumstances, whether in danger or not." [14]

Killer he was, but not the cold-blooded killer of one of his stereo-types in legend. "He done some things I can't endorse," com-mented Meadows. "But Kid certainly had good feelings." [15] In two killings, he regretted the deed but, to himself, easily defended the necessity.

In fact, one of his dominant characteristics was self-justification. He rationalized everything he did as right, or at least as necessary even if unfortunate. In his mind, all his killings could be excused as self-defense or the demands of war.

Legend would credit the boy with twenty-one killings, one for each year of his life. The actual tally fell far short of that count. For certain he shot and killed four men—Windy Cahill, Joe Grant, Bob Olinger, and Jim Bell. In the Lincoln County War he shared with others the slaying of five more men—Billy Morton, Frank Baker, William McCloskey, Sheriff Brady, and Manuel Segovia ("Indian"). Finally, in the shootout at Greathouse ranch, Jim Carlyle died from a bullet that the Kid may or may not have fired.

Except in the last fatal encounter with Pat Garrett, the Kid took other men's lives with instinctive suddenness and untroubled abandon. This casual attitude toward violent death, however, was not unique. The Kid reflected the values of the frontier society that nurtured him. Nearly everyone carried firearms, and few shrank from using them when they thought someone needed killing. In a milieu full of suffering and death, the extinction of a life aroused only fleeting compassion or sorrow. Usually the killer went free, uncondemned and often even excused by his peers, rarely brought to trial, even more rarely convicted by the crude system of frontier justice.

As killer, so as outlaw the real Billy failed to match any of the Kid's personae of legend. While still a teenager, he stole some horses in Arizona. Later, he ran for a month with the outlaw gang of Jesse Evans but quickly dropped out and laid plans to take up ranching. The Lincoln County War of 1878 dashed those plans.

That violent clash of selfish interests gave the Kid a cause in which he could fight as a soldier rather than an outlaw. The fighters on both sides could kill, injure, destroy, and steal under the guise of legitimate war and thus avoid the taint of criminality. Looking back from his later notoriety, even wartime comrades tended to refer to "Billy the Kid's bunch." But he was never chief of the Regulators, however daringly and effectively he performed. He did not change the course of the war; it would have turned out the same if he had never taken part. Had he been incinerated in the blazing McSween house on July 19, 1878, the world would not remember him today.

In the Lincoln County War, the Kid reached his peak of excitement and adventure. Afterward, he wavered between going straight and returning to outlawry, at length slipping into crime without ever wholly giving up the quest for a life of respectable toil. For a year, 1880, he pursued an erratic course of cattle rustling and horse theft—not a heinous offense in the values of the time and place. He was never a large-scale rustler, although the pace of his depredations quickened as the months slipped by.

Nor did the Kid captain a big gang of outlaws, or even a little gang. The outlaw temperament did not lend itself to a formal command structure, and few organized gangs existed. When the Kid outlawed, he did it with a few buddies. By force of personality, he probably dominated them. But they did not form "his gang," instantly obedient to his orders.

Except in its final months, therefore, the Kid's career did not measure up to his reputation. Although a superb gunman and arresting personality, he was a quite ordinary outlaw, of uncertain commitment, narrow practice, and ambiguous purpose. In truth, he seems to have had no particular purpose at all, but rather youth's penchant for submerging long-term goals in the pleasures of the moment. After the Lincoln County War, during the months of his reputed outlawry, he was a drifter psychologically as well as geographically.

Even so, in the flesh and in legend, Billy the Kid embodies the frontier's affinity for violence. He also stands for much more, however, as evinced by his steadfast appeal to generation after generation. His life both reflects and reproaches not only frontier society but the entire nation. The Gilded Age that blossomed as the nation industrialized in the last years of the frontier featured attitudes and values that the Kid would have clearly recognized and that embedded themselves in the ethic of American society.

All around him the Kid saw corruption, both personal and institutional. As the Lincoln County War so vividly dramatized, the institutions of government, law, and business served selfish interests and personal ambitions. Governors, prosecutors, judges, sheriffs and marshals, army officers, Indian agents, attorneys, cattle barons, mercantile czars—all perverted political, legal, and economic systems for individual benefit. If Billy took what he wanted without regard for the rights of others, so on a much grander scale did Murphy, Dolan, Chisum, and Tunstall. And so in the territorial capital did the malodorous Santa Fe Ring.

In New Mexico as elsewhere on the frontier, such pillars of the establishment provided the examples of success. Billy's actions mirrored their muddy ethics.

Despite his superior abilities, however, the Kid met failure at almost every turn. He failed because he lacked powerful friends and because he did not shed the wartime habits of open rebellion. Dolan, Mathews, the Coes, even Doc Scurlock and John Middleton, eventually donned the mantle of respectability.

For the Kid, Governor Wallace briefly held forth the promise of a pathway to respectability. If a pardon or other form of clemency had been forthcoming, a ranch on the Peñasco or a similar enterprise might well have provided Billy with a base for legitimate prosperity. But those hopes collapsed either in the governor's contempt for the brash young desperado or simply in his preoccupation with other matters.

Another difference distinguished Billy from many of his wartime friends and enemies. Although the newly respectable did not suddenly acquire scruples and cleanse society of its iniquities, they did rely less on violence to advance their fortunes. But Billy remained a gunman, coiled to defend himself or project his will through violence.

Failing in his bid for respectability, the Kid remained the consistent rebel. His criminal escapades, especially as they began to gain him notoriety, affronted and challenged the establishment. In contrast to Dolan, Riley, Mathews, and the others who had initially created such turmoil, Billy continued to make trouble. Perhaps men like Bristol, Rynerson, and even Governor Wallace saw in the Kid's contempt for conventions and defiance of authority a disquieting reminder of their own pliant ethics and questionable actions. Whatever their motives, they singled him out for special treatment and ultimately, together with his comrades Bowdre and O'Folliard, saw that he paid for his insolence with his life.

Billy the Kid died as America enthusiastically plunged into the Gilded Age. The transformation of an agrarian nation into an industrial giant launched a frenzy of material aquisitiveness that corrupted national institutions with the same ethical laxity so conspicuous on the frontier. Jimmy Dolan and his friend District Attorney Rynerson would have felt entirely at home in Boss Tweed's Tammany Hall or even in U. S. Grant's White House. Only in a quick reliance on violence did the frontier differ from the nation as a whole in the relentless quest for power and wealth, and then it was largely a difference of degree.

The twin specters of corruption and violence remained embedded in American culture, periodically to surface separately or in tandem. Whether originating in the frontier experience or in some dark stain in the American character, they continue to find ambiguous expression in the legend of the youth who lived both. More than a century after his death, Billy the Kid still rides boldly across America's mental landscape, symbolizing an enduring national ambivalence toward corruption and violence.

For a life that ended at twenty-one, that is a powerful and disturbing legacy.

ABBREVIATIONS

AAAG	Acting Assistant Adjutant General
AAG	Assistant Adjutant General
ACP	Appointments, Commissions, Promotions
AGO	Adjutant General's Office
AHS	Arizona Historical Society, Tucson
BIA	Bureau of Indian Affairs
CO	Commanding Officer
DFRC	Denver Federal Records Center
DM	Department of Missouri, Fort Leaven-worth, KS
DNM	District of New Mexico, Santa Fe
HHC	Haley History Center, Midland, TX
HL	Huntington Library, San Marino, CA
HQ.	Headquarters
IHS	Indiana Historical Society, Indianapolis
LR	Letters Received
LS	Letters Sent
LSM	Lincoln State Monument, NM
NARA	National Archives and Records Admin-istration, Washington, DC
NMSRCA	New Mexico State Records Center and Archives, Santa Fe
PHPHM	Panhandle-Plains Historical Museum, Canyon, TX
RG	Record Group
TANM	Territorial Archives of New Mexico
UAL	University of Arizona Library, Tucson
WPA	Works Progress Administration

1. THE KID

1   Among students of Billy's roots, the pioneers are Philip J. Rasch and Robert N. Mullin, who, despite the demands of professions unrelated to history, devoted their lifetimes to the pursuit. Mullin is now dead, but his collection of historical materials may be consulted at the Haley History Center in Midland, Texas (hereafter HHC). Rasch, who resides in California, donated his collection to the Lincoln State Monument in Lincoln, New Mexico. Pertinent here are Rasch and Mullin, "New Light on the Legend of Billy the Kid," *New Mexico Folklore Record* 7 (1952–53): 1–5; Rasch and Mullin, "Dim Trails: The Pursuit of the McCarty Family," ibid. 8 (1954): 6–11; and Mullin, *The Boyhood of Billy the Kid*, Southwestern Studies Monograph No. 17 (El Paso: Texas Western Press, 1967): 7–10.

     The Antrim-McCarty marriage is listed in the Santa Fe County Book of Marriages, A, and in the church's record book of marriages performed by Reverend McFarland. Photocopies are in the Research Files, Mullin Collection, HHC. Henry and "Josie" McCarty are named as witnesses, together with members of the McFarland family.

2   The astute and tenacious researcher who succeeded in connecting Indianapolis with Santa Fe via Kansas is Waldo Koop, *Billy the Kid: Trail of a Kansas Legend* (Kansas City: Kansas City Westerners, 1965). Important in this process was the work of Philip J. Rasch in tracking stepfather William Antrim and brother Joseph

Antrim. See Rasch's "A Man Named Antrim," *Los Angeles Westerners Brand Book* 6 (1956): 48–54, and "The Quest for Joseph Antrim," *NOLA Quarterly* 6 (July 1981): 13–17.

3 The former theory is best set forth by Jack DeMattos, "The Search for Billy the Kid's Roots—Is Over!" *Real West* 23 (January 1980): 20–25. The latter theory is advanced in Donald Cline, *Alias Billy the Kid: The Man Behind the Legend* (Santa Fe: Sunstone Press, 1986), chapter 1. The problem is complicated by the sloppy record keeping of the times and by the superabundance, in New York and all other cities, of McCartys, McCarthys, and McCartneys named Patrick, Michael, Henry, Joseph, and Catherine. As a further complication, Billy's use of the alias of William H. Bonney has sent trackers in pursuit of all the Bonneys who ever immigrated from Ireland. No theory yet advanced is without its holes, although advocates can plug most of them with arguments. Rather than convince, however, the arguments usually lead to more arguments. Students interested in following the esoterica of this immensely complex and unyielding puzzle will be rewarded by the works cited in these footnotes.

The date usually given for Billy's birth is November 23, 1859. It first appeared in a book that will be cited frequently in the following pages, both to deny its assertions and to serve as a source for my assertions. This book is Pat F. Garrett, *The Authentic Life of Billy the Kid* (Santa Fe: New Mexico Printing and Publishing Co., 1882). The history and significance of this book will be treated in chapter 18, but its prominent place in my notes requires a brief introduction here. Although Garrett is credited as author, much of the book was written by Marshall Ashmun Upson, a wandering journalist who was Roswell postmaster at the time of the Lincoln County War. Upson wrote the first fifteen chapters, Garrett the final eight. Upson's contributions are mostly (but not exclusively) sensationalist fabrications. Garrett's are excellent firsthand sources. Since generations of subsequent writers turned to Upson-Garrett for their facts, the Upson fantasies have become embedded in the literature of Billy the Kid. Any authentic life of the Kid, therefore, must confront, step by step as it unfolds, the *Authentic Life of Billy the Kid*. I have done this in my notes.

The original edition of the *Authentic Life*, of course, is exceedingly scarce and commands a high price. There have been several subsequent editions, of which the most notable are one by the Macmillan Company, edited by Maurice G. Fulton (1927), and one by the University of Oklahoma Press, edited by Jeff C. Dykes (1954). The latter, now in its twelfth printing, is still available. Wherever the *Authentic Life* is cited in my notes, I have used the Dykes edition. The introductions of Fulton and of Dykes contain much of value relating to the book and its authors, with Dykes's being the more informative and authoritative.

4   Koop, *Billy the Kid*, 7–12. Koop unearthed the land records and newspaper items that documented the Antrim-McCarty stay in Wichita, shedding light on the past and present relationship of the two.

5   The Colorado connection appears in Garrett, *Authentic Life*, 7. Also, Billy himself mentioned a brief residence in Denver to Frank Coe: *El Paso Times*, September 16, 1923. Finally, an old man generally believed to have been Billy's brother, Joe, surfaced in Denver in 1928, and he said the family had lived for a time in Denver: *Denver Post*, April 1, 1928.

6   The code is excellently treated in two books by C. L. Sonnichsen: *"I'll Die Before I'll Run": The Story of the Great Feuds of Texas* (New York: Devin-Adair, 1962) and *Tularosa: Last of the Frontier West*, 2d ed. (Albuquerque: University of New Mexico Press, 1980). The theme is prevalent throughout the historical literature of Texas and New Mexico.

7   *Arizona Weekly Star* (Tucson), November 11, 1880.

8   Quoted in Conrad Keeler Naegle, "Silver City, New Mexico's Frontier Paradox, 1870–1890" (MS, Santa Fe, n.d.), 15.

9   Quoted in Mullin, *Boyhood of Billy the Kid*, 10.

10 Mrs. Patience Glennon of Silver City, quoting her mother, Englishwoman Mary Richards, to Robert N. Mullin, May 15, 1952, quoted in ibid., 12. See also *The Southwesterner* (Columbus, N. Mex.), June 1962.

11 *Silver City Enterprise*, September 18, 1874; *Mining Life* (Silver City, N. Mex.), September 19, 1874.

12 Anthony B. Connor, interview in *Independent* (Silver City, N. Mex.), March 22, 1932. See also Connor to Maurice G. Fulton, April 29 and June 22, 1932, Billy the Kid Binder, Mullin Collection, HHC.

13 Chauncey O. Truesdell, interview with Robert N. Mullin, Phoe-

nix, Ariz., January 9, 1952, Billy the Kid Binder, Mullin Collection, HHC. For another Truesdell interview, see Roscoe G. Wilson, "Billy the Kid's Youth is Topic for Argument," *Arizona Republic*, December 30, 1951.

14 Recollections of Henry Whitehill, in Notes by Mrs. Helen Wheaton, Silver City, from Gilbert Cureton Collection, Billy the Kid Binder, Mullin Collection, HHC.

15 Connor, *Independent*, March 22, 1932.

16 Harvey C. Whitehill, interview in *Silver City Enterprise*, January 3, 1902.

17 Louis Abraham, in Notes by Mrs. Helen Wheaton, Silver City, from Gilbert Cureton Collection, Billy the Kid Binder, Mullin Collection, HHC.

18 Whitehill, Mullin Collection, HHC.

19 Truesdell, January 9, 1952, Mullin Collection, HHC. Truesdell remembered that Henry did not even participate in the theft but hid the loot at Shaffer's request, which is also implied by the newspaper item quoted below.

20 Connor, *Independent*, March 22, 1932.

21 Whitehill, Mullin Collection, HHC.

22 *Silver City Enterprise*, January 3, 1902.

23 *Grant County Herald* (Silver City, N. Mex.), September 26, 1875.

2. THE ADOLESCENT

1 Ash Upson crowded the first five chapters of the *Authentic Life* with wild tales of Billy's adventures. They are unbelievable and without any confirming evidence. All may be confidently tossed on the trash heap of fable.

A widely credited explanation of Billy's activities in these two years was a long account given to a newspaper reporter by Thomas Dwyer, a New York policeman, shortly after the Kid's death. Dwyer was certain that New Mexico's celebrated bandit was Michael McCarty, a juvenile delinquent well known to the officers of the Oak Street Station. McCarty had disappeared in September 1876 after stabbing a friend to death in a drunken brawl. The Dwyer story illustrated a tendency that would become increasingly common with the passing years. Oldtimers remembered all manner of thrilling exploits by a nameless young fellow who they later decided must have been Billy the Kid.

The Dwyer account, in the *New York Sun*, July 22, 1881, is the cornerstone of Donald Cline's reconstruction not only of the two-year void but also of the Kid's family origins. *Alias Billy the Kid: The Man Behind the Legend* (Santa Fe: Sunstone Press, 1987), 14–21, 37–41. It requires us to throw out the Kid's connections with Kansas and Indiana altogether and to believe that he fled from Silver City to New York rather than to Arizona. The brutal knifing described by Dwyer did occur, as documented by newspaper accounts reproduced by Cline. But to accept Michael McCarty as Henry Antrim badly strains logic, plausibility, reasonably well-established facts, and the evidence itself.

2   For much of the contents of this chapter I am indebted to Jerry Weddle of Tucson, Arizona, whose diligent researches into the Kid's Arizona years give promise of important results. Although Weddle will soon publish a book setting forth his findings, he has generously allowed me to make use of them. Employment records of the Hooker ranch establish Antrim's connection with Hooker but at this writing remain unavailable to researchers.

3   According to Jerry Weddle, citing personal communications with the Hooker and the Whelan families.

4   There are three short reminiscences by Wood, the first in 1911 and the others in the 1920s. Each contains details lacking in the others, but all three are internally consistent. These have generously been made available by Jerry Weddle.

5   John Mackie's background appears in two pension applications, in 1911 and 1912, unearthed by Jerry Weddle and made available to me. The shooting is recounted in *Arizona Weekly Citizen* (Tucson), September 25 and October 9, 1875.

6   Miles L. Wood reminiscences, courtesy of Jerry Weddle.

7   The complaint, February 16, 1877, details the circumstances of the theft. The Fort Grant post returns, November 1876, document Lewis Hartman's pursuit of the thieves. Both documents were provided by Jerry Weddle. The apprehension of Antrim by the soldiers near Globe was related by storekeeper Pat Shanley and appears in Clara T. Woody and Milton L. Schwartz, *Globe, Arizona* (Tucson: Arizona Historical Society, 1977), 31.

8   Miles L. Wood reminiscences. Wood's formal request to put the

two in the post guardhouse, March 25, 1877, is in the Camp Grant Letters Received (hereafter LR), Record Group (hereafter RG) 98, National Archives and Records Administration, Washington, D.C. (hereafter NARA). Both documents are courtesy of Jerry Weddle.

9   Miles L. Wood reminiscences, courtesy of Jerry Weddle.

10 J. Fred Denton, "Billy the Kid's Friend Tells for First Time of Thrilling Incidents," *Tucson Daily Citizen*, March 28, 1931.

11 Ibid.

12 *Arizona Weekly Star* (Tucson), August 23, 1877; *Arizona Citizen* (Tucson), August 25, 1877.

13 Major C. E. Compton to U.S. Deputy Marshal W. J. Osborn, August 23, 1877, reproduced in Cline, *Alias Billy the Kid*, 51.

14 *Independent* (Silver City, N. Mex.), March 22, 1932.

15 The following is according to Ash Upson in Garrett, *Authentic Life*, 6, 8–9, 22–24. Although Upson's tales of Henry's escapades during this period are bogus, his description and characterization of the seventeen-year-old who reappeared in 1877 stem from personal acquaintance and find confirmation in the testimony of others who knew the boy.

3. THE OUTLAW

1   A solid history of Lincoln County is John P. Wilson, *Merchants, Guns & Money: The Story of Lincoln County and Its Wars* (Santa Fe: Museum of New Mexico Press, 1987).

2   Robert M. Utley, *High Noon in Lincoln: Violence on the Western Frontier* (Albuquerque: University of New Mexico Press, 1987), chapter 2.

3   *Las Vegas Gazette*, November 25, 1875, quoted in William A. Keleher, *The Fabulous Frontier: Twelve New Mexico Items* (Albuquerque: University of New Mexico Press, 1962), 60.

4   Philip J. Rasch, "The Pecos War," *Panhandle-Plains Historical Review* 29 (1956): 101–11. For Chisum, see Harwood P. Hinton, "John Simpson Chisum, 1877–84," *New Mexico Historical Review* 31 (July 1956): 177–205; 31 (October 1956): 310–37; 32 (January 1957): 53–65.

5   Upson's role in Kid historiography is discussed in chapter 18. See also note 1 in chapter 2. Upson describes Roswell and its founder

in a long letter to his father: Roswell, August 30, 1876, Fulton Collection, Box 11, Folder 6, Special Collections, University of Arizona Library, Tucson (hereafter UAL).

6   Quoted in Milton W. Callon, *Las Vegas, New Mexico . . . The Town That Wouldn't Gamble* (Las Vegas: Las Vegas Daily Optic, 1962), 116–17. See also Lynn W. Perrigo, *Gateway to Glorieta: The History of Las Vegas, New Mexico* (Boulder, Colo.: Pruett Press, 1982).

7   James D. Shinkle, *Fort Sumner and the Bosque Redondo Indian Reservation* (Roswell, N. Mex.: Hall-Pourbough Press, 1965), 77–81; William A. Keleher, *The Maxwell Land Grant: A New Mexico Item* (Santa Fe: Rydal Press, 1942), 36–37.

8   *Mesilla Valley Independent*, October 13, 1877. Carpenter's identification furnishes the only known documentation for the Kid's whereabouts before he turned up on the Pecos River about two weeks later. If Carpenter named the wrong man, we do not know where the Kid was or what he did in the weeks following the killing of Cahill unless we credit the wild tale concocted by Ash Upson for Garrett's *Authentic Life*, which I am unwilling to do. Robert N. Mullin (*The Boyhood of Billy the Kid* [El Paso: Texas Western Press, 1967]: 18–19) does not think the Kid rode with the Evans gang during this period or any other. I do, for these reasons: (1) the Carpenter identification; (2) evidence cited below tying the Kid closely to Evans's known whereabouts; (3) evidence cited in the next chapter making it plain that the Kid and Evans knew each other with considerable intimacy at the time of John H. Tunstall's death three months later. There is no other time when the relationship could have taken root. Evans, Baker, and others of the bunch that stole the horses at Pass Coal Camp are named in the *Independent*, October 6, 1877.

9   *Mesilla Valley Independent*, July 21, 1877. For Evans, see Grady E. McCright and James H. Powell, *Jessie Evans: Lincoln County Badman* (College Station, Texas: Creative Publishing Co., 1983); and Philip J. Rasch, "The Story of Jessie J. Evans," *Panhandle-Plains Historical Review* 33 (1960): 108–21. For Kinney, see Philip J. Rasch, "John Kinney: King of the Rustlers," English Westerners *Brand Book* 4 (October 1961): 10–12; Jack DeMattos, "John Kinney," *Real West* 27 (February 1984): 20–25; and Robert N. Mullin, "Here Lies John Kinney," *Journal of Arizona History* 14 (Autumn 1973): 223–42.

10 Quoted in Philip J. Rasch, "Death at the Baile," Potomac Western-
    ers *Corral Dust* 6 (August 1961): 30. See also Rasch and DeMattos,
    "John Kinney."

11 Rasch, "Story of Jessie J. Evans," 109.

12 A. B. Connor to Maurice G. Fulton, April 29, 1932, Billy the Kid
    Binder, Mullin Collection, HHC: "The school kids used to call him
    Bonney, but why I don't know."

13 As conceded in n. 8, the only documentary evidence that places
    Billy with the Evans gang at this time is Carpenter's identification
    of him as one of the Pass Coal Camp thieves. But when Evans was
    on the lower Pecos in late October, so was Billy; and when Evans
    was in jail in Lincoln in November, Billy was nearby and, as we
    shall see, helped him escape from jail. I think it highly likely, there-
    fore, that Billy rode across the mountains with the Evans gang and
    shared their adventures. The following account of those adven-
    tures is drawn from various news items in the *Mesilla Valley Inde-
    pendent*, October 6 and 13, 1877.

    The usual version of Billy's journey to the Pecos is, of course, Up-
    son's in Garrett, *Authentic Life*, 36–44. In this tale, the Kid, with
    friend Tom O'Keefe, takes a direct route across the Sacramento
    and Guadalupe mountains, endures terrible hardships, engages in
    some fantastic Indian combats, loses his mount and becomes sepa-
    rated from his buddy, and finally lands, exhausted and footsore, at
    the Jones ranch near Seven Rivers. This story resembles all the
    other sensations that Upson's creative pen attributed to Billy's
    early life and cannot be taken any more seriously than the others.
    Tom O'Keefe is otherwise unknown to history.

14 *Mesilla Valley Independent*, October 6, 1877.

15 Ibid.

16 Frank Coe, interview with J. Evetts Haley, San Patricio, N. Mex.,
    August 14, 1927, HHC.

17 I have dealt with the Murphy-Dolan establishment, known as
    "The House," in greater depth in *High Noon in Lincoln*. For the
    connection between The House and The Boys, see pp. 29, 32–33.
    The "Fence Rail" letter appears in the *Mesilla Valley Independent*,
    October 13, 1877, along with a detailed account of the progress of
    The Boys from the Rio Grande to the summit above the Indian
    agency. The economics of federal beef contracts are authoritatively
    probed in Wilson, *Merchants, Guns & Money*, 58–60.

18   Philip J. Rasch and Lee Myers, "The Tragedy of the Beckwiths,"
      English Westerners *Brand Book* 5 (July 1963): 1–6.

19   Eve Ball, *Ma'am Jones of the Pecos* (Tucson: University of Arizona
      Press, 1969), tells the story of the Jones family. For the historian
      imbued with proper skepticism, this book poses a dilemma. On
      the one hand, Eve Ball obtained the story from the Jones boys
      (mostly Sam) in the 1940s and 1950s, and their recollections must
      be taken seriously. On the other hand, the story is presented in
      grossly romanticized fashion replete with contrived conversation.
      Separating the Jones boys and Eve Ball is impossible. I have used
      the book for color and characterizations, but not for events unless
      supported in other sources.

      Billy Bonney's arrival at the Jones ranch in October 1877, related
      in Ball's chapter 17, is a case in point. Billy's presence there at this
      time is confirmed in other sources, notably the recollections of Lily
      Casey and her brother Robert, cited below, and I believe that he
      was in fact there. But the account of his arrival, presented chiefly
      in theatrical dialogue, strains credulity. He arrives horseless,
      broken-down, and with almost useless feet after the perilous cross-
      ing of the Guadalupe Mountains described so breathtakingly by
      Upson in Garrett's *Authentic Life*. Ever since the first appearance of
      the Jones-Ball version (Eve Ball, "Billy Strikes the Pecos," *New
      Mexico Folklore Record* 4 [1949–50]: 7–10), students have regarded
      it as substantiation of the Upson yarn. It seems more likely to me
      that the Upson account, published in 1882, colored the Joneses'
      memory of Billy's stay at the ranch. For her rendering of the story,
      Ball cites "almost identical accounts" of Bill, Sam, Frank, and Nib
      Jones. In 1877 these brothers were, respectively, fourteen, eight,
      six, and five years old. Given the mysterious workings of memory,
      one may easily reject this version without regarding the Joneses or
      Eve Ball as dishonest. The birth dates of all the Joneses are re-
      corded in the family Bible; a copy is in the New Mexico Biograph-
      ical Notes, Mullin Collection, HHC.

20   *Mesilla Valley Independent*, September 22 and October 27, 1877;
      Frederick W. Nolan, ed., *The Life and Death of John Henry Tunstall*
      (Albuquerque: University of New Mexico Press, 1965), 243–44. I
      have dealt with these events in *High Noon in Lincoln*, 333–34.

21   Tunstall's acquisition of the Casey cattle and the beginnings of his
      ranch on the Feliz are detailed in Utley, *High Noon in Lincoln*, 27.

22   Adherents of the Upson-Jones-Ball story may wonder where Billy, horseless after his ordeal in the Guadalupes, acquired or stole a horse so quickly after his arrival at the Jones ranch.

23   Lily (Casey) Klasner, *My Girlhood among Outlaws*, ed. Eve Ball (Tucson: University of Arizona Press, 1972), 169–70. Lily Casey Klasner is a more reassuring historical source than the Jones brothers, and the student wishes that Eve Ball had been able to do as well by them as she did by Lily. Where susceptible to corroboration in other sources, Lily turns out to be unusually reliable. In addition, her memory of various personalities is acute, and she is indispensable in aiding the historian to get a feel for them as people rather than mere names. With Lily and the Joneses placing Billy here at this time, and Add remembering him here too (see n. 24), we may feel confident that Billy was indeed at the Jones ranch.

24   Ibid., 174; Robert A. Casey, interview with J. Evetts Haley, Picacho, N. Mex., June 25, 1937, HHC.

25   Not surprisingly, Lily says nothing about Tunstall's cows or their recovery by Brewer. Tunstall, however, describes the episode in detail in a letter to his parents of November 29, 1877, in Nolan, ed., *Life and Death of Tunstall*, 248–49. See also Florencio Chavez, interview with J. Evetts Haley, Lincoln, N. Mex., August 15, 1927, HHC. Chavez was one of Brewer's men. The Brewer mission, undertaken on October 20 or 21 and probably completed within ten days, allows us to place almost exact dates on the Caseys' stay at the Jones ranch and thus on Billy Bonney's presence there, which in turn ties in nicely with the documented presence of Evans and his henchmen at the nearby Beckwith ranch. In both the Casey and the Jones accounts, the time is vague.

26   Lily Casey Klasner placed Billy in Lincoln: *My Girlhood among Outlaws*, 174. So did Florencio Chavez: "I knew the Kid from the first time *he first came to Lincoln with Jesse Evans, Frank Baker, . . .*" (italics mine), as quoted in Eugene Cunningham, "Fought with Billy the Kid," *Frontier Times* 9 (March 1932): 244. And so did Francisco Trujillo, who later rode with the Kid, as cited below in n. 27.

     Billy's movements at this time are thinly documented. A few scattered scraps of evidence hint that he may have been arrested at Seven Rivers or Roswell for some offense and confined in the Lincoln jail himself. Released for want of evidence, possibly with the

218

aid of Tunstall, he then went to work for Tunstall. The evidence behind this theory is not persuasive enough to warrant my substituting it for the account I present in the following paragraphs.

27 Francisco Trujillo, interview with Edith L. Crawford, San Patricio, N. Mex., May 10, 1937, translated by A. L. White, WPA Files, Folder 212, New Mexico State Records Center and Archives (hereafter NMSRCA), and printed in Robert F. Kadlec, ed., *They "Knew" Billy the Kid: Interviews with Old-Time New Mexicans* (Santa Fe: Ancient City Press, 1987), 68. Trujillo later rode with Bonney in the Lincoln County War and knew him well. At first glance, this interview seems the incoherent rambling of a senile old man. Once the phonetically rendered names are accurately translated, however, and the framework of his narrative substantiated from other sources, the result is an important tool in reconstructing some key aspects of the Lincoln County War. Trujillo's narrative of his encounter with Billy Bonney finds corroboration in a letter from Lincoln dated December 3, 1877, that appeared in the *Mesilla Valley Independent*, December 15, 1877: "On their way to the Feliz, they met Juan Trujillo, and *borrowed* his saddle, gun and pistol for Don Lucas Gallegos." (Italics mine.) Gallegos, not part of the Evans gang, was the fifth prisoner liberated.

28 I have dealt with the escape in more detail in *High Noon in Lincoln*, 34–35 and notes. Each faction accused the other of aiding the escape, and the exact truth cannot be recovered. Principal sources are Tunstall's account in Nolan, ed., *Life and Death of Tunstall*, 253–56; *Mesilla Valley Independent*, November 24 and December 13, 1877; and depositions of Alexander McSween and Juan Patrón, in Frank Warner Angel, "Report on the Death of John H. Tunstall," File 44–4–8–3, RG 60, Records of the Department of Justice, NARA (hereafter cited as Angel Report). The case against Tunstall is best stated in "Cowboy" to Ed., Rio Pecos, April 8, 1878, *Weekly New Mexican* (Santa Fe), April 20, 1878; and the case against Dolan is best stated in McSween to Ed., Lincoln, April 27, 1878, which appeared in the *Cimarron News and Press* and is reproduced in Maurice G. Fulton, *History of the Lincoln County War*, ed. Robert N. Mullin (Tucson: University of Arizona Press, 1968), 189–92. Both Evans and Andrew Boyle, soon to become prominent in the anti-McSween forces, implicated McSween in the escape: Depositions of Evans and Boyle, Report of Inspector E. C.

Watkins, Report no. 1981, June 27, 1878, RG 75, Records of the
Bureau of Indian Affairs, Inspectors' Reports, 1873–80, NARA
(hereafter Watkins Report). This report concerns allegations made
by McSween of fraudulent relations between Indian Agent Frederick C. Godfroy and Dolan & Co. Godfroy lost his job as a result.

4. THE RANCH HAND

1   George Coe wrote a book that has become a minor classic: *Frontier
     Fighter: The Autobiography of George W. Coe*, as related to Nan Hil-
     lary Harrison (Boston and New York: Houghton Mifflin Co., 1934;
     2d ed., Albuquerque: University of New Mexico Press, 1951;
     Lakeside Classics ed., ed. Doyce B. Nunis, Jr., Chicago: R. R.
     Donnelley and Co., 1984). The book suffered from the interven-
     tion of Harrison and is of limited value as source material. Far more
     valuable are interviews with both Frank and George conducted by
     J. Evetts Haley in the 1920s and 1930s, the notes and transcripts of
     which are now housed in the Haley History Center in Midland,
     Texas. Both also contributed articles and letters to newspapers.
     Frank and George had a poor memory for chronology, but they
     provide excellent local color and characterizations and good detail
     for certain events.

2   Frank Coe, "A Friend Comes to the Defense of Notorious Billy the
     Kid," *El Paso Times*, September 16, 1923.

3   Ibid.

4   William Chisum, interview with Allen A. Erwin, Los Angeles,
     1952, Arizona Historical Society, Tucson (hereafter AHS). This
     source consists of a dozen tapes recorded by Erwin in a series of
     conversations in Chisum's Los Angeles home during August and
     September 1952. The son of James Chisum, Will was a nephew of
     John Simpson Chisum, for whom he worked at the South Spring
     ranch near Roswell beginning in December 1877. For frontier fire-
     arms in general, and Billy's in particular, see Louis A. Garavaglia
     and Charles G. Worman, *Firearms of the American West, 1866–1894*
     (Albuquerque: University of New Mexico Press, 1985).

5   Coe, *Frontier Fighter*, 49. I have used the Lakeside Classics edition.

6   Frank Coe, interview with J. Evetts Haley, San Patricio, N. Mex.,
     March 20, 1927, HHC.

7   William Wier, interview with J. Evetts Haley, Monument, N.

Mex., June 22, 1937, Barker History Center, University of Texas. For a biographical sketch of Scurlock, see Philip J. Rasch, Joseph E. Buckbee, and Karl K. Klein, "Man of Many Parts," English Westerners *Brand Book* 5 (January 1963): 9–12.

8   Coe, *Frontier Fighter*, 50. Quotation from Frank Coe, interviews with J. Evetts Haley, San Patricio, N. Mex., March 20, 1927, and February 20, 1928, HHC. The latter interview is penciled jottings on slips of paper and apparently was never transcribed and edited.

9   Frederick W. Nolan, ed., *The Life and Death of John Henry Tunstall* (Albuquerque: University of New Mexico Press, 1965), 213.

10   Sue (McSween) Barber, interview with J. Evetts Haley, White Oaks, N. Mex., August 16, 1927, HHC.

11   Nolan, ed., *Life and Death of Tunstall*, 259.

12   Ibid., 249; New Mexico Biographical Notes, Mullin Collection, HHC.

13   Frank Coe, February 20, 1928, HHC; deposition of Henry Brown, Angel Report, NARA; New Mexico Biographical Notes, Mullin Collection, HHC. Because of his later notoriety in Kansas, Brown has attracted more attention than other gunmen. Consult the following: Bill O'Neal, *Henry Brown, the Outlaw Marshal* (College Station, Texas: Creative Publishing Co., 1980); Colin W. Rickards, "Better for the World That He is Gone," English Westerners *Brand Book* 2 (April 1960): 2–8; and Philip J. Rasch, "A Note on Henry Newton Brown," Los Angeles Westerners *Brand Book* 5 (1953): 58–67. I cannot be sure that Brown worked for Tunstall. The above publications have him hiring on with John Chisum after the break with The House in December 1877. By his own testimony, however, as well as that of Godfrey Gauss, William Bonney, Jacob B. Mathews, and John Hurley (Angel Report, NARA), Brown was at the Tunstall ranch on February 13–18, 1878, at the time of the attachment proceedings that led to Tunstall's death, treated below. His deposition does not indicate whom he worked for after leaving Murphy, but his presence at the Tunstall ranch and his subsequent career as one of the Regulators lead me to think that he went to work for Tunstall at about the same time as Bonney. In any event, these associations seem inconsistent with employment on the Chisum ranch, more than fifty miles to the east.

14   Frank Coe, February 20, 1928, HHC; New Mexico Biographical Notes, Mullin Collection, HHC. The latter consist mainly of some

useful correspondence Maurice G. Fulton conducted with people who knew Waite in Paul's Valley, Oklahoma.

15   Carlota Baca Brent, interview with Frances E. Totty, December 6, 1937, WPA Files, Folder 212, NMSRCA.

16   Deposition of Andrew Boyle, June 17, 1878, Watkins Report, NARA.

17   Depositions of William H. Bonney and Robert A. Widenmann, Angel Report, NARA.

18   Robert A. Casey, interview with J. Evetts Haley, Picacho, N. Mex., June 25, 1937, HHC.

19   I have dealt with these events in greater detail in *High Noon in Lincoln: Violence on the Western Frontier* (Albuquerque: University of New Mexico Press, 1987), 38–43.

20   Deposition of Robert A. Widenmann, Angel Report, NARA; Brady to Rynerson, March 5, 1878, in *Mesilla Valley Independent*, March 30, 1878. The inventories are in Lincoln County, District Court, Docket Book F, NMSRCA.

21   Nolan, ed., *Life and Death of Tunstall*, 252; depositions of Bonney, Widenmann, and James Longwell (a posseman in the store), Angel Report, NARA.

22   Depositions of Widenmann, Bonney, Mathews, and Hurley, Angel Report, NARA. The sources also mention one McCormick, who is otherwise unidentified.

23   Depositions of Gauss and Bonney, Angel Report, NARA. According to Gauss, "It was reported by Alex Rudder that the posse was agoing to kill us." Since Gauss later says that Brewer sent Rudder on to the Peñasco to get a load of corn, I assume Rudder (known locally as "Crazy Alex") gave this information at the ranch rather than in Lincoln. Bonney says, "Having been informed that said deputy sheriff and posse were going to round up all the cattle and drive them off and kill the persons at the ranch, the persons at the ranch cut portholes in the walls of the house and filled sacks with earth so that they . . . could defend themselves." Widenmann also tells of these defensive measures, and they were noted by a member of the second posse on February 18: depositions of Widenmann and Pantaleón Gallegos, Angel Report, NARA.

24   Deposition of Mathews, Angel Report, NARA.

25   The Mimbres raid is reported in the *Mesilla Valley Independent*,

January 26, 1878. The meeting with Dolan is covered in the deposition of Dolan, Angel Report, NARA. The Dolan and the McSween-Tunstall parties met at Shedd's Ranch in San Augustín Pass east of Mesilla. With Evans looking on, Dolan tried to provoke Tunstall into a shootout, but the Englishman refused to go for his gun.

26 Depositions of Mathews and Hurley, Angel Report, NARA. Evans's explanation may have been genuine, or it may have been a screen for other purposes. As will become apparent, Billy did have a spare horse, and it could have been borrowed from Evans. In any event, the explanation, whether truthful or not, establishes a prior relationship between the two that could have occurred only since the killing of Cahill. As suggested in chapter 3, I believe that Bonney rode with the Evans gang in October and helped spring Evans from the Lincoln jail in November. Mathews identifies Evans's companion at Blazer's Mills as Rivers rather than Hill. Hurley names Hill. Because Evans and Hill were especially close, I favor Hurley's memory. In any event, all four were present at Paul's ranch.

27 Those present who later gave depositions for the Angel Report were Mathews, Hurley, Middleton, Widenmann, Bonney, and Gauss. Brown's deposition dealt only with the events of February 18.

28 Depositions of Widenmann, Bonney, and Gauss, Angel Report, NARA. Evans, Baker, Hill, and two others had been indicted for larceny by a federal grand jury on November 21, 1877; this was the basis for the warrant Widenmann carried. U.S. District Court, Third Judicial District, Record Book, 1871–79, pp. 659 and 663, RG 21, Records of the District Court of the United States, Territory of New Mexico, NARA, Denver Federal Records Center (hereafter DFRC).

29 In his Angel Report deposition, McSween, whose dates were usually imprecise, says that Widenmann came in "on or about" February 14 and that Tunstall had already decided not to fight. Because Tunstall was still behaving belligerently three days later, however, I infer a similar attitude in the meeting on the night of February 13.

30 For the organization and movement of the expanded posse, see

depositions of Mathews, Hurley, Gallegos, and Samuel R. Perry, Angel Report, NARA. The Lincoln possemen were Mathews, Hurley, Gallegos, George Hindman, Andrew Roberts, Manuel Segovia, Alexander Hamilton Mills, Thomas Moore, Ramón Montoya, E. H. Wakefield, Felipe Mes, and Pablo Pino y Pino. From Seven Rivers were Billy Morton, Perry, Charles Wolz, Charles Kruling, Charles Marshall, John Wallace Olinger, Robert W. Beckwith, Thomas Green, Thomas Cochran, and George Kitt.

31   Depositions of Longwell and McSween, Angel Report, NARA.

32   Depositions of McSween, Widenmann, Bonney, Middleton, and Gauss, Angel Report, NARA.

33   The scene at the ranch is described in the depositions of Dolan, Mathews, Gauss, Gallegos, Perry, and Kruling, Angel Report, NARA. Perry and Gallegos tell of the exchange with Evans. The Morton quotation is from Gauss. The subposse consisted of Morton, Gallegos, Perry, Kruling, Hurley, Segovia ("Indian"), Hindman, Olinger, Beckwith, Montoya, Green, Cochran, Kitt, and Marshall. Perry and Dolan both mention meeting Henry Brown on the approach from the Peñasco, and Brown's deposition also describes the meeting. Perry notes that Bonney had *a* horse of Evans's, whereas all the rest refer to more than one.

34   The experiences of the Tunstall party are reconstructed from the depositions of Widenmann, Middleton, and Bonney, Angel Report, NARA; from an undated Widenmann draft on stationery of Tunstall's Lincoln County Bank, HHC; and from Widenmann's testimony before Judge Bristol as reported in the *Mesilla News*, July 6, 1878.

35   Deposition of Middleton, Angel Report, NARA.

36   The experiences of Morton's subposse are reconstructed from the depositions of Perry, Cochran, Beckwith, Olinger, Gallegos, Hurley, and Kruling, Angel Report, NARA.

37   Evans's testimony in a hearing before Judge Bristol is reported in the *Mesilla News*, July 6, 1878.

38   Longwell, still holding the Tunstall store next door for Brady, testified that these men had gathered well before word arrived of Tunstall's death. Therefore, they must have come in response to Tunstall's daylong ride through the countryside on February 16. Deposition of Longwell, Angel Report, NARA.

1   Frank Coe, interview with J. Evetts Haley, San Patricio, N. Mex., August 14, 1927, HHC.

2   My reconstruction of the events of February 18–23, based chiefly on depositions in the Angel Report, differs from previous chronologies. I have also dealt with the sequence in *High Noon in Lincoln: Violence on the Western Frontier* (Albuquerque: University of New Mexico Press, 1987), 52–56 and notes.

3   An affidavit of Middleton, and another of Brewer and Bonney, February 19, 1878, together with an explanatory affidavit of Justice Wilson, August 31, 1878, are Exhibits 10a and 13 appended to McSween's deposition in the Angel Report, NARA. Middleton's affidavit named only Hindman. The Brewer-Bonney affidavit named Dolan, Baker, Evans, Davis, Mills, Morton, Moore, Hindman, Frank Rivers (another Evans associate), and Gallegos. Curiously, Wilson issued warrants for the arrest, as a copyest took the names from his docket book the following August, of "John [James] J. Dolan, J. Conovar [Thomas Cochran?], Frank Baker, Jessie Evans, Tom Hill, George Davis, O.[A.] L. Roberts, P. Gallegos, T. Green, J. Awley [John Hurley?], 'Dutch Charley' proper name unknown [Kruling], R. W. Beckwith, William Morton, George Harmon [Hindman], J. B. Mathews and others." Considering Wilson's execrable handwriting, the confused rendering of the names is understandable. In addition to Dolan, others of those named were at the ranch on the Feliz rather than with the Morton subposse.

4   Exhibit 14 appended to McSween's deposition in the Angel Report is a certified copy of an entry of February 20, 1878, in Wilson's docket book, which says that the warrant based on the larceny charge was issued on February 19. Brady's request for military protection, February 18, is annexed to Purington to Angel, June 25, 1878, in the Angel Report, NARA.

5   Deposition of Longwell, Angel Report, NARA. Longwell's dating is imprecise. My reconstruction of Billy's whereabouts leaves this as the only day on which the event could have happened.

6   Deposition of Widenmann, Angel Report, NARA; Widenmann to Purington, February 20 [about 1:00 A.M., according to the deposition], 1878, Angel Report, NARA. U.S. Marshal John Sherman

to Colonel Edward Hatch, Santa Fe, December 3, 1877; 1st end., Loud to Purington, December 10; 2d end., Purington to Loud, March 14, 1878, RG 393, LR, Hq. District of New Mexico (hereafter DNM), NARA (M1088, roll 30).

7   The rest of the possemen were Tunstall store clerk Sam Corbet, Lincoln's black handymen George Washington and George Robinson, Josiah G. Scurlock, Frank McNab, Sam Smith, Ygnacio Gonzalez, Jesús Rodriguez, Esequio Sanchez, Roman Barregon, and one Edwards. Since Brady later charged the Martínez posse with riot, the names appear in court records: Lincoln County, District Court Journal, 1875–79, April 1878 term, pp. 264–91, NMSRCA. They are also named in an affidavit of George W. Peppin, sworn before clerk of the district court, April 18, 1878, Fulton Collection, Box 12, Folder 2, UAL. According to Peppin, the deputies in the store were himself, Longwell, John Long, Charles Martin, and John Clark.

8   Depositions of Longwell, Martínez (2), Widenmann (2), and Goodwin; affidavit of Wilson, Exhibit 14 to McSween's deposition; all in Angel Report, NARA. Longwell's deposition is the most informative, although he dates the episode February 23, which is contradicted by Wilson's docket book as well as other evidence.

9   Purington to Acting Assistant Adjutant General (hereafter AAAG) DNM, Fort Stanton, February 21, 1878, encl. to Pope to Assistant Adjutant General (hereafter AAG) Military Division of the Missouri, April 24, 1878, RG 94, Adjutant General's Office (hereafter AGO) LR (Main Series) 1878–80, File 1405 AGO 1878, NARA (M666 Rolls 397 and 398) (hereafter cited as File 1405 AGO 1878); Purington to Bristol, February 21, 1878, RG 393, Post Records, Fort Stanton, N. Mex., Letters Sent (hereafter LS), vol. 18, 1876–78, NARA.

10   Deposition of Goodwin, Angel Report, NARA.

11   Depositions of Goodwin and Widenmann, Angel Report, NARA.

12   Depositions of Martínez, Widenmann, and McSween, Angel Report, NARA.

13   Purington to AAAG DNM, February 21, 1878, File 1405 AGO 1878, and Purington to Bristol, same date, RG 393, Post Records, Fort Stanton, N. Mex., LS, vol. 18, 1876–78, NARA. Deposition of Goodwin, and Purington to Angel, June 25, 1878, Angel Report, NARA.

14   Depositions of Gonzalez and John Newcomb (the fourth member of the group), Angel Report, NARA.

15   Depositions of McSween and Adolph Barrier, Angel Report, NARA. The bond, with Rynerson's disapproving endorsement, is Exhibit 15 to McSween's deposition.

16   Affidavit of Wilson, August 31, 1878, attesting to entry in his docket book of February 22, 1878, Exhibit 13 to McSween's deposition, Angel Report, NARA.

17   The standard authority on vigilantism is Richard Maxwell Brown, *Strain of Violence: Historical Studies of American Violence and Vigilantism* (New York: Oxford University Press, 1975), pt. 3.

18   New Mexico Biographical Notes, Mullin Collection, HHC.

19   Frank Coe, interview with J. Evetts Haley, San Patricio, N. Mex., February 20, 1928, HHC.

20   New Mexico Biographical Notes, Mullin Collection, HHC.

21   Details of the chase are given in Morton to H. H. Marshall (Richmond, Va.), South Spring River, March 8, 1878, printed in *Mesilla Valley Independent*, April 13, 1878. The story is told in greater detail in Garrett's *Authentic Life*, 54–57. Except for the hyperbole and the effort to place Billy at the center of events, I credit this part of the *Authentic Life*. Ash Upson was Roswell postmaster. He received Morton's letter, cited above, and talked with him as well as the Regulators. More than anyone else outside the Regulators, he was in a position to know what happened. He identifies Billy as the Regulator who wanted to kill Morton. Upson's account tallies well with reports that appeared in the *Mesilla Valley Independent*, March 16, 1878, and the *Weekly New Mexican* (Santa Fe), May 4, 1878, the information for which he himself furnished.

22   Morton to Marshall, as cited in n. 21.

23   William Chisum, interview with Allen A. Erwin, Los Angeles, 1952, AHS.

24   *Weekly New Mexican* (Santa Fe), May 4, 1878.

25   Upson to My Dear Niece, Roswell, March 15, 1878, Fulton Collection, Box 11, Folder 4, UAL.

26   Dispatch from Roswell, March 10, 1878, almost certainly written by Upson, *Mesilla Valley Independent*, March 16, 1878; deposition of McSween, Angel Report, NARA. John Middleton recounted this version in his deposition in the Angel Report, NARA.

27   Depositions of McSween and David P. Shield, Axtell responses to

Angel "interrogatories," and Montague R. Leverson to President Hayes, March 16, 1878, Angel Report, NARA. The proclamation is Exhibit 16 to McSween's deposition. Widenmann to Ed., March 30, 1878, *Cimarron News and Press*, April 11, 1878.

The justice of the peace elected in November 1876 had resigned, and the county commissioners had appointed Wilson, who had been justice in the past, to serve pending another election. Although the appointment was in accord with the 1876 act of the territorial legislature creating county commissions, it contravened the New Mexico organic act, which required justices to be elected and which took precedence. Technically, therefore, Axtell was right. But he himself had sponsored the 1876 law, and his proclamation suggests more of a desire to back Dolan than to uphold the law.

28   Deposition of McSween, Angel Report, NARA.

29   Garrett, *Authentic Life*, 56.

30   In Garrett, *Authentic Life*, 55–57, Upson gives a detailed account of this version, derived, he says, from Billy himself and confirmed by "several of his comrades." In this rendering, McNab killed Mc-Closkey, then all the Regulators pursued the fleeing Morton and Baker, and Billy fired the shots that felled them both. It is possible that Billy told Upson the story, but one must look on this claim with healthy skepticism. At the same time, Upson was close enough to the event to have learned what happened in its essentials, and his report deserves respect.

Florencio Chavez told J. Evetts Haley that he was one of the Regulators, that Henry Brown killed McCloskey, and that the other two fled and were killed as related by Upson: Florencio Chavez, interview with J. Evetts Haley, Lincoln, N. Mex., August 15, 1927, HHC. Upson, in the account in the *Weekly New Mexican* (Santa Fe), May 4, 1878, says the bodies bore eleven wounds, one for each Regulator. (He saw the bodies brought into Roswell, according to his letter to his niece cited in n. 25.) Morton, in his letter to Marshall of March 8 (cited in n. 21), names ten Regulators: Brewer, Scurlock, Bonney, Bowdre, Waite, Middleton, Brown, McNab, French, and Smith. The eleventh, if there was an eleventh, could have been Chavez. Given the attitudes of the time and place, a Hispanic among the Regulators might not have registered on Morton or might not have been known to him by name.

Although not claiming to have been present, Francisco Trujillo knew what was going on and talked with Billy in San Patricio immediately afterward. Trujillo's version also has McCloskey killed first and the other two then executed. Francisco Trujillo, interview with Edith L. Crawford, San Patricio, N. Mex., May 10, 1937, WPA Files, Folder 212, NMSRCA.

31   *New Mexico State Tribune* (Albuquerque), July 27, 1928.

6. THE ASSASSIN

1   A biography is Donald R. Lavash, *William Brady: Tragic Hero of the Lincoln County War* (Santa Fe: Sunstone Press, 1987). For his military record, see his enlistment papers, RG 94, Appointments, Commissions, Promotions (ACP) File, NARA, and the pension application of Bonafacia Brady, 555976, August 28, 1892, NARA.

2   Garrett, *Authentic Life*, 60–61.

3   Of all the participants in that meeting, only Francisco Trujillo left an account: interview with Edith Crawford, San Patricio, N. Mex., May 10, 1937, WPA Files, Folder 212, NMSRCA. The account is chronologically confused and somewhat incoherent, but it unmistakably credits McSween with offering a reward for Brady's slaying.

     As I indicated in chapter 3, n. 27, certain portions of Trujillo's account ring true and where susceptible to cross-checking are generally supported in other sources. One reminiscent account fifty-nine years after the fact is pretty thin evidence on which to base such a major allegation, however, and so the question must remain open. My own feeling is that McSween at least implied, seriously or not, that Brady's demise would be welcome, and that the assassins believed they were doing what McSween wanted and, possibly, would pay for.

4   Deposition of McSween, Angel Report, NARA; Montague Leverson to President Hayes, Lincoln, April 2, 1878, in Frederick W. Nolan, ed., *The Life and Death of John Henry Tunstall* (Albuquerque: University of New Mexico Press, 1965), 308–10.

5   Deposition of McSween, Angel Report, NARA.

6   Taylor F. Ealy, "The Lincoln County War As I Saw It," MS, c. 1927, Ealy Collection, UAL. There are three versions, each differing slightly from the others. All three, therefore, should be consulted. Portions of the Ealy papers have been published: Norman

J. Bender, ed., *Missionaries, Outlaws, and Indians: Taylor F. Ealy at Lincoln and Zuni, 1878–1881* (Albuquerque: University of New Mexico Press, 1984).

7   Deposition of McSween, Angel Report, NARA; Ealy, "Lincoln County War." Brady's purpose in walking down the street draws no less than three explanations, and there is dispute over whether he was walking east or west.

In addition to my explanation, which represents my reading of the evidence, another is that, as a ruse to draw Brady into the trap, Henry Brown staged a drunken disturbance near the Ellis store on the east edge of town (George Coe, interview with J. Evetts Haley, Glencoe, N. Mex., March 20, 1927, HHC; and Juan Peppin, interview with Maurice G. Fulton, c. 1930, Mullin Collection, HHC).

Reverend Ealy's explanation, representing the McSween point of view, was that Brady was on the way to the east end of town to intercept McSween, known to be coming in for court, seize him and throw him in the cellar jail (Ealy, "Lincoln County War").

Brady's biographer believes that Brady, coming in from his home east of town, had arranged to meet his deputies at the courthouse, proceed to the Tunstall store to await the arrival of McSween, and there arrest him and once more invoke the writ of attachment. Thus he has the Brady party, not having been at the Dolan store at all that morning, proceeding *west* on the street (Lavash, *Sheriff William Brady*, 105–6). Fulton also has Brady walking west, having reached the courthouse and begun the return to the Dolan store (Maurice G. Fulton, *History of the Lincoln County War*, ed. Robert N. Mullin [Tucson: University of Arizona Press, 1968], 158–59).

Fulton cites no authority. Lavash's authority is Brady's grandson, who is thus reflecting family tradition. Ealy, of course, saw the party walking east, but this is not inconsistent with its reaching the courthouse and starting back before the killings. The son of George Peppin, Juan ran to the scene immediately after hearing the firing.

The relationship of the wall and the east face of the store is another reason for believing that Brady was headed west. Walking east, the victims could not be seen until they were opposite the killers; walking west, they could be tracked for some distance before reaching the store.

8   Frank Coe, interview with J. Evetts Haley, San Patricio, N. Mex., March 20, 1927, HHC.

The original writ of attachment has survived: Lincoln County, District Court, Civil Case no. 141, NMSRCA. The writ bears a notation that it was retrieved from the body of Sheriff Brady. The arrest warrant must have been there too, for Deputy Peppin tried to serve it on McSween later in the day.

The basic facts of the Brady killing are set forth in the *Mesilla Valley Independent*, April 13 and 27 and May 4, 1878, and in the *Weekly New Mexican* (Santa Fe), May 4, 1878. Reminiscent accounts are Robert Brady (the sheriff's young son), interview with Edith L. Crawford, Carrizozo, N. Mex., c. 1937; Gorgonio Wilson (son of Justice Wilson), interview with Edith L. Crawford, Roswell, N. Mex., 1938; and Carlota Baca Brent (daughter of Saturnino Baca), interview with Frances E. Totty, December 6, 1937; all in WPA Files, Folder 212, NMSRCA. These also appear in Robert F. Kadlec, ed., *They "Knew" Billy the Kid: Interviews with Old-Time New Mexicans* (Santa Fe: Ancient City Press, 1987). See also Ealy, "Lincoln County War."

9   Carlota Baca Brent, December 6, 1937, NMSRCA.

10   Ealy, "Lincoln County War." Most accounts identify Billy's companion in the bolt to Brady's body as Fred Waite and the man treated by Ealy as Billy himself. In the passage here quoted, Ealy does not name the man he treated. But in another of his three versions of this manuscript he does name French. In addition, Mary Ealy later declared that French "was pretty badly wounded and the Dr. dressed his wounds." Mary R. Ealy to Maurice G. Fulton, January 16, 1928, Fulton Collection, Box 1, Folder 8, UAL. Frank Coe agrees: "Someone—Mathews said he did it—shot the Kid just above the hip, and the same bullet went through French's leg. Kid and his crowd rode out of town, but French could not run." Frank Coe, March 20, 1927, HHC.

11   Ealy, "Lincoln County War."

12   Ibid. Frank Coe says Corbet put French and the two pistols in the basement of the Tunstall store and dragged a carpet over the trapdoor. Frank Coe, March 20, 1927, HHC. The Tunstall store did not have a cellar either, but it had enough space between floor and ground for French to have hidden. Since Corbet had clerked in the

Tunstall store and knew it well, and since the search centered on the McSween house, I favor the store.

13   The events of the afternoon of April 1 are treated in more detail in Robert M. Utley, *High Noon in Lincoln: Violence on the Western Frontier* (Albuquerque: University of New Mexico Press, 1987), 62–63 and notes.

14   Frank Coe, March 20, 1927, HHC. Waite was indicted for the murder of Hindman. The original indictment, badly water stained, is in the Research Files, Mullin Collection, HHC, and was probably among documents that Mullin retrieved from a trash barrel in Lincoln in 1914. The indictment lists seven witnesses to Hindman's slaying by Waite: Rob Widenmann, Isaac Ellis, Saturnino Baca, Bonifacio Baca, J. B. Mathews, Ike Stockton, and once again the elusive McCormick.

15   Gene Rhodes to Maurice G. Fulton, Santa Fe, May 12, 1927, Fulton Collection, Box 4, Folder 3, UAL.

7. THE SHOOTOUT

1   Much that is known about the events of this day, and some that is erroneous, comes from Almer Blazer and Paul Blazer, son and grandson respectively of Dr. Joseph H. Blazer, proprietor of the sawmill and gristmill. Almer was a boy of thirteen in 1878, and Paul was born twelve years later. Almer's account appeared in the *Alamogordo News*, July 16, 1928, and was reprinted as "The Fight at Blazer's Mill in New Mexico," *Frontier Times* 16 (August 1939): 461–66. Paul's account is "The Fight at Blazer's Mill: A Chapter in the Lincoln County War," *Arizona and the West* 6 (Autumn 1964): 203–10. Almer also gave important details in letters to Maurice G. Fulton, Mescalero, N. Mex., April 24, 1931, and August 27, 1937, Fulton Collection, Box 1, Folder 7, UAL. The Blazers' explanation for Roberts's presence at South Fork is much more persuasive than the story embraced by the Coe cousins and other McSween adherents. According to the latter group's version, the Lincoln County commissioners had posted a reward of either one or two hundred dollars a head for each Regulator, and Roberts had appointed himself a bounty hunter to collect the prize by killing as many as he could. Given the destitute state of the county treasury and the paralysis of the county government, such a reward seems highly un-

likely. I have seen no contemporary documentation for it and doubt that any exists. Nor does it make much sense. The Regulators were not widely enough perceived as outlaws to prompt the county commission to put a price on their heads.

That Roberts was employed by Dolan at the South Fork branch store is testified to by Mathews in his deposition for the Angel Report, NARA.

An excellent synthesis of the evidence is Colin Rickards, *The Gunfight at Blazer's Mill*, Southwestern Studies Monograph No. 40 (El Paso: Texas Western Press, 1974).

2   George W. Coe, *Frontier Fighter: The Autobiography of George W. Coe*, as related to Nan Hillary Harrison, Lakeside Classics ed., ed. Doyce B. Nunis, Jr. (Chicago: R. R. Donnelley and Co., 1984), 90; Frank Coe in Walter Noble Burns, *The Saga of Billy the Kid* (New York: Grosset and Dunlap, 1926), 95–100. Burns's book, so influential in advancing the Kid legend, will not often be cited in these pages as a source. However, Frank Coe's account to Burns, reproduced verbatim, is detailed and generally supported in other sources. See also Frank Coe, interview with J. Evetts Haley, San Patricio, N. Mex., March 20, 1927, HHC, for another good Coe reminiscence. Still another account by Frank Coe appeared in the *New Mexico State Tribune* (Albuquerque), July 23, 1928. The *Mesilla Valley Independent*, April 13, 1878, reported that the Regulators were at Blazer's Mills searching for Roberts. For the ambush plot, see Murphy to CO Fort Stanton, Lincoln, April 4, 1878, and Lt. Col. Nathan A. M. Dudley to Judge Warren Bristol, Fort Stanton, April 5, 1878, Exhibits 77–3 and 77–4, Records Relating to the Dudley Inquiry (QQ 1284), RG 153, Judge Advocate General's Office, NARA (hereafter cited as Dudley Court Record). See also *Mesilla Valley Independent*, April 13, 1878. Colonel Dudley assumed command of Fort Stanton, superseding Captain Purington, on April 4.

3   The others were "Dirty Steve" Stevens, John Scroggins, "Tiger Sam" Smith, and Ygnacio Gonzalez. According to the *Mesilla Valley Independent*, April 13, 1878, Smith and Gonzalez did not stop at Blazer's Mills and thus did not participate in the fight.

4   The gunfight has been reconstructed from the Blazer and Coe accounts cited in nn. 1 and 2, from the account in the *Mesilla Valley Independent*, April 13, 1878, and from the testimony of David M.

Easton, a Blazer employee, at the Dudley Court of Inquiry, in the Dudley Court Record, NARA. The Blazer accounts, which depart in some important ways from the version given here, draw on Billy Bonney himself. After his murder conviction in Mesilla in April 1881, the deputies escorting Billy to Lincoln for execution paused for the night at Blazer's Mills. Here the Kid gave his version of the fight, even acting it out on site in pantomime. The Coe accounts draw substantiation in their essentials from the contemporary report in the *Independent*, which was probably written by Albert J. Fountain. Besides being editor of the *Independent*, Fountain was clerk of the district court and among the party the Regulators allegedly plotted to ambush. Thus he would have been at Blazer's Mills only a day or so after the fight. My reconstruction closely follows that of Rickards, *Gunfight at Blazer's Mill*.

5 These quotations and those that follow are from Coe's *New Mexico State Tribune* account. In the Haley interview, Coe explains the personal enmity behind Roberts's remark as stemming from a scrap the week before. According to Coe, Roberts said, "If it was you, George Coe, and Brewer, I would surrender to you. But there is the Kid and Bowdre, and if we had got them last week we would have killed them, and I won't surrender." Coe adds, "The week before they had had a running fight with the Kid and Bowdre down below San Patricio but they got up a side canyon and got away." Coe also alludes to this episode in the account included in Burns's *Saga of Billy the Kid*. This encounter, if it occurred, is otherwise undocumented.

6 Joe Buckbee (grandson of Scurlock, quoting Scurlock), interview with Philip J. Rasch, Austin, Texas, July 20, 1963, Scurlock File, Rasch Collection, Lincoln State Monument, N. Mex. (hereafter LSM).

7 In the *New Mexico State Tribune* account, but not in his others, Frank Coe includes Billy with Bowdre, Middleton, and George Coe in the initial group that descended on Roberts. David Easton, however, testified, "I was standing in front of the house conversing with Billy Bonnie alias 'Kid' [when] some three or four men of the party passed around the corner of the house to where Roberts was sitting and immediately some eight or ten shots were fired in succession." Easton said that Roberts, just before dying, identified these men as Bowdre, Middleton, McNab, and Brown and that he

234

named Bowdre as the one who fired the fatal shot (Dudley Court Record, NARA).

8   This is part of the story the Kid told and acted out at Blazer's Mills in April 1881. Blazer, "Fight at Blazer's Mill." Almer Blazer was present. The Kid, in fact, thought he had inflicted the fatal wound on Roberts and so boasted at the time and during the telling at Blazer's Mills three years later. This story is not corroborated by any other participant.

9   Testimony of Easton, Dudley Court Record, NARA. The Blazers name the Kid as the one who threatened Blazer and Godfroy, but Coe identifies Brewer, which is more believable, since he was the leader.

10   Ealy, "Lincoln County War."

8. THE WARRIOR

1   For the session of district court, see Lincoln County, District Court Journal, 1875–79, April 1878 term, April 8–24, 1878: 164–91, NMSRCA. Judge Bristol's charge to the grand jury is given verbatim in a supplement to the *Mesilla Valley Independent*, April 20, 1878. Two reports of the grand jury are printed in ibid., April 27 and May 4, 1878, and in the *Weekly New Mexican* (Santa Fe), May 4, 1878.

2   *Mesilla Valley Independent*, March 16 and 23, 1878; U.S. Marshal John Sherman to Lt. Col. N.A.M. Dudley, Fort Stanton, April 8, 1878, File 1405 AGO 1878, NARA; Grady E. McCright and James H. Powell, *Jessie Evans: Lincoln County Badman* (College Station, Texas: Creative Publishing Co., 1983), 109–13.

3   The *Mesilla Valley Independent*, May 4, 1878, prints a "card to the public," dated April 23, in which Dolan and Riley give notice of the closing of their store.

4   Diary of Reverend Ealy, March 10, 1878, Ealy Papers, Special Collections, UAL.

5   A photocopy of McNab's surety bond as deputy constable, April 27, 1878, is in the Research Files, Mullin Collection, HHC. That McNab obtained his commission at San Patricio is speculation, but Wilson had not been reelected in Lincoln, and the inference seems reasonable. Justice Trujillo proved a consistently reliable McSween supporter.

A revealing chronicle of Copeland's activities during the last week of April, replete with excitement, confusion, and heavy drinking, is the report of a soldier detailed to aid him: Cpl. Thomas Dole to CO Fort Stanton, May 1, 1878, File 1405 AGO 1878, NARA. See also "J" to Ed., Lincoln, May 3, 1878, *Weekly New Mexican* (Santa Fe), May 18, 1878; and *Mesilla News*, May 18, 1878.

6   Mary Ealy to Maurice G. Fulton, c. 1927, Fulton Collection, Box 1, Folder 8, UAL.

7   Like Mathews's February posse, this one consisted of both a Lincoln and a Seven Rivers contingent. From Lincoln were Mathews, Peppin, John Hurley, John Long, and Manuel Segovia ("Indian"). From Seven Rivers were William H. Johnson (Hugh Beckwith's son-in-law), Robert and John Beckwith, Robert and Wallace Olinger, Lewis Paxton, Milo Pearce, Thomas B. "Buck" Powell, Joseph Nash, Samuel Perry, Thomas Cochran, Thomas Green, Richard Lloyd, Charles Kruling, Reuben Kelly, Charles Martin, John Galvin, and one Perez. See *Mesilla Valley Independent*, May 11, 1878.

8   Frank Coe, interview with J. Evetts Haley, San Patricio, N. Mex., August 14, 1927, HHC, gives a detailed account of this event. See also "Outsider" to Ed., Fort Stanton, May 1, 1878, *Mesilla Valley Independent*, May 11, 1878.

9   George Coe, interview with J. Evetts Haley, Glencoe, N. Mex., March 20, 1927, HHC, describes the shot in loving detail. The following sources are the basis for my account: *Weekly New Mexican* (Santa Fe), May 11, 1878; "El Gato" to Ed., Fort Stanton, May 10, 1878, ibid., June 1, 1878; "Van" to Ed., Lincoln, May 3, 1878, *Mesilla News*, May 18, 1878; and "Outsider" to Ed., Fort Stanton, May 1, 1878, *Mesilla Valley Independent*, May 11, 1878. "Outsider," whose account is the most reliable and objective, was probably Edgar Walz, Catron's agent. Military sources are Dudley to AAAG, DNM, Fort Stanton, May 4, 11, and 15, 1878, with enclosures (including Lt. George W. Smith's informative report of May 1) in File 1405 AGO 1878, NARA. Frank and George Coe left detailed and graphic reminiscences in interviews with J. Evetts Haley, HHC. Also, George Coe gives an account in *Frontier Fighter*, 113–24.

10   Dudley to AAAG, DNM, Fort Stanton, May 4, 1878, with enclosures, File 1405 AGO 1878, NARA; Dudley to Justice of the Peace

David Easton, May 1, 1878, RG 393, Post Records, Fort Stanton, LS, Vol. 19: 15–16, NARA. McSween's arrest in San Patricio is described in Lieutenant Goodwin's deposition, June 25, 1878, in the Angel Report, NARA. He erroneously dates it May 6, but other documents show it to have been May 2. See also "El Gato" to Ed., Fort Stanton, May 10, 1878, *Weekly New Mexican* (Santa Fe), June 1, 1878.

11   "El Gato" to Ed., Fort Stanton, May 23, 1878, *Weekly New Mexican* (Santa Fe), June 1, 1878.

12   Francisco Trujillo, interview with Edith L. Crawford, San Patricio, N. Mex., May 10, 1937, WPA Files, Folder 212, NMSRCA. See also Florencio Chavez, interview with J. Evetts Haley, Lincoln, N. Mex., August 15, 1927, HHC. Chavez got the killing of Indian badly mixed up with the killings of Morton, Baker, and McCloskey. He says he was present, however, and adds, "Billy the Kid told him if he would tell the truth [about the slaying of McNab] he would turn him loose. The Navajo told him the truth. Billy told him to get on his pinto mare and run away, and he could go. The Indian got on and just got started, and the Kid shot him in the back, and four or five men shot him." Other sources bearing on the cow camp raid are *Mesilla News*, June 1, 1878; *Cimarron News and Press*, June 6, 1878; and *Weekly New Mexican* (Santa Fe), June 8, 1878.

13   Dudley to AAAG DNM, Fort Stanton, May 25, 1878, with enclosures, File 1405 AGO 1878, NARA.

14   Catron to Axtell, May 30, 1878; Axtell to Hatch, May 30, 1878; Hatch to AAG, Department of the Missouri (hereafter DM), June 1; Loud to CO Fort Stanton, June 1; endorsement by Brig. Gen. John Pope, June 7; all in File 1405 AGO 1878, NARA.

15   Compare the two depositions in Angel Report, NARA.

16   *Weekly New Mexican* (Santa Fe), June 1, 1878; Executive Record Book No. 2, May 31, 1878, TANM, Roll 21, Frame 502, NMSRCA. For Dolan's letters to the newspaper, see issues of May 25 and June 1. Catron's anger over the Regulator raid of May 15, which scattered cattle that now belonged to him, had nothing to do with Axtell's action. Catron did not learn of the raid until two days later.

17   Frank Coe, interview with J. Evetts Haley, February 20, 1928, HHC. For the advent of Sheriff Peppin, see *Mesilla News*, June 15, 1878; "Scrope" to Ed, Fort Stanton, June 18, 1878, and Lincoln,

June 22, 1878, both in ibid., June 29, 1878 ("Scrope" was probably Dolan); Andrew Boyle to Ira Bond, Lincoln, August 2, 1878, *Grant County Herald* (Silver City, N. Mex.), August 24, 1878. See also Peppin to Dudley, Fort Stanton, June 18, 1878; Goodwin to Post Adjutant, Fort Stanton, June 22, 1878; Dudley to AAAG, DNM, Fort Stanton, June 22, 1878; all in File 1405 AGO 1878, NARA. Also Special Order 44, Hq. Fort Stanton, June 16 [*sic*, June 18], 1878; and Dudley to Axtell, Fort Stanton, June 20, 1878, Exhibits 77–34 and 77–28, Dudley Court Record, NARA.

18   The warrant and subsequent indictments named Henry Antrim, Charles Bowdre, Doc Scurlock, Henry Brown, John Middleton, Stephen Stevens, John Scroggins, George Coe, Fred Waite, and Richard Brewer. U.S. District Court, Third Judicial District, Record Book 1871–79, Criminal Case 411, June 22, 1878, p. 687, RG 21, Records of the District Court of the United States, Territory of New Mexico, DFRC.

19   George Washington named the men in this contingent as McSween, Copeland, Bonney, Waite, Bowdre, French, Scroggins, Stevens, Jesús Rodriguez, Atanacio Martínez, and Esequio Sanchez. *Weekly New Mexican* (Santa Fe), July 6, 1878.

20   The clash of June 27 has been reconstructed from *Weekly New Mexican* (Santa Fe), July 6, 1878; *Mesilla News*, July 6, 1878; "Julius" (probably Dolan) to Ed., Lincoln, June 27, 1878, ibid.; Andrew Boyle to Ed., Lincoln, August 2, 1878, *Grant County Herald* (Silver City, N. Mex.), August 24, 1878. Also Dudley to AAAG DNM, Fort Stanton, June 29, 1878, with enclosures; Capt. Henry Carroll to Post Adjutant, July 1, 1878; both in File 1405 AGO 1878, NARA. Also Special Order 48, Fort Stanton, June 27, 1878; Dudley to Carroll, Fort Stanton, June 27, 1878; and Special Order 49, Fort Stanton, June 28, 1878: Exhibits 77–43, 77–44, and 78–2 respectively, Dudley Court Record, NARA. Fort Stanton Post Returns, June 1878, NARA (M617, Roll 1218).

21   George Coe, March 20, 1927, HHC. Other sources are *Mesilla News*, July 13, 1878; Andrew Boyle to Ed., Lincoln, August 2, 1878, *Grant County Herald* (Silver City, N. Mex.), August 24, 1878; and Dudley to AAAG, DNM, Fort Stanton, July 6, 1878, with enclosures, File 1405 AGO 1878, NARA.

22   A scattering of entries in Sallie's cryptic diary through July and August 1878 suggests more than a casual relationship. Excerpts from

238

the original in Chaves County Historical Society in Roswell, N. Mex., provided by Harwood P. Hinton. An authoritative treatment is Marilyn Watson, "Was Sallie Billie's Girl?" *New Mexico Magazine* (January 1988): 57–60.

23   *Weekly New Mexican* (Santa Fe), June 27, 1878; George Coe, interviews with J. Evetts Haley, Glencoe, N. Mex., March 20, 1927, and Ruidoso, N. Mex., June 12, 1939, HHC; Robert Beckwith to Josie Beckwith, Lincoln, July 11, 1878, Mullin Collection, HHC.

9. THE FIRE

1   *El Paso Times*, September 16, 1923.

2   Frank Coe, interview with J. Evetts Haley, San Patricio, N. Mex., August 14, 1927, HHC. See also Jack Shipman, "Brief Career of Tom O'Folliard, Billy the Kid's Partner," *Voice of the Mexican Border* 1 (January 1934): 216–19; and Philip J. Rasch, "The Short Life of Tom O'Folliard," Potomac Westerners *Corral Dust* 6 (May 1961): 9–11, 14.

3   Sue (McSween) Barber to Maurice G. Fulton, White Oaks, N. Mex., March 21 and 24, 1926, and October 12, 1928, Fulton Collection, Box 1, Folder 4, UAL.

4   Testimony of Appel, Dudley Court Record, NARA; Mary Ealy to Maurice G. Fulton, December 7, 1927, Fulton Collection, Box 1, Folder 8, UAL.

5   Testimony of David Easton, George Peppin, José María de Aguayo, Saturnino Baca, and John Long, Dudley Court Record, NARA. Easton watched the scene from the Dolan store, across the street from the Wortley Hotel. I recount the Five-Day Battle in *High Noon in Lincoln: Violence on the Western Frontier* (Albuquerque: University of New Mexico Press, 1987), 87–111. See also Philip J. Rasch, "Five Days of Battle," Denver Westerners *Brand Book* 11 (1955): 295–323.

6   Unaccounted for is Fred Waite. Whether he was at the Ellis store, or not even present, is not known.

7   U.S. District Court, Third Judicial District, Record Book, 1871–79, p. 696 (June 28, 1878), RG 21, Records of the District Court of the United States, Territory of New Mexico, DFRC; *Mesilla News*, July 6, 1878.

Possemen identifiable by name are Robert and John Beckwith,

Andrew Boyle, Roscoe L. Bryant, John Chambers, José Chavez y Baca, Thomas Cochran, John Collins, Charles Crawford, James J. Dolan, "Dummy," Jesse Evans, Pantaleón Gallegos, John Galvin, Charles Hart, John Hurley, John Irvin, William H. Johnson, John and James Jones, John Kinney, John Long, Jacob B. Mathews, James McDaniels, "Mexican Eduardo," Lucio Montoya, Joseph H. Nash, Robert and Wallace Olinger, W. R. "Jake" Owens, L. R. Parker, Milo L. Pearce, George W. Peppin, Samuel Perry, Thomas B. "Buck" Powell, James B. Reese, George A. Rose (Roxie), John Thornton, Marion Turner, and Buck Waters.

8 Taylor F. Ealy, "The Lincoln County War As I Saw It," MS, c. 1927, Ealy Papers, UAL; Mary Ealy to Maurice G. Fulton, c. 1928, Fulton Collection, Box 1, Folder 8, UAL.

9 Pink Simms to Maurice G. Fulton, Great Falls, Mont., April 18, 1932, Fulton Collection, Box 4, Folder 5, UAL.
The incidents involving the military are reported in Dudley to AAAG DNM, Fort Stanton, July 16, 17, and 18, 1878, with enclosures, File 1405 AGO 1878, NARA. See also testimony of Capt. George A. Purington, Asst. Surgeon Daniel Appel, and Saturnino Baca, and affidavits of John Long, November 9, 1878, and George Peppin, November 6, 1878, Exhibits 6C and 8, all in Dudley Court Record, NARA.

10 Testimony of José María de Aguayo, Dudley Court Record, NARA.

11 Testimony of Lt. Millard F. Goodwin (Dudley's adjutant), Dudley Court Record, NARA; Fort Stanton Post Returns, July 1878, NARA (M617, roll 1218).

12 Testimony of Sue McSween and William H. Bonney, Dudley Court Record, NARA.

13 The message to Dudley is enclosed with Dudley to AAAG DNM, Fort Stanton, July 20, 1878, File 1405 AGO 1878, NARA. The reply was given from memory by Dudley's adjutant, Lieutenant Goodwin, in his testimony, Dudley Court Record, NARA. Bonney's testimony in ibid. says McSween showed his note to him after writing it. Although McSween's carelessly phrased message literally states his intention to blow up his own house, surely he had reference to Dudley's artillery. The constable was still Atanacio Martínez. By "here," McSween may have meant Lincoln rather than

his house, for Martínez's name does not anywhere appear as one of the defenders of the McSween house.

14   Testimony of Peppin, Dudley Court Record, NARA.

15   Testimony of Isaac Ellis, George Washington, Martín Chavez, Sgt. Houston Lusk, Pvt. James Bush, George Peppin, Sgt. O. D. Kelsey, Capt. George A. Purington, Dr. Daniel Appel, Samuel Corbet, Sgt. Andrew Keefe, Lt. M. F. Goodwin, Theresa Philipowski, Sebrian Bates, and Francisco Romero y Valencia, Dudley Court Record, NARA.

16   Pink Simms to Maurice G. Fulton, Great Falls, Mont., April 18, 1932, Fulton Collection, Box 4, Folder 5, UAL.

17   Testimony of George Peppin, David M. Easton, Andrew Boyle, Robert Olinger, Joseph Nash, Milo Pearce, and Marion Turner, Dudley Court Record, NARA.

18   A parade of witnesses, including Dudley and Sue, gave conflicting and partisan versions of this conversation, Dudley Court Record, NARA. For the encounter with Peppin, see his testimony and hers, ibid.

19   Testimony of John Long, Andrew Boyle, and Thomas B. Powell, Dudley Court Record, NARA; George Coe, interview with J. Evetts Haley, Glencoe, N. Mex., March 20, 1927, HHC.

20   Testimony of John Long, Andrew Boyle, and Joseph Nash, Dudley Court Record, NARA.

21   Sue (McSween) Barber, interview with J. Evetts Haley, White Oaks, N. Mex., August 16, 1927, HHC.

22   Testimony of Purington, Dudley Court Record, NARA; notes of Dr. D.M. Appel, July 20, 1878, Exhibit B6, ibid.

23   The account that follows is reconstructed from the following sources: testimony of William H. Bonney, José Chavez y Chavez, Joseph Nash, and Andrew Boyle, Dudley Court Record, NARA; and affidavit of Yginio Salazar, Lincoln, July 20, 1878, encl. to Dudley to AAAG DNM, Fort Stanton, July 20, 1878, File 1405 AGO 1878, NARA.

Billy's testimony before the Dudley Court is disappointing. Doubtless at the urging of Sue McSween and her attorney, he was more intent on supporting her thesis that soldiers participated in the fighting than in describing what actually happened. The testimony yields many important clues valuable in reconstructing the sequence, but the historian wishes it had been fuller and less partisan. Soldiers did not participate in the fighting.

24   George Coe, March 20, 1927, HHC.

25   Ibid.

10. THE DRIFTER

1   George Coe, interview with J. Evetts Haley, Glencoe, N. Mex., March 20, 1927, HHC. The Casey brothers, though not Ellen and Lily, seem to have returned from Texas by this time. Coe identified his victims as Caseys.

2   Dudley to AAAG DNM, Fort Stanton, August 3 and 22, 1878, with enclosures, File 1405 AGO 1878, NARA.

3   Godfroy to Post Adjutant Fort Stanton, August 3, 1878, encl. to Dudley to AAAG DNM, Fort Stanton, August 3, 1878, File 1405 AGO 1878, NARA. For the past friction, see McSween to Schurz, February 13, 1878, and McSween to Lowrie, February 25, 1878, RG 75, Office of Indian Affairs, LR, NARA (M234, roll 576). The investigation revealed that Godfroy had been "lending" flour and other supplies to The House to meet temporary shortages. Apparently the loans were repaid in kind, but such casual handling of government stores led to Godfroy's dismissal. See Watkins Report, NARA.

4   A party of "wild" Indians—that is, unattached to the agency—had been seen in the vicinity, and at first some thought the firing meant these Indians were fighting with agency Indians. These roamers, apt to be more trigger-happy than the agency people, may have been the Indians the Hispanics encountered.

5   George Coe, March 20, 1927, HHC. Frank Coe was also present and told much the same story. See his interview with J. Evetts Haley, San Patrico, N. Mex., August 14, 1927, HHC. Other sources bearing on this incident are Dudley to AAAG DNM, Fort Stanton, August 6, 7, 8, and 10, 1878, with enclosures, File 1405 AGO 1878, NARA. A rich source, enclosure to Dudley's of August 10, is a lengthy report of an investigation by Capt. Thomas Blair, which includes the accounts of Godfroy, Dr. Blazer, and Interpreter José Carillo. See also *Mesilla Valley Independent*, August 15, 1878; and *Cimarron News and Press*, September 19, 1878.

6   Frank Coe, August 14, 1927, HHC.

7   These notes are from Sallie's diary in the Chaves County Historical Society, Roswell, N. Mex., excerpts provided by Harwood P. Hinton. These take the form of a document assembled by Maurice G. Fulton, who added pertinent entries from other sources as well. Sallie recorded that she received a letter from Billy on July 20 and that her father received one from Charley Bowdre on July 21 telling of the burning of the McSween house. Available from another source is a letter Joe Smith wrote from the Tunstall store on July 19, Fulton Collection, Box 11, Folder 7, UAL. The Five-Day Battle does not seem to have interfered with the U.S. mail. See also Marilyn Watson, "Was Sallie Billy's Girl?" *New Mexico Magazine* (January 1988): 57–60.

8   Frank Coe, interview with J. Evetts Haley, San Patricio, N. Mex., February 20, 1928, HHC. See also George Coe, March 20, 1927. As usual, the Coes' chronology is confused, and they differ somewhat on the sequence of the Regulator wanderings. Frank even has them riding as far west as Los Lunas, on the Rio Grande, but within the known time constraints this seems doubtful. I have adjusted their chronology and sequence to fit what is known from other sources.

9   This quotation and those that follow are from the Frank Coe interview, February 20, 1928, HHC. George Coe tells much the same story, although more briefly.

10   Dudley to AAAG DNM, Fort Stanton, 3 P.M., September 7, 1878, File 1405 AGO 1878, NARA. Fritz recognized only Sam Smith and Joe Bowers, but Tom O'Folliard later came under indictment for this theft. At the least, I think the thieves were Kid, O'Folliard, Smith, and Bowers, and there were probably others.

11   Dudley to AAAG DNM, Fort Stanton, September 7, 1878, File 1405 AGO 1878, NARA. This dispatch was prepared before the one cited in ibid.

12   Garrett, *Authentic Life*, 78. Other sources tend to confirm the version given by Upson-Garrett.

13   The opening of the Staked Plains to cattlemen is well told by J. Evetts Haley in two books: *Charles Goodnight, Cowman and Plainsman* (Boston, 1936; reprint, Norman: University of Oklahoma Press, 1949); and *George W. Littlefield, Texan* (Norman: University of Oklahoma Press, 1943). See also John L. McCarty, *Maverick Town: The Story of Old Tascosa* (Norman: University of Oklahoma Press, 1946).

14   A. B. McDonald, "Tascosa's Lone Settler [Mrs. Mickie Mc-Cormick] Recalls Wild Days," *Frontier Times* 8 (February 1931): 235. Reprint from *Kansas City Star*.

15   Henry Hoyt, *A Frontier Doctor* (New York: Houghton-Mifflin Co., 1929). I have used the Lakeside Classics edition, ed. Doyce B. Nunis, Jr. (Chicago: R. R. Donnelley & Sons, 1979), 148. Hoyt exaggerated Billy's notoriety in October 1878, forgetting that he did not become a celebrity until later, but his recollections are otherwise authoritative.

16   Ibid., 153.

17   Ibid., 149, 154.

18   Hoyt later presented the document to J. Evetts Haley, and it is now in the Panhandle-Plains Historical Museum in Canyon, Texas.

19   Garrett, *Authentic Life*, 81. Fred Waite ended up back home in the Indian Territory, where he served as a tax collector and died naturally in 1895. Henry Brown, after returning for a stint as Tascosa's first marshal, became a respected Kansas lawman, but he also developed a covert sideline as a bank robber, and in 1884 a lynch mob ended both careers. John Middleton punched cows in Kansas, married an heiress, wrote complaining letters to the elder Tunstall in London, and died in 1885 from the effects of his wound at Blazer's Mills.

20   Dudley to AAAG DNM, Fort Stanton, December 9, 1878, File 1405 AGO 1878, NARA; General Order 62, Fort Stanton, December 20, 1878, Exhibit 45, Dudley Court Record, NARA.

21   Garrett, *Authentic Life*, 82, 85, says that Billy was arrested in Lincoln, confined in the jail, and escaped. He adds that Billy penciled an inscription on the oak door of his cell stating that he had been imprisoned here on December 22, 1878. This is corroborated nowhere else, and the inscription, which Garrett says he copied in 1881, could not have been on an oak door to a cell. Lincoln still made do with the old cellar jail, reached through a trapdoor. I think this is more Upson apocrypha.

11. THE BARGAIN

1   S. R. Corbet to John Middleton, Lincoln, February 3, 1880, Fulton Collection, Box 11, Folder 8, UAL.

2   New Mexico Biographical Notes, Mullin Collection, HHC. I have

dealt with this background in greater detail in *High Noon in Lincoln: Violence on the Western Frontier* (Albuquerque: University of New Mexico Press, 1987), 125–31.

3   Dudley to AAAG DNM, Fort Stanton, February 19, 1879, File 1405 AGO 1878, NARA. Dudley was shown the letter and told of the reply.

4   Dudley to AAAG DNM, Fort Stanton, February 21, 1879, Exhibit 79–43, Dudley Court Record, NARA. Three parties to the agreement told Dudley its terms.

5   The most detailed and authoritative evidence for reconstructing the events of this night is a newspaper account summarizing the testimony of participants and witnesses in Judge Bristol's court in Mesilla in July 1879: *Mesilla Valley Independent*, July 5, 1879. See also ibid., March 9 and 22, 1879; *Mesilla News*, March 1, 1879; *Las Vegas Gazette*, March 1, 1879; *Las Cruces Thirty-Four*, March 6 and 19 and April 9, 1879; and Dudley to AAAG DNM, Fort Stanton, February 19, 1879, with enclosures, File 1405 AGO 1878, NARA. Edgar Walz, Tom Catron's brother-in-law and agent in Lincoln, who was present, wrote a graphic reminiscent account: "Retrospection," MS, October 1931, in Museum of New Mexico Historical Library, Santa Fe. For a synthesis of the evidence, see Philip J. Rasch, "The Murder of Huston I. Chapman," Los Angeles Westerners *Brand Book* 8 (1959): 69–82.

6   Kimball to CO Fort Stanton, February 18, 1879, and Lt. Byron Dawson to Post Adjutant, February 19, 1879, both encl. to Dudley to AAAG DNM, Fort Stanton, February 19, 1879, File 1405 AGO 1878, NARA.

7   Walz, "Restrospection."

8   Wallace to Hatch, Lincoln, March 7, 1879; Special Field Order No. 2, Hq. DNM, March 8, 1879; Wallace to Hatch, Lincoln, March 9, 1879; all in Lew Wallace Papers, Indiana Historical Society, Indianapolis (hereafter IHS).

9   Wallace to Carroll, Lincoln, March 11 and 12, 1879, Wallace Papers, IHS.

10   Wallace to Hatch, Lincoln, March 5, 1879; Wallace to Carroll, Lincoln, March 10, 1879; Carroll to Wallace, March 11, 1879; Wallace to Secretary of the Interior Carl Schurz, Lincoln, March 21, 1879; all in Wallace Papers, IHS. Special Order 34, Fort Stanton, March 6, 1879, Exhibit 79–58, Dudley Court Record, NARA.

11   Wallace to Schurz, Lincoln, March 31, 1879, Wallace Papers, IHS;
      "Rio Bonito" to Ed., Fort Stanton, April 8, 1879, *Mesilla Valley In-
      dependent*, April 12, 1879.

12   Wallace to Hatch, Lincoln, March 6, 1879, Wallace Papers, IHS.

13   The exchange of letters is in the Wallace Papers, IHS. This first let-
      ter from Billy, however, is not there, nor is another that is critical to
      the events of chapter 15. The two are available because Maurice G.
      Fulton obtained copies from Lew Wallace's son. The one here
      cited appears in Fulton's *History of the Lincoln County War*, ed.
      Robert N. Mullin (Tucson: University of Arizona Press, 1968),
      336.

14   Wallace did not describe this meeting in his memoirs but told the
      story to a reporter. Between Wallace's tendency to romanticize and
      the reporter's inclination to embellish, it may not have come out
      exactly faithful to factual detail. The spirit and the substance, how-
      ever, appear reliable, and my account is drawn from this report.
      See *Indianapolis World*, June 8, 1902.

15   For the escape of Evans and Campbell, see *Mesilla Valley Indepen-
      dent*, April 5, 1879; and Carroll to COs Forts Bayard, Craig, and
      Bliss, Fort Stanton, March 19, 1879, RG 393, Post Records, Fort
      Stanton, N. Mex., LS, Vol. 20: 241, NARA.

16   Wallace to Schurz, Lincoln, March 31, 1879, Wallace Papers, IHS.

17   "Statement by Kid, made Sunday night March 29, 1879," Wallace
      Papers, IHS.

18   Capt. Juan Patrón to Wallace, Fort Sumner, April 12, 1879, Wal-
      lace Papers, IHS. For the Rifles, see Campaign Records, Lincoln
      County Rifles, 1879, TANM, Roll 87, Frames 185–202, NMSRCA.

19   Leonard to Wallace, Lincoln, May 20, 1879, Wallace Papers, IHS.

20   Lincoln County, District Court Journal, 1875–79, April 1879
      term: 333–35 (April 28, 1879), NMSRCA. The indictment of Ev-
      ans, Criminal Case File 229, is also in NMSRCA. A photostat of the
      indictment of Dolan and Campbell, Criminal Case 280, is in the
      Fulton Collection, Box 12, Folder 2, UAL.

21   *Mesilla Valley Independent*, May 10, 1879.

22   Leonard to Wallace, April 20, 1879, Wallace Papers, IHS; Lincoln
      County, District Court Journal: 316–18 (April 21, 1879),
      NMSRCA.

23   *Mesilla Valley Independent*, May 10, 1879; *Mesilla News*, May 1,
      1879, in *New Mexican* (Santa Fe), May 17, 1879.

24   The voluminous transcript and appended exhibits are in RG 153, Judge Advocate General's Office, Records Relating to the Dudley Inquiry (QQ 1284), NARA.

    In his memoirs, published in 1906, Lew Wallace reproduced a number of letters written by his wife, Susan Wallace, from New Mexico during his governorship. One that she penned at Fort Stanton during the Dudley inquiry mentioned Billy Bonney and has been cited frequently by Kid students. In one passage, she wrote, "The Lincoln County reign of terror is not over, and we hold our lives at the mercy of desperadoes and outlaws, chief among them 'Billy the Kid,' whose boast is that he has killed a man for every year of his life. Once he was captured, and escaped after overpowering his guard, and now he swears when he has killed the sheriff and the judge who passed sentence upon him, and Governor Wallace, he will surrender and be hanged."

    This letter is not in the Wallace Papers, and I am led to believe that Wallace or his wife manufactured the quoted passage many years later, after Billy the Kid had become a celebrity. Everything in it, including the appellation "Billy the Kid," dates from *after* May 11, 1879. Certainly at this time he had yet to develop such intense animosity toward the governor.

    See Susan E. Wallace to Henry L. Wallace, Fort Stanton, May 11, 1879, in Lew Wallace, *Lew Wallace: An Autobiography*, 2 vols. (New York and London: Harper and Bros., 1906), 2: 920–21.

25   *Mesilla Valley Independent*, June 21, 1879.

26   *Mesilla News*, June 21, 1879.

27   San Miguel County, District Court Records, Criminal Case 1005, Territory v. The Kid: Keeping a Gaming Table, NMSRCA.

28   Henry Hoyt, *A Frontier Doctor*, Lakeside Classics edition, ed. Doyce B. Nunis, Jr., (Chicago: R. R. Donnelley & Sons, 1979), 183–87. This incident displays all the implausibilities of the typical Ash Upson tale, but Hoyt's credibility in other respects makes one hesitate to toss it in the bin of Upsonian fantasies. In an appendix Editor Nunis discusses the issue, showing that James's presence in Las Vegas in July 1879 is not precluded by other evidence of his whereabouts. Under the name Thomas Howard, he and his family lived in Nashville, Tennessee, from 1875 to 1881, but he traveled extensively. The railroad had just reached Las Vegas, and he may well have been exploring possibilities. Also, according to the *Las*

Vegas Optic, December 6, 1879, "Jessie James was a guest at Las Vegas Hot Springs, July 26th to 29th. Of course it was not generally known."

29   Purington to AAAG DNM, Fort Stanton, August 17, 1879, RG 93, LR, Hq. DNM, NARA (M1088, Roll 38).

30   Frank Coe, interview with J. Evetts Haley, San Patricio, N. Mex., February 20, 1928, HHC.

31   *Las Vegas Gazette*, December 28, 1880.

12. THE RUSTLER

1   William Wier, interview with J. Evetts Haley, Monument, N. Mex., June 22, 1937, Vandale Collection 2H482, Barker History Center, University of Texas.

2   Quoted in Walter Noble Burns, *The Saga of Billy the Kid* (New York: Grosset and Dunlap, 1926), 185–86.

3   The quotations of Paulita Maxwell Jaramillo are from Burns, *Saga of Billy the Kid*, 180–90. Burns interviewed Mrs. Jaramillo in Fort Sumner. In its first version, his account identified Mrs. Jaramillo as an object of Billy's affections, but his publisher's lawyers, fearing libel, forced him to rewrite it. The true story, as developed by his research, is set forth in Burns to Judge William H. Burges (El Paso), Chicago, June 3, 1926, Research Files, Mullin Collection, HHC. Burns's findings are enlarged by the researches of Maurice G. Fulton as set forth in the Billy the Kid Binder, Mullin Collection, HHC. Fulton's information came principally from Charles Foor, a Fort Sumner old-timer in the 1920s who had been on the scene in 1880. This documentation states that Burns's Abrana García was really Serina Segura, who was given a false name to protect her identity. Since the 1880 census lists Abrana García, twenty-two, and her husband, Martín García, thirty-three, this seems to be in error. Nasaria Yerby is listed in the 1880 census as unmarried and the mother of a son, three, and a daughter, Florintina, aged one; see New Mexico Biographical Notes, Mullin Collection, HHC. For another, confirming source citing Foor, see Leslie Traylor, "Facts Regarding the Escape of Billy the Kid," *Frontier Times* 13 (July 1936): 512. Celsa Gutierrez also presents a problem, which I can resolve only by assuming that her maiden and married names were both Gutierrez, a common Hispanic surname. The 1880 cen-

sus lists her as twenty-four and the wife of Sabal Gutierrez, with a son, aged three. This census also lists Dolores and Feliciana Gutierrez, ages fifty-two and thirty-six, living with their six-year-old grandson, Candido. In later years, according to the Fulton-Mullin documentation, Candido stated that he was the son of Sabal and Celsa Gutierrez, although there is also some indication that he was born to Celsa out of wedlock. Pat Garrett's marriage record reveals that his bride, Apolinaria Gutierrez, was also the daughter to Dolores Gutierrez and thus was Celsa's sister. See William A. Keleher, *The Fabulous Frontier: Twelve New Mexico Items*, 2d ed. (Albuquerque: University of New Mexico Press, 1992), 68.

4   The pattern is well described in John L. McCarty, *Maverick Town: The Story of Old Tascosa* (Norman: University of Oklahoma Press, 1946), 81ff.

5   John Meadows, interview with J. Evetts Haley, Alamogordo, N. Mex., June 13, 1936, HHC. Coghlan's story is graphically told in C. L. Sonnichsen, *Tularosa: Last of the Frontier West*, 2d ed. (Albuquerque: University of New Mexico Press, 1980), 245–59. See also New Mexico Biographical Notes, Mullin Collection, HHC.

6   *Las Vegas Gazette*, December 28, 1880.

7   F. Stanley, *Dave Rudabaugh: Border Ruffian* (Denver: World Press, 1961); Bill O'Neal, *Encyclopedia of Western Gun-Fighters* (Norman: University of Oklahoma Press, 1979), 269–71; William A. Keleher, *Violence in Lincoln County, 1869–1881: A New Mexico Item* (Albuquerque: University of New Mexico Press, 1957), 281–82. For the escape, see *Weekly New Mexican* (Santa Fe), April 5 and 12, 1880.

8   Philip J. Rasch, "He Rode with the Kid: The Life of Tom Pickett," *English Westerners Tenth Anniversary Publication* (London, 1964), 11–15; O'Neal, *Encyclopedia*, 154–55; *Las Vegas Morning Gazette*, January 10, 1884; New Mexico Biographical Notes, Mullin Collection, HHC.

9   Philip J. Rasch, "Amende Honorable—The Life and Death of Billy Wilson," West Texas Historical Association *Year Book* 34 (1958): 97–111.

10   The usual version, drawn from Garrett, *Authentic Life*, 86–89, has all the marks of another Upson yarn. In this instance, however, the Upson version is confirmed in all essentials by William Chisum, interview with Allen A. Erwin, Los Angeles, 1952, AHS. Although

Will's memory may have been heavily influenced by the *Authentic Life*, he surely heard the story many times from his father, James Chisum, who was a witness. Adding to Will's credibility, his account contains details absent from the Upson rendering. See also Harwood P. Hinton, "John Simpson Chisum, 1877–84," *New Mexico Historical Review* 31 (October 1956): 332–33. In addition to the Erwin interview, Hinton drew on correspondence with Will Chisum. Despite the improbabilities, therefore, I am inclined to credit the accepted version, from which the following account is drawn.

11   A cryptic notice appeared in the *Weekly New Mexican* (Sante Fe), January 17, 1880: "Billy Bonney, more extensively known as 'the Kid,' shot and killed Joe Grant. The origin of the difficulty was not learned." In his letter of February 3, 1880, to John Middleton, Sam Corbet referred to the shooting: "Bill Boney shot and killed a man at Ft. Sumner not long since, by the name of Grant, do not know the cause." Fulton Collection, Box 11, Folder 8, UAL.

12   *Las Vegas Daily Optic*, February 22, 1881.

13   William Chisum, 1952, AHS. See also Hinton, "John Simpson Chisum," 333.

14   San Miguel County, District Court Records, Criminal Case 1185, Territory v. William Bonney: Stealing Cattle, NMSRCA.

15   Pat Garrett and his deputy, John William Poe, described the transaction for reporters when Coghlan's bout with the law ground to a close in the spring of 1882: *Daily New Mexican* (Santa Fe), April 22, 1882; *New Mexico News and Press* (Raton), May 6, 1882.

The pattern, and Billy's role in it, were exposed in the winter of 1880–81 by Charley Siringo and other agents of the Panhandle stockmen. Siringo tells the story in *A Texas Cowboy; or, Fifteen Years on the Hurricane Deck of a Spanish Pony* (Chicago: M. Umbdenstock & Co., 1885), chapter 23.

According to my construction, Billy was busy during May 1880 at Los Portales and on the Staked Plains. Some writers, however, say that he participated in an escapade in Albuquerque in May 1880 in which he and one John Wilson stole a horse and a mule, only to be captured by a posse and lodged in the county jail. Promptly indicted, tried, and convicted, he was sentenced to five years in the penitentiary. He dug his way through the cell wall, however, and made good his escape. For example, see Donald Cline, *Alias Billy the Kid: The Man Behind the Legend* (Santa Fe: Sunstone Press, 1986), 88–91.

This adventure is recorded in the Bernalillo County Court Docket Book for the May 1880 term, NMSRCA; and in press items in the *Albuquerque Advance*, May 8 and 22, and the *Albuquerque Review*, May 20, 1880. In neither the court records nor the newspapers is the culprit identified by any name other than "Kid" or "Kidd." Moreover, a newspaper item observes that this Kid had previously been confined in jails at Trinidad, Las Vegas, and Santa Fe. Since Billy Bonney had been in none of these jails at this time, since no other source places him anywhere near Albuquerque throughout 1880, and since he was well enough known by May 1880 to have been recognized as Antrim or Bonney, I am convinced that the Albuquerque Kid is not our Kid.

16   McCarty, *Maverick Town*, 82–85.

17   Wild submitted daily reports to the Chief of the U.S. Secret Service from his arrival in Santa Fe in September 1880 until his return to his New Orleans headquarters early in January 1881. See U.S. Treasury Department, Secret Service Division, New Orleans District, Reports of Special Operative Azariah F. Wild (T915, Roll 308), RG 87, Records of U.S. Secret Service Agents, 1875–1936, NARA (hereafter Secret Service Records).

18   Albert E. Hyde, *Billy the Kid and the Old Regime in the Southwest* (Ruidoso, N. Mex.: Frontier Book Co., n.d.), 19.

19   A biography is Leon Metz, *Pat Garrett: The Story of a Western Lawman* (Norman: University of Oklahoma Press, 1973). See also William A. Keleher, *The Fabulous Frontier: Twelve New Mexico Items* (Albuquerque: University of New Mexico Press, 1962), 67–101. With the advent of Pat Garrett in this story, his *Authentic Life of Billy the Kid* becomes an authentic historical source. Beginning with chapter 16, the tone changes dramatically, the narrative shifts to first person, and much of the content is corroborated in other sources. Upson occasionally prettified the prose, but the writing is now essentially Garrett's, and for succeeding events he knew whereof he wrote. Henceforth the *Authentic Life* will be cited in these pages without apology.

20   George Curry, *An Autobiography* (Albuquerque: University of

New Mexico Press, 1958), 18–19. Curry, later a Rough Rider and territorial governor, related a much-quoted anecdote of Billy's political activities. See also Keleher, *Fabulous Frontier*, 72–73.

21 Metz, *Pat Garrett*, 57.

22 Azariah F. Wild, report for January 2, 1881, Secret Service Records, NARA.

23 Henry Hoyt, *A Frontier Doctor*, Lakeside Classics ed., ed. Doyce B. Nunis, Jr. (Chicago: R. R. Donnelley & Sons, 1979), 185; *Daily New Mexican* (Santa Fe), December 17, 1880.

24 Azariah F. Wild, daily reports for October 20, 22, and 28, November 1 and 6, 1880, Secret Service Records, NARA.

13. THE CELEBRITY

1 Azariah F. Wild, daily reports for October 6 and 9, 1880, Secret Service Records, NARA.

2 Ibid., daily report for January 14, 1881.

3 For Grzelachowski, a fascinating character in New Mexico's history, see Francis C. Kajencki, "Alexander Grzelachowski: Pioneer Merchant of Puerto de Luna, New Mexico," *Arizona and the West* 26 (Autumn 1984): 243–60.

4 William Chisum, interview with Allen A. Erwin, Los Angeles, 1952, AHS; Mason's affidavit, March 18, 1881, and related documents, including indictment of the grand jury, in San Miguel County, District Court Records, Criminal Case 1200, Territory v. William Wilson, Samuel Cook, Thomas Pickett, and William Bonney: Larceny of Horses, NMSCRA. Mason's affidavit gives November 18 as the date, but that does not fit well with later known dates. November 15 is the date given in Garrett, *Authentic Life*, 91.

5 San Miguel County, District Court Records, Criminal Cases 1276 and 1278, Territory v. Barney Mason: Altering Brands, NMSRCA.

6 For a sketch of Mason, see Philip J. Rasch, "Garrett's Favorite Deputy," Potomac Westerners *Corral Dust* 9 (Fall 1964): 3–5.

7 The quotation is from the *Socorro Sun*, December 20, 1881, quoted in F. Stanley, *Notes on Joel Fowler* (Pep, Texas: n.p., 1963), 10. See also New Mexico Biographical Notes, Mullin Collection, HHC; Philip J. Rasch, "Alias 'Whiskey Jim,'" *Panhandle-Plains Historical Review* 36 (1963): 103–14; and W. H. Hutchinson and Robert N. Mullin, *Whiskey Jim and a Kid Named Billie* (Clarendon, Texas:

Clarendon Press, 1967). The Greathouse ranch was located a mile or more southwest of the present town of Corona.

8   Garrett, *Authentic Life*, 92, says the provisions were purchased. According to Wild's daily report for Monday November 22, 1880, Secret Service Records, NARA, "Information has just reached me through a reliable source that Billy Kid had been driven out of the Canadian River country and was now at Greathouse ranch with twenty five armed men, and a bunch of stolen horses. On Saturday night [November 20] seven of Kids men went to White Oaks and attempted to rob one or two places and stole a lot of blankets, over coats, rifles and provisions."

9   Garrett, *Authentic Life*, 91–92. Garrett dates this event November 20. Operative Wild, however, in his report for November 21, 1880, records Mason's journey from Lincoln to White Oaks as occurring on November 21; Secret Service Records, NARA.

10   The best account is in Garrett, *Authentic Life*, 91–92. This account, however, has Billy riding back to White Oaks—where the horse came from is unspecified—and circulating unrecognized in a saloon containing members of the posse. Then the next night he is said to have taken a shot at a townsman in front of the Hudgens saloon. That Billy would have gone back to White Oaks at all seems improbable to me. He was afoot, without provisions, and a marked man in town. I think he told the truth when he later said, "After mine and Billie Wilsons horses were killed we both made our way to a Station forty miles from the Oaks kept by Mr. Greathouse." Bonney to Wallace, Fort Sumner, December 12, 1880, Wallace Papers, IHS. This also coincides with the statement of Joe Steck, a hand at the Greathouse ranch, cited in n. 11 below: "One day the cowboys [Billy and friends] went away, returning after three days."

11   The detailed account by Steck, an employee at the ranch, appeared in the *Lincoln County Leader* (White Oaks), December 7, 1889, and was reprinted in William A. Keleher, *The Fabulous Frontier: Twelve New Mexico Items* (Albuquerque: University of New Mexico Press, 1962), 70–72. The standard and apparently authoritative version is Garrett, *Authentic Life*, 94–97. A press report obtained from posse members, datelined Las Vegas December 20, appeared in the *New York Sun*, December 27, 1880. A fourth account, although twice removed from the action, also merits citation; it was obtained by Frank Stewart, the Panhandle Stock Association's de-

tective, from members of the posse and was passed on to Pink Simms, who in turn sent it to Maurice G. Fulton in a letter of May 16, 1932, Fulton Collection, Box 4, Folder 5, UAL.

12   Bonney to Wallace, December 12, 1880, Wallace Papers, IHS. The Steck and Garrett accounts do not mention an ultimatum or a shot. Both the *New York Sun* and Stewart accounts support Billy's version.

13   *Las Vegas Daily Optic*, January 21, 1881.

14   *New York Sun*, December 27, 1880.

15   Garrett, *Authentic Life*, 96.

16   *Las Vegas Gazette*, December 3, 1880, in William A. Keleher, *Violence in Lincoln County, 1869–1881* (Albuquerque: University of New Mexico Press, 1957), 286–88. Key runs of the *Gazette*, including this issue, exist only in the Keleher Collection, which is not presently open to the public.

17   Bonney to Wallace, Fort Sumner, December 12, 1880, Wallace Papers, IHS.

18   Executive Record Book No. 2, 1867–82, p. 473, December 13, 1880, TANM, Roll 21, Frame 565, NMSRCA. W. S. Koogler to Wallace, November 30, 1880; Wallace to Koogler, December 4, 1880; Wallace to Secretary of the Interior Carl Schurz, December 7 and 14, 1880; all in Wallace Papers, IHS.

14. THE CAPTURE

1   San Miguel County, District Court Records, Civil Case 1100, John Deolevara v. Fredrike Deolevara: Divorce, NMSRCA. The file contains letters written by the estranged wife, together with her husband's commentary, indicating that outlaws, including "Billy Kid," often visited the house where she lived and threatened the plaintiff when he tried to get custody of the children.

2   The plan unfolds in Wild's daily reports from November 4 through the balance of the month, Secret Service Records, NARA.

3   Wild had also remained in Roswell. His daily reports contain some details of the "raid," but the best source is Garrett, *Authentic Life*, 101–4. For the raid on the Diedrick ranch, see *Weekly New Mexican* (Santa Fe), December 13, 1880.

4   Garrett, *Authentic Life*, 105–6.

5   Ibid., 114–15, says they moved into town. Brazil, in a newspaper

interview, says they also spent time at the two ranches: *Las Vegas Gazette*, December 27, 1880.

6   Bowdre to Lea, Fort Sumner, December 15, 1880, Ritch Collection, Huntington Library, San Marino, Calif. (hereafter HL), microfilm copy in NMSRCA; Garrett, *Authentic Life*, 115.

7   The most authoritative account of these and subsequent events is Garrett, *Authentic Life*, 110ff. Accounts of three participants are James H. East, interview with J. Evetts Haley, Douglas, Ariz., September 27, 1927, HHC; Louis P. Bousman, interview with J. Evetts Haley, October 23, 1934, HHC; and Charles Frederick Rudulph, *"Los Bilitos": The Story of "Billy the Kid" and His Gang* (New York: Carlton Press, 1980), 206–54. See also James H. East to Charlie Siringo, Douglas, Ariz., May 1, 1920, in Charles A. Siringo, *History of "Billy the Kid"* (Santa Fe: n.p., 1920), 97–105. Siringo, who headed one of the two parties, told his story first in *A Texas Cowboy; or, Fifteen Years on the Hurricane Deck of a Spanish Pony* (Chicago: M. Umbdenstock & Co., 1885); again in *A Lone Star Cowboy* (Santa Fe: n.p., 1919); and still again in *Riata and Spurs* (Boston and New York: Houghton Mifflin Co., 1927). As a result of these books, Siringo became something of an icon in the historiography of the Southwest. His penchant for romanticizing, however, gravely weakens his reliability; and anyway he did not join his comrades in volunteering for Garrett's expedition to Fort Sumner, a decision for which he must have bitterly reproached himself throughout a lifetime of self-glorification. Although somewhat garbled, another firsthand account was given a reporter by M. S. Brazil, a peripheral actor in the events: *Las Vegas Gazette*, December 27, 1880. For East, see also J. Evetts Haley, "Jim East, Trail Hand and Cowboy," *Panhandle-Plains Historical Review* 4 (1931): 48–61. The story is also told in Leon Metz, *Pat Garrett: The Story of a Western Lawman* (Norman: University of Oklahoma Press, 1973), 71ff.; and John L. McCarty, *Maverick Town: The Story of Old Tascosa* (Norman: University of Oklahoma Press, 1946), 84ff. A number of the original sources are reprinted in James H. Earle, ed., *The Capture of Billy the Kid* (College Station, Texas: Creative Publishing Co., 1988).

8   The six, besides Stewart, were "Tenderfeet Bob" Williams, Louis "The Animal" Bousman, "Poker Tom" Emory, James East, Lee Hall, and Lon Chambers.

One of those who continued to White Oaks with Siringo was Cal Polk. As Jim East observed, "Cal Polk was just a kid and I did not blame him for not going." But Cal Polk himself said that he went with Garrett, describing his adventures in elaborate detail in a manuscript "Life of Cal Polk, commenced January 25, 1896," now preserved in the Panhandle-Plains Historical Museum at Canyon, Texas (hereafter PHPHM). It is a curious document, not only for its amusing phonetic spelling but also for its combination of wild fancy with demonstrable fact. Polk clearly knew much that occurred on the Garrett expedition. By 1896 Garrett and Siringo were the only participants who had published their accounts. Polk may have obtained some of his material from their books, and very likely he absorbed a lot by talking with the other Texans such as East. Since no other authority places Polk with Garrett, I do not believe he went, which leaves this part of his autobiography, at least, a phony.

9   Rudulph, *"Los Bilitos,"* 207.

10   Roybal's mission is recounted by Garrett, *Authentic Life*, 114–15, and by his fellow townsman Rudulph, *"Los Bilitos,"* 208.

11   So Rudabaugh's friend John J. Webb told Garrett when arrested at Bosque Grande on November 30: *Weekly New Mexican* (Santa Fe), December 13, 1880.

12   My account of the ambush substantially follows Garrett, *Authentic Life*, 118–19. Surprisingly, for events so thoroughly worked over, the chronology of the Garrett expedition is hopelessly muddled or entirely nonexistent both in the sources and the secondary works. A close reading of the *Authentic Life* discloses a reasonably satisfactory sequence, beginning with the posse's arrival in Fort Sumner on the morning of December 18. Garrett, however, telescopes into one day, the eighteenth, events that I have spread over two days; as a result, Garrett has O'Folliard's death on December 18 and the capture at Stinking Springs on December 22. This not only leaves him with a day unaccounted for in his own calendar but also contradicts most other sources, which give the two dates as December 19 and 23. Both Rudulph and East support me in placing the posse in Sumner one night before the night of O'Folliard's death.

13   James H. East, September 27, 1927, HHC. I find East's account of the deathbed scene more believable than the melodramatic conver-

sation among Garrett, Mason, and O'Folliard given in *Authentic Life*, 120, which I suspect owed more to Upson than Garrett.

14 Garrett, *Authentic Life*, 121.

15 Rudulph, *"Los Bilitos,"* 210.

16 Garrett, *Authentic Life*, 122.

17 So Brazil related to Garrett: ibid., 126.

18 The sources disagree on who went with whom. East names only himself, Emory, Chambers, and Hall as accompanying Garrett, while relegating Stewart, whom he obviously did not like, to the position of horse tender. Both Rudulph and Bousman include themselves with Garrett, and Mason was there. Garrett says only that he divided his force between Stewart and himself.

19 Garrett says he gave no warning; Rudulph and Bousman agree; East says Garrett shouted "Throw up your hands!" Garrett and Rudulph say everyone fired; East says only Garrett and Lee Hall fired; Bousman says he, Garrett, and Chambers fired.

20 This according to Garrett, *Authentic Life*, 125. Others gave slightly different versions. For example, Rudulph, East, and Bousman name Bonney as the one who shouted that Bowdre wanted to come out. East quotes the Kid as saying, "Charley, you are going to die anyway, so go out and see if you can't get some of them." East also says that Bowdre had his six-shooter in hand but was too weak to cock it. Bousman says that the pistol remained in its holster and that he, Bousman, took hold of Bowdre and laid him on a blanket.

21 Rudulph, Brazil, and East support Garrett's version. Bousman says he killed the horse in the doorway and Garrett severed the other ropes, although Bousman, erroneously assuming that Rudabaugh had not been remounted, counts only one other horse.

22 *Las Vegas Gazette*, December 28, 1880.

23 Garrett makes no reference to this incident. East tells the story both in his Haley interview and his letter to Charley Siringo. Bousman noted: "Mason said, 'Now Pat, let's kill the sons-a-bitches.' We threw down on him and said, 'You dirty son-of-a-bitch, just try that and we'll cut you in two and Pat too.'"

24 Rudulph, *"Los Bilitos,"* 214.

25 East to Siringo, May 1, 1920, in Siringo, *History of "Billy the Kid,"* 105.

26 East to Siringo, April 20, 1920, in ibid., 105–7. East also tells the

story in East to William H. Burges, Douglas, Ariz., May 20, 1926, Research Files, Folder labeled "Saga of Billy the Kid," Mullin Collection, HHC. Probably because Paulita was still alive and denied any liaison with the Kid, East's letter to Siringo, as printed, named her Dulcinea Toboso. The unpublished letter to Burges used correct names.

27 Rudulph, *"Los Bilitos,"* 214; East to Siringo, May 1, 1920, in Siringo, *History of "Billy the Kid,"* 97–105; Louis P. Bousman, interviews with J. Evetts Haley, September 7 and October 23, 1934, HHC.

28 Lea to Wallace, Roswell, December 24, 1880, Ritch Collection, HL, Microfilm Reel 9 in NMSRCA.

29 As previously mentioned, Garrett's chronology is flawed, as are those of almost all other sources and commentators. Garrett has the posse and prisoners leaving the Wilcox-Brazil ranch for Las Vegas immediately after the surrender, spending the night neither at the ranch nor in Fort Sumner but reaching Puerto de Luna on Christmas afternoon. Since he also dates the surrender on December 22, this leaves two and one-half days and two nights for a journey that in fact required a day and a night. Most of the other sources agree that the party passed the night of the surrender, December 23, at the Wilcox-Brazil ranch, reached Sumner shortly before noon on the twenty-fourth and departed shortly after noon, and arrived at Grzelachowski's store in Puerto de Luna after noon on the twenty-fifth, where they were treated to a hearty Christmas dinner. They were in Las Vegas by late afternoon, December 26.

15. THE SENTENCE

1 *Las Vegas Gazette,* December 27, 1880 (extra). Rudulph, Wilson, and the Roybal brothers had returned to their homes in Puerto de Luna. The rest of the Texans (Williams, Bousman, Hall, and Chambers) had taken the road to White Oaks to rejoin Siringo and the others who had declined to go with Garrett.

2 Albert E. Hyde, *Billy the Kid and the Old Regime in the Southwest* (Ruidoso, N. Mex.: Frontier Book Co., n.d.), 20–22 (reprint of an article, "The Old Regime in the Southwest: The Reign of the Revolver in New Mexico," *Century Magazine* 63 [March 1902]).

3   These quotations and those that follow are from *Las Vegas Gazette*, December 28, 1880.

4   Ibid.; Garrett, *Authentic Life*, 129.

5   Garrett, *Authentic Life*, 129, says he dismissed all but Stewart and Mason and enlisted the help of a friend, mail contractor Mike Cosgrove. The *Las Vegas Gazette*, December 30, 1880, identifies the guards as I have given them, and Jim East testifies to his presence and Emory's in interview with J. Evetts Haley, Douglas, Ariz., September 27, 1927, HHC.

6   Garrett, *Authentic Life*, 130. East says Garrett shoved a six-shooter into the leader's stomach and pushed him off: James H. East, September 27, 1927, HHC.

7   *Las Vegas Gazette*, December 28, 1880.

8   Ibid.; *Daily New Mexican* (Santa Fe), December 29, 1880.

9   James H. East, September 27, 1927, HHC.

10 Ibid. Another firsthand account is Hyde, *Billy the Kid*, 24–28.

11 *Daily New Mexican* (Santa Fe), December 28, 1880.

12 Leon Metz, *Pat Garrett: The Story of a Western Lawman* (Norman: University of Oklahoma Press, 1973), 89–91.

13 This and subsequent missives from Billy to Wallace are in the Wallace Papers, IHS.

14 *Las Vegas Gazette*, January 4 and March 12, 1881; *Daily New Mexican* (Santa Fe), January 6, 1881.

15 *Daily New Mexican* (Santa Fe), March 1, 1881.

16 This letter is not in the Wallace Papers but was obtained from Wallace's son by Maurice G. Fulton. Its text appears in Fulton's *History of the Lincoln County War*, ed. Robert N. Mullin (Tucson: University of Arizona Press, 1968), 336, and in William A. Keleher, *Violence in Lincoln County, 1869–1881: A New Mexico Item* (Albuquerque: University of New Mexico Press, 1957), 300.

    Nearly twenty years later, in a newspaper interview, Wallace said of this letter, "I knew what he meant. He referred to the note he received from me and in response to which he appeared at the hut on the mesa [Squire Wilson's hut in Lincoln]. He was threatening to publish it if I refused to see him. I thwarted his purpose by giving a copy of the letter and a narrative of the circumstances connected with it to the paper published in the town. It was duly printed and upon its appearance a copy was sent to 'Billy' in his cell. He had nothing further to say." *Indianapolis World*, June 8, 1902. No such item has been found in Santa Fe newspapers, and of course Billy had much more to say.

17 *Las Vegas Gazette*, March 30, 1881; *Daily New Mexican* (Santa Fe), April 2, 1881. Both Rudabaugh and Wilson were convicted, and both escaped from jail. Rudabaugh disappeared into Mexico, where he made himself so obnoxious that at Parral, in 1886, residents killed him and cut off his head. Wilson supposedly went to Texas, lived respectably under an assumed name, and ultimately won a presidential pardon. However, Donald R. Lavash, biographer of Sheriff William Brady, is presently researching the life of Billy Wilson and is convinced that the man pardoned in Texas was not the man convicted in New Mexico.

18 *Daily New Mexican* (Santa Fe), April 3, 1881.

19 Helen Irwin, "When Billy the Kid Was Brought to Trial," *Frontier Times* 6 (March 1929): 214–15, based on recollections of George Bowman, clerk of the court, and originally appearing in *Fort Worth Star-Telegram*, December 2, 1928.

20 The proceedings against Billy in Mesilla, both federal and territorial, are thinly documented, both in official records and the newspapers. Surviving records of the federal trial are in Criminal Case 411, U.S. v. Charles Bowdre, Dock Scurlock, Henry Brown, Henry Antrim, John Middleton, Stephen Stevens, John Scroggins, George Coe, Frederick Wait: murder. U.S. District Court, 3d Judicial District, RG 21, Records of the District Court of the United States, Territory of New Mexico, DFRC.

21 In addition to official sources, consult the secondary accounts in Keleher, *Violence in Lincoln County*, 305–15; and Philip J. Rasch, "The Hunting of Billy, the Kid," English Westerners *Brand Book* 11 (January 1969): 6.

22 A biography is A. M. Gibson, *The Life and Death of Colonel Albert Jennings Fountain* (Norman: University of Oklahoma Press, 1965). Curiously, the book is silent on Fountain's role as the Kid's attorney.

23 Surviving records are Criminal Cases 531 and 532, Territory v. William Bonney alias Kid: murder; and Doña Ana County, District Court Journal: 384–91, 406–07, 411, NMSRCA. The case was tried in Doña Ana County on a change of venue from Lincoln County, where the identifying numbers were 243 and 244. These records are printed as an appendix to C. L. Sonnichsen and Wil-

liam V. Morrison, *Alias Billy the Kid* (Albuquerque: University of New Mexico Press, 1955), 98–107.

24 *Mesilla News*, April 16, 1879.

25 *Las Vegas Gazette*, April 28, 1881.

16. THE ESCAPE

1 Bell Hudson, quoted by his daughter in Mary Hudson Brothers, *A Pecos Pioneer* (Albuquerque: University of New Mexico Press, 1943), 71–72. See also Philip J. Rasch, "The Olingers, Known Yet Forgotten," Potomac Westerners *Corral Dust* 8 (February 1963): 1, 4–6.

2 Gildea to Maurice G. Fulton, Pearce, Ariz., January 16, 1929, New Mexico Notebook, Mullin Collection, HHC; W. R. (Jake) Owens, interview with J. Evetts Haley, Carlsbad, N. Mex., June 24, 1937, HHC; Lily (Casey) Klasner, *My Girlhood among Outlaws*, ed. Eve Ball (Tucson: University of Arizona Press, 1972), 188; *Weekly New Mexican* (Santa Fe), May 1, 1881.

3 *Daily New Mexican* (Santa Fe), May 3, 1881; Garrett, *Authentic Life*, 134.

4 *Newman's Semi-Weekly* (Las Cruces), April 17, 1881.

5 Paul Blazer, "The Fight at Blazer's Mill: A Chapter in the Lincoln County War," *Arizona and the West* 6 (Autumn 1964): 210; Garrett, *Authentic Life*, 132.

6 Garrett, *Authentic Life*, 132.

7 Bonney to Caypless, Mesilla, April 15, 1881, copy in LSM. The text also appears in William A. Keleher, *Violence in Lincoln County, 1869–1881: A New Mexico Item* (Albuquerque: University of New Mexico Press, 1957), 320–21.

8 John P. Meadows, in collaboration with Maurice G. Fulton, "Billy the Kid as I Knew Him," MS, c. 1931, Rasch Collection, LSM. There is also a Meadows interview with J. Evetts Haley, Alamogordo, N. Mex., June 13, 1936, HHC, and a newspaper interview, "My Personal Recollections of 'Billy, the Kid,'" *Alamogordo News*, June 11, 1936.

Meadows's reminiscences challenge the historian. Internal evidence and other sources leave little question in my mind that he knew the Kid well, perhaps as well as he says. In April 1881 Meadows and a partner operated a little spread on the Peñasco south of

Lincoln. According to Meadows, after Billy escaped from confinement in Lincoln, he came to the cabin and stayed over one night, during which he related the story of his incarceration and breakout. If true, this is the only source in which Billy's own testimony is given. That Billy visited the Meadows cabin cannot be corroborated in other sources, but neither do other sources foreclose the possibility. To me, the Meadows recollections, allowing for fifty years' dimming of memory and the inevitable exaggerations of the old-timer, ring true. With a faintly nagging hesitation, I have chosen to use them as source material.

9   Garrett, *Authentic Life*, 134.

10 Ibid., 133.

11 Ibid., 138.

12 *Daily New Mexican* (Santa Fe), May 3, 1881.

13 I have combined Garrett's and Billy's similar versions of this incident to present what seems to me most likely. Garrett, *Authentic Life*, 137; and Meadows and Fulton, "Billy the Kid as I Knew Him."

The reconstruction that follows is drawn from several firsthand sources. They agree in some respects, disagree in others, and (usually the case) describe an incident in differing detail. In evaluating these sources, I have considered closeness to the event in time and place and, admittedly a highly personal judgment, plausibility— what most likely happened given the people, the setting, and the evidence. In addition to Garrett and Meadows, as cited above, the sources are an anonymous letter from Lincoln in *Daily New Mexican* (Santa Fe), May 3, 1881; two anonymous letters from White Oaks, April 30, 1881, in ibid.; account in *Golden Era* (White Oaks), May 5, 1881; anonymous letter from Lincoln, April 29, 1881, in *New Southwest and Grant County Herald* (Silver City, N. Mex.), May 14, 1881; anonymous letter from Seven Rivers, N. Mex., May 11, 1881, in *Tombstone Epitaph*, June 6, 1881; account in *Las Vegas Morning Gazette*, May 10, 1881; account of Godfrey Gauss, Lincoln, January 15, 1890, in *Lincoln County Leader* (White Oaks), March 1, 1890; and Yginio Salazar, interview with J. Evetts Haley, Lincoln, N. Mex., August 17, 1927, HHC.

The account in the *Grant County Herald* deserves special mention. The writer had a sleeping room on the first floor of the courthouse and, when the break occurred, had just left the building with Ben

Ellis to walk down the street to Ike Ellis's store for dinner. The two heard the firing but attributed no significance to it. When they returned, they witnessed the final stages of the escape. Both in time and place, therefore, this account has immediacy.

Immediacy of place but nine years distance in time marks the account of Godfrey Gauss, who knew Billy from their weeks in Tunstall's employ and who played a direct role in the escape.

Garrett was not in Lincoln, but obviously he took pains to find out what had happened and why, then wrote his account some five months later.

Finally, there is the Meadows account, previously discussed, which purports to give Billy's own version but is separated in time from the event by fifty years.

14   Herman B. Weisner, "The Prisoners Who Saw the Kid Kill Olinger," *Rio Grande History* 9 (Las Cruces: New Mexico State University Library, 1978): 6–7. The five men were Alexander Nunnelly, Charles Wall, John Copeland (not the Copeland of Lincoln County War note), Augustin Davalas, and Marejildo Torres.

Some accounts have Olinger taking these men out for the noon meal. However, the contemporary sources, and Garrett, specify evening.

15   Thus I credit the Meadows account of the killing of Bell. There are several others, but the only witness to the killing was the killer, and if Meadows told the truth, this is Billy's own version.

The first press accounts, which had to be based on surmise, reported that Billy and Bell were playing cards when Billy hit him with the handcuffs and grabbed his revolver.

In Garrett's rendering, Billy got so far ahead of Bell coming up the steps that he hobbled to the armory, shoved open the locked door, scooped up a pistol, and returned to the top of the stairs in time to shoot Bell as he came up. Bell was undoubtedly careless, but that careless?

In still another version, Billy's friend Sam Corbet planted, or caused to be planted, in the privy a pistol wrapped in a newspaper and slipped word of it to Billy. This story, current among Lincoln old-timers in the 1920s and 1930s, was credited to Bonifacio Baca, Corbet's brother-in-law. See Leslie Traylor, "Facts Regarding the Escape of Billy the Kid," *Frontier Times* 13 (July 1936): 509. The respected historian of the Lincoln County War, Maurice G. Fulton, subscribed to this version. See his *History of the Lincoln County War*, ed. Robert N. Mullin (Tucson: University of Arizona Press, 1968), 394–95. Fulton, who never bothered to cite sources, said that Judge Lucius Dills, a turn-of-the-century New Mexico attorney with a passion for history, had proved that after the shooting Bell's pistol was still in his holster, fully loaded. I have not seen this "proof"; but if it resembles other Dill essays in history that I have seen, it is highly suspect. Until such proof is forthcoming, the recital that Meadows attributed to Billy seems to me the more plausible.

16 Gauss account in *Lincoln County Leader* (White Oaks), March 1, 1890, as confirmed by the account in *Grant County Herald* (Silver City, N. Mex.), May 14, 1881. A letter from Lincoln in the *Daily New Mexican* (Santa Fe), May 3, 1881, reported that "Bell lay dead in the back yard with one bullet through him and two gashes on his head, apparently cut by a blow from the handcuffs."

17 All the sources are in essential agreement about the details of this event. My account combines mainly Gauss, Garrett, and the Kid (Meadows). Some accounts (including the Meadows account) identify Alex Nunnelly, one of the men held in the Tularosa killings, as the one who told Olinger that the Kid had killed Bell. This does not make sense, for Nunnelly would have been on the other side of the street with Olinger. Nunnelly did figure in subsequent events, which probably led later to the erroneous ascription of this and other actions to him.

18 Kid (Meadows) and Gauss accounts. Again, Meadows wrongly attributes Gauss's role to Nunnelly.

19 *Las Vegas Daily Optic*, May 3, 1881.

20 Anonymous from Lincoln, April 29, 1881, in *Grant County Herald* (Silver City, N. Mex.), May 14, 1881.

21 Ibid. There are variations of what Billy said and when he said it, but the quotation is from an eyewitness writing the next day. The same observer stated that Billy also threw his handcuffs at Bell with a similar expletive. Since Bell's body lay in the backyard, this is less easy to credit.

22 This is according to Gauss.

23 Garrett, *Authentic Life*, 138. Finally, we have a logical role for Nunnelly to play in the story. All others, in my judgment, were distortions of this act.

264

24 Ibid., 138.

25 Ibid., 138–39.

26 *Las Vegas Optic*, May 4, 1881.

27 *Daily New Mexican* (Santa Fe), May 3, 1881.

28 Ibid.; Executive Record Book No. 2, 1867–82, April 30, 1881, pp. 507–8, TANM, Microfilm Reel 21, Frame 581, NMSRCA. Legal documents of this period were full of misspelled words. Bonney was often spelled Bonny, and William Antrim was occasionally substituted for Henry Antrim as an alias.

29 Executive Record Book No. 2, 1867–82, June 30, 1881, p. 515, Frame 586, TANM, NMSRCA.

17. THE EXECUTION

1 As related by Francisco Gómez in Leslie Traylor, "Facts Regarding the Escape of Billy the Kid," *Frontier Times* 13 (July 1936): 510. Gómez incorrectly remembers the escape as at noon rather than in the evening. He also has Billy going up Baca Canyon rather than Salazar Canyon. But Baca Canyon lies east of Lincoln and would not have offered a logical route over the mountains to Las Tablas. Following up Salazar Canyon, Billy would have reached the Capitan summit near the head of Las Tablas Creek.

2 Yginio Salazar, interview with J. Evetts Haley, Lincoln, N. Mex., August 17, 1927, HHC; Garrett, *Authentic Life*, 140; Godfrey Gauss in *Lincoln County Leader* (White Oaks), March 1, 1890.

3 John P. Meadows, in collaboration with Maurice G. Fulton, "Billy the Kid as I Knew Him," MS, c. 1931, Rasch Collection, LSM. I have discussed this source in chapter 16, n. 8. Barney Mason, who claimed that he trailed the Kid, gives his route as Agua Azul, Newcomb's Ranch (on the Ruidoso), "Consios" Springs (probably Conejos), and Buffalo Arroyo: *Las Vegas Morning Gazette*, June 16, 1881. Thus Mason mentions neither Las Tablas nor the Peñasco, but does not necessarily preclude them either. Conejos and Buffalo are near Fort Sumner and do not rule out the Peñasco. In addition to the Meadows account, I think the reports of Mathews's death lend support to Billy's presence on the Peñasco.

4 Barney Mason interview, *Las Vegas Gazette*, June 16, 1881. Mason calls the site of the stampede Consios Springs, which I think is a reporter's or printer's corruption of Conejos. Mason also says Billy

went from these springs to Buffalo Arroyo, stole another horse, and made his way to Sumner. Buffalo Arroyo would have taken him to Sumner by a longer route, which does not seem logical.

5   Garrett, *Authentic Life*, 140–41; *Las Vegas Gazette*, May 12 and June 16, 1881.

6   *Tombstone Epitaph*, June 16, 1881.

7   Garrett, *Authentic Life*, 142.

8   *Daily New Mexican* (Santa Fe), July 21, 1881.

9   Garrett, *Authentic Life*, 142–43.

10   Poe's wife wrote an admiring but informative biography of her husband. Sophie A. Poe, *Buckboard Days*, 2d ed., introduction by Sandra L. Myres (Albuquerque: University of New Mexico Press, 1981).

11   John W. Poe, *The Death of Billy the Kid*, introduction by Maurice G. Fulton (Boston and New York: Houghton Mifflin Co., 1933), 12–15. Poe wrote this account sometime early in the twentieth century, and it was first published in a British magazine in 1919. A Roswell bank president, Poe died in 1923.

     Poe portrays Garrett as so incredulous of the report that only with the greatest difficulty could he be persuaded to go to Fort Sumner. Garrett says he acted on the strength of Brazil's letter, and he does not even mention Poe's tip. I think that both reports prompted the decision and that, despite apprehension that it would be wasted effort, Garrett made the decision without any resistance.

     The son of Tip McKinney, another Garrett deputy, stated in 1969 that Poe's information really came from Pete Maxwell, who wanted Billy removed from influence on his sister Paulita. Thus the story of the informant in the hay loft was concocted to protect Maxwell from retaliation by Billy's friends. See Leon Metz, *Pat Garrett: The Story of a Western Lawman* (Norman: University of Oklahoma Press, 1973), 98. This is hard to credit, if for no other reason than that time is a relentless enemy to conspiracies. Sooner or later, they tend to unravel. Even the Kid's staunchest friends would have been unlikely to harm Maxwell, who was not only well liked but also an economic power in the Fort Sumner area. Moreover, Poe was a stranger recently arrived from Texas. Maxwell did not know him, or he Maxwell, as Poe himself divulged. Had Maxwell wanted to squeal on Billy, it would surely have been to Garrett. Finally, by the time Poe wrote his account, he would have had no reason to preserve such a fiction. It is not even hinted in any other credible source.

12   Garrett says McKinney was in Lincoln. Poe says he joined at Roswell.

Many and detailed accounts of the happenings of July 14, 1881, have been printed, a few with documentation, most without. Besides Garrett and Poe, who were indisputably firsthand witnesses and participants, the sources, when identified, are mostly Fort Sumner residents, and they represent almost as many versions as there were residents. Poe wrote some thirty years afterward, but he had a good memory and a reputation for honesty. Garrett left three accounts, two at the time and the third within a year: (1) Garrett's report to the governor of New Mexico, Fort Sumner, July 15, 1881, widely printed in the press (I have used the *Rio Grande Republican* [Las Cruces], July 23, 1881); (2) Garrett interviews with newsmen in *Las Vegas Optic*, July 18, 1881, and *Daily New Mexican* (Santa Fe), July 21, 1881; and (3) *Authentic Life*, 143–49. Garrett may have had reasons for tampering with the truth, but until credible evidence can be presented to show that he did, and to show how he did, his testimony must be given more weight than anyone else's. Without apology, therefore, I lean primarily on Garrett and secondarily on Poe. Tracing the many accounts of Billy's activities on this day is like chasing a prairie zephyr. I shall indulge it in restrained moderation.

13   Garrett, *Authentic Life*, 144, says they went in to talk with Maxwell; Poe, *Death of Billy the Kid*, 28, says that they intended to watch the house. I think both were motives, as logically they should have been. Again Poe portrays Garrett as the negativist, convinced that Billy was nowhere about and ready to give up. Poe takes credit for the idea of consulting Maxwell and then only after the three had watched the town plaza from hiding for a couple of hours. Since Poe did not know Maxwell or his reputation and Garrett did, I think Poe's memory played tricks on him.

14   Garrett mentions this man, but strangely Poe does not. His wife Sophie, however, does refer to him in *Buckboard Days*, 109–10.

15   The house to be watched is usually assumed to have been where Celsa Gutierrez lived with her husband, Sabal. This could have been kept under observation from a point behind and slightly to the west of Bob Hargrove's saloon (see map), although the view of

other buildings would have been narrowly restricted. A point farther east would have afforded a wider view, but chiefly of the rear
of the old barracks, which would have blocked direct sight of Celsa's apartment. Another possibility is that Garrett may have intended to keep watch on Manuela Bowdre's place. If she still lived
in the old hospital building, this latter location in the orchard
would have been a perfect point of observation. And finally, the
Maxwell house itself, where Paulita Maxwell lived, cannot be altogether discounted.

16   Garrett, *Authentic Life*, 145. Poe does not mention this incident.

17   Lobato and Silva gave their stories to former New Mexico Governor Miguel Otero, who reproduced them within quotation marks
in *The Real Billy the Kid: With New Light on the Lincoln County War*
(New York: Rufus Rockwell Wilson, 1936), 154–58. Their recollections are entitled to consideration, but Otero's book is so bad
that one hesitates to believe anything in it.

18   A belief persists that Billy was armed only with a butcher knife. Besides being highly uncharacteristic of him to be caught anywhere
without a gun, both Garrett and Poe say he had a pistol (his Colt .41
"self-cocker," according to both Garrett and a letter from Sunnyside dated July 15, 1881, that appeared in the *Las Vegas Optic*, July
18). Although Garrett and Poe had reason to want the world to believe that Billy carried a pistol, their testimony that he did can be
disqualified only by equally persuasive evidence that he did not. I
am not aware of any.

19   Poe, *Death of Billy the Kid*, 31–35.

20   *Daily New Mexican* (Santa Fe), July 21, 1881.

21   Poe's account of what happened after the shooting (*Death of Billy
the Kid*, 39–44) is more detailed and persuasive than any of
Garrett's.

22   Ibid., 40–41. Deluvina Maxwell also described the scene: "Pete
took a candle and held it around in the window and Pat stood back
in the dark where he could see into the room. When they saw that
he was dead, they both went in." Deluvina denied the prevalent
story that Garrett sent her inside with the candle to see if Billy was
dead. Deluvina Maxwell interview with J. Evetts Haley, Fort Sumner, N. Mex., June 24, 1927, PHPHM.

23   This is from Charles Frederick Rudulph, *"Los Bilitos": The Story
of "Billy the Kid" and His Gang* (New York: Carlton Press, 1980),

252. This is an "interpretive translation" by Louis L. Branch of
Rudulph's manuscript in Spanish and therefore must be handled
with caution. Rudulph, however, brings two elements of authority
to his account. First, as a nineteen-year-old, he came to Fort Sumner the next day with his father, Milnor Rudulph, who headed the
coroner's jury. Second, through his mother and, later, through his
own wife, he was part of the Hispanic community and was in a better position than most to know how they reacted.

24   Poe, *Death of Billy the Kid*, 44.

25   Rudulph, "*Los Bilitos*," 252–53, which also reproduces the report
of the coroner's jury.

26   Poe, *Death of Billy the Kid*, 42. Both Poe and Rudulph have the
body moved the night before, after the shooting. However, the coroner's report, executed on July 15, explicitly states that the jurors
proceeded to a room in the Maxwell house where they examined
the body.

27   *Daily New Mexican* (Santa Fe), July 21, 1881.

18. THE LEGEND

1   *New Southwest and Grant County Herald* (Silver City, N. Mex.),
July 23, 1881; *New York Sun*, July 22, 1881.

2   "Billy the Kid's Exploit," *National Police Gazette*, May 21, 1881.

3   These and more than four hundred additional outpourings over
the next seventy years are described in J. C. Dykes, *Billy the Kid:
The Bibliography of a Legend* (Albuquerque: University of New
Mexico Press, 1952).

4   Most of my biographical details come from sketches in William A.
Keleher, *Violence in Lincoln County, 1869–1881: A New Mexico
Item* (Albuquerque: University of New Mexico Press, 1957), 73–
75; and idem, *The Fabulous Frontier: Twelve New Mexico Items* (Albuquerque: University of New Mexico Press, 1962), 144–49. The
characterization is from Lily (Casey) Klasner, *My Girlhood among
Outlaws*, ed. Eve Ball (Tucson: University of Arizona Press, 1972),
116–23. Lily knew him well. Upson's letters to relatives are in the
Fulton Collection, UAL.

5   *Las Vegas Gazette*, October 22, 1881, stated that the book had already been written and would soon be published, which means

that it was completed in record time after the death of the Kid. Quoted in Keleher, *Violence in Lincoln County*, 75.

6   Letter quoted in Keleher, *Fabulous Frontier*, 147.

7   The thesis of the social bandit was propounded as an English phenomenon in Eric J. Hobsbawm, *Social Bandits and Primitive Rebels* (Glencoe, Ill.: The Free Press, 1959). For its application to the American West, see Richard White, "Outlaw Gangs of the Middle Border: American Social Bandits," *Western Historical Quarterly* 12 (October 1981): 387–408.

8   Paul A. Hutton, "Billy the Kid as Seen in the Movies," *Frontier Times* 57 (June 1985): 24–29.

9   For scholarly assessments of the legend, see especially Stephen Tatum, *Inventing Billy the Kid: Visions of the Outlaw in America, 1881–1981* (Albuquerque: University of New Mexico Press, 1982); Kent Ladd Steckmesser, *The Western Hero in History and Legend* (Norman: University of Oklahoma Press, 1965); Jon Tuska, *Billy the Kid: A Handbook* (Lincoln: University of Nebraska Press, 1986); Alfred Adler, "Billy the Kid: A Case Study in Epic Origins," *Western Folklore* 10 (April 1951): 143–52; and J. Frank Dobie, "Billy the Kid," *Southwest Review* 14 (Spring 1929): 314–20. Dykes, *Billy the Kid*, surveys the published literature to 1952, but of course there has been much since that has not been systematically recorded.

10   "Brushy Bill" was the most vocal and persistent claimant. He even appeared in person before the governor of New Mexico to ask for a pardon. His case is stated, although not widely regarded as proved, in C. L. Sonnichsen and William V. Morrison, *Alias Billy the Kid* (Albuquerque: University of New Mexico Press, 1955). Advocates of conspiracy seize upon perceived suspicious circumstances to convert possibility into fact. The theoretical possibility exists that Billy the Kid was not killed at Fort Sumner in 1881. To prove that he was not, however, demands hard evidence that has yet to be revealed. Until that day arrives, we must believe that if Billy does not rest beneath the sod in the old Fort Sumner cemetery, it is not because he was not buried there on July 15, 1881.

11   John P. Meadows, in collaboration with Maurice G. Fulton, "Billy the Kid as I Knew Him," MS, c. 1931, Rasch Collection, LSM; Henry Hoyt, *A Frontier Doctor*, Lakeside Classics ed., ed. Doyce B. Nunis, Jr. (Chicago: R. R. Donnelley & Sons, 1979), 154.

12   William Chisum, interview with Allen A. Erwin, Los Angeles, 1952, AHS.

13   Meadows and Fulton, "Billy the Kid as I Knew Him."

14   Deluvina Maxwell, interview with J. Evetts Haley, Fort Sumner, N. Mex., June 24, 1927, PHPHM; *Daily New Mexican* (Santa Fe), July 21, 1881.

15   Meadows and Fulton, "Billy the Kid as I Knew Him."

SOURCES

Any modern student who follows Billy the Kid quickly meets several in-
defatigable researchers who have scouted the trail in the past. The Kid commands a devoted following of aficionados, many of whom have spent a lifetime searching for material bearing on his life and death. Those who made
today's trail substantially easier to follow were Maurice Garland Fulton,
Robert N. Mullin, and Philip J. Rasch.

An English professor at New Mexico Military Institute in Roswell, Fulton for three decades collected and studied material relating to the Kid and
the Lincoln County War. He interviewed and corresponded with many who
knew of Billy's exploits through firsthand experience. Although he made
poor use of his collection, he left a rich legacy for subsequent researchers.
The Fulton Collection may now be consulted at the University of Arizona
Library in Tucson. Also at this repository are the papers of Rev. Taylor F.
Ealy, an observant witness of happenings in Lincoln during the war.

Mullin, an oil executive whose hobby drew him to Fulton, amassed a
huge body of material. It is of uneven quality and often difficult to trace to
origins, but it contains much of value. Mullin corresponded regularly with
Fulton, and abundant Fultonia survives in the Mullin Collection. It is
housed at the Haley History Center in Midland, Texas.

Philip J. Rasch also spent years pursuing the Kid, sometimes in collaboration with Mullin. He wrote many articles on the subject and donated
his extensive collection to the Lincoln State Monument in Lincoln, New
Mexico.

A special value of these three collections is the shortcut they offer researchers. These men labored for years to assemble Kid items from con-

ventional sources, such as newspapers. Their efforts save long hours sifting through huge stacks of material or endless frames of eye-straining microfilm.

Uniquely valuable are the pioneering researches of J. Evetts Haley, premier historian of Texas cows and cowmen. In the 1920s and 1930s Haley interviewed many participants in the Lincoln County War and the hunt for Billy the Kid. He intended to write a biography of the Kid, but turned to other projects when Walter Noble Burns published *The Saga of Billy the Kid*. The transcripts of the interviews are housed in the Haley History Center at Midland, Texas. They are more carefully organized and recorded than Fulton's and thus more useful. Not least of their importance is the personal perspective offered by Haley himself, a venerable fixture of the Center.

The reminiscent accounts are all of interest, but have to be used carefully. By the time they were transcribed, the subjects suffered from bad memory and were influenced by the romanticization that had suffused the literature. (The vivid writing of Burns's *Saga* affected the memory even of participants.) These recollections are better for local color and characterization of people than for chronology or events. For some features of the story, however, they are the only source. Consulted in conjunction with contemporary sources, they can contribute importantly.

A storehouse of original documentation is the New Mexico State Records Center and Archives in Santa Fe, which contains the Territorial Archives of New Mexico, a scattering of county records, and the records of the territorial district courts. Pertinent are court records for Lincoln, Doña Ana, and Socorro counties in the Third Judicial District and San Miguel County in the First Judicial District. Court records consist of docket books recording the sequence of actions in individual cases, journals chronologically recording courtroom actions, and case files containing various documents relating to individual cases, such as indictments and arrest warrants. Court records are aggravating to use, both because most of the key case files have not survived and because of extraordinary verbosity that yields the most minimal information. Even so, they are indispensable. The territorial district court also functioned as federal district court. Records of federal cases are housed at the Denver Federal Records Center of the National Archives.

The NMSRCA also contains copies of the WPA interviews conducted in the 1930s and copies of important historical documents collected and au-

274

thored by Territorial Secretary William G. Ritch. The original Ritch Collection is in the Huntington Library, San Marino, California.

Federal records are critical to understanding the Lincoln County War and occasionally throw light on the doings of Billy the Kid. Preserved in the National Archives and Records Administration in Washington, D.C., most are available on microfilm.

The most important federal document is the voluminous report of Frank Warner Angel, investigator for the Departments of Justice and the Interior, submitted in October 1878. The Angel Report contains forty-three depositions sworn by active participants on both sides of the Lincoln County War, including the Kid. The citation is "Report on the Death of John H. Tunstall," File 44-4-8-3, RG 60, Records of the Department of Justice. A complete copy is in the Victor Westphall Collection, NMSRCA.

Also valuable are military documents, especially a special file relating to the Lincoln County War: RG 94, AGO LR (Main Series), 1871–80, File 1405 AGO 1878, available on microfilm as M666, Rolls 397 and 398. Essential too is the record of the Dudley Court of Inquiry, featuring the testimony of more than sixty witnesses (including the Kid) together with annexed documents. The Dudley Court Record is Records Relating to the Dudley Inquiry (QQ 1284), RG 153, Judge Advocate General's Office. Other military records include RG 393, LR, Hq. District of New Mexico, on microfilm as M1088; the same, LS, M1072; and LR and LS of the post of Fort Stanton, RG 393, not on microfilm.

Pertinent civilian records include RG 48, Interior Department Territorial Records: New Mexico (M364); and Interior Department Appointment Papers (M750). Indian Bureau records, which throw light on civilian affairs in Lincoln County, are RG 75, Office of Indian Affairs, LR (M234); Records of the New Mexico Superintendency, 1849–80 (T21); Report of Inspector E. C. Watkins, Report No. 1981, June 27, 1878, Inspectors' Reports, 1873–80 (containing affidavits of thirty-five witnesses); and Special Case 108, Reduction of the Mescalero Reservation.

Throwing crucial light on the doings of Billy the Kid in the last part of 1880 are the daily reports of Secret Service Agent Azariah F. Wild, who was sent to New Mexico to investigate a counterfeiting ring: U.S. Treasury Department, Secret Service Division, New Orleans District, Reports of Special Operative Azariah F. Wild (T915, Roll 308), RG 87, Records of U.S. Secret Service Agents, 1875–1936.

For Governor Lew Wallace, his personal papers at the Indiana Historical Society in Indianapolis are unusually rich in documenting his role in the concluding stages of the Lincoln County War, including his exchange of missives with Billy the Kid. The New Mexico portion of the Wallace Papers may be consulted on microfilm.

Newspapers are important sources if handled properly. They feature letters from the scene, usually by anonymous correspondents, and when shorn of bias they help in establishing the chronology and course of events. The most helpful are the *Mesilla Valley Independent*, *Mesilla News*, Silver City *Grant County Herald*, Santa Fe *New Mexican*, *Las Vegas Gazette*, and *Las Vegas Optic*.

MISCELLANEOUS MANUSCRIPTS

Chisum, Sallie. Diary. Chavez County Historical Society, Roswell, N. Mex.

Ealy, Taylor F. "The Lincoln County War as I Saw It." MS, c. 1927. Ealy Papers, UAL.

Meadows, John P., in collaboration with Maurice G. Fulton. "Billy the Kid as I Knew Him." MS, c. 1931. Rasch Collection, LSM.

Naegle, Conrad Keeler. "Silver City, New Mexico's Frontier Paradox." MS, n.d., New Mexico State Library, Santa Fe.

Polk, Cal. "Life of Cal Polk, Commenced January 25, 1896." MS, PHPHM.

Walz, Edgar. "Retrospection." MS, October 1931. Museum of New Mexico Historical Library, Santa Fe.

Wood, Miles. Reminiscences. MS, c. 1911–23. In collection of Jerry Weddle, Tucson, Arizona.

INTERVIEWS

Abraham, Louis. With Helen Wheaton. HHC (Mullin Collection).

Barber, Sue (McSween). With J. Evetts Haley. HHC.

Bousman, Louis P. With J. Evetts Haley. HHC.

Brady, Robert. With Edith L. Crawford. NMSRCA.

Brent, Carlota Baca. With Frances E. Totty. NMSRCA.

Buckbee, Joe. With Philip J. Rasch. LSM.

Casey, Robert A. With J. Evetts Haley. HHC.

Chavez, Florencio. With J. Evetts Haley. HHC.

Chisum, William. With Allen A. Erwin. AHS.

Coe, Frank. *El Paso Times*, September 16, 1923.

———. *New Mexico State Tribune* (Albuquerque), July 23, 1928.

———. With J. Evetts Haley. HHC.

Coe, George. With J. Evetts Haley. HHC.

Connor, Anthony B. *Independent* (Silver City, N. Mex.), March 22, 1932.

East, James H. With J. Evetts Haley. HHC.

Gauss, Godfrey. *Lincoln County Leader* (White Oaks), March 1, 1890.

Gildea, A. M. *Daily Citizen* (Tucson), March 28, 1931.

Maxwell, Deluvina. With J. Evetts Haley. PHPHM.

Meadows, John P. *Alamogordo News* (N. Mex.), June 11, 1936.

———. With J. Evetts Haley. HHC.

Owens, W. R. (Jake). With J. Evetts Haley. HHC.

Peppin, Juan. With Maurice G. Fulton. HHC (Mullin Collection).

Salazar, Yginio. With J. Evetts Haley. HHC.

Steck, Joseph. *Lincoln County Leader* (White Oaks), December 7, 1889.

Truesdell, Chauncey O. *Arizona Republic* (Phoenix), December 30, 1951.

———. With Robert N. Mullin. HHC (Mullin Collection).

Trujillo, Francisco. With Edith L. Crawford. NMSRCA.

Wallace, Lew. *Indianapolis World*, June 8, 1902.

Whitehill, Harvey C. *Enterprise* (Silver City N. Mex.), January 3, 1902.

Whitehill, Henry. With Helen Wheaton. HHC (Mullin Collection).

Wier, William. With J. Evetts Haley. Vandale Collection, Barker History
    Center, University of Texas.

Wilson, Gorgonio. With Edith L. Crawford. NMSRCA.

NEWSPAPERS

Albuquerque Advance

Albuquerque Review

Arizona Daily Citizen (Tucson)

Arizona Weekly Citizen (Tucson)

Arizona Weekly Star (Tucson)

Cimarron News and Press (N. Mex.)

Daily New Mexican (Santa Fe)

Grant County Herald (Silver City, N. Mex.)

Las Vegas Gazette (N. Mex.)

Las Vegas Optic (N. Mex.)

Mesilla News (N. Mex.)

Mesilla Valley Independent (Mesilla, N. Mex.)

Mining Life (Silver City, N. Mex.)

New York Sun

Newman's Semi-Weekly (Las Cruces, N. Mex.)

Rio Grande Republican (Las Cruces, N. Mex.)

Silver City Enterprise (N. Mex.)

Weekly New Mexican (Santa Fe)

PUBLISHED MATERIAL

Adams, Ramon F. *A Fitting Death for Billy the Kid*. Norman: University of
Oklahoma Press, 1960.

Adler, Alfred. "Billy the Kid: A Case Study in Epic Origins." *Western Folklore* 10 (April 1951): 143–52.

Ball, Eve. "Billy Strikes the Pecos." *New Mexico Folklore Record* 4 (1949–
50): 7–10.

———. *Ma'am Jones of the Pecos*. Tucson: University of Arizona Press,
1969.

Ball, Larry D. *The United States Marshals of New Mexico and Arizona,
1846–1912*. Albuquerque: University of New Mexico Press, 1978.

Bender, Norman J., ed. *Missionaries, Outlaws, and Indians: Taylor F. Ealy
at Lincoln and Zuni, 1878–1881*. Albuquerque: University of New Mexico Press, 1984.

Blazer, Almer. "The Fight at Blazer's Mill in New Mexico." *Frontier Times*
16 (August 1939): 461–66.

Blazer, Paul. "The Fight at Blazer's Mill: A Chapter in the Lincoln County
War." *Arizona and the West* 6 (Autumn 1964): 203–10.

Brothers, Mary Hudson. *A Pecos Pioneer* [Bell Hudson]. Albuquerque:
University of New Mexico Press, 1943.

Brown, Richard Maxwell. *Strain of Violence: Historical Studies of American
Violence and Vigilantism*. New York: Oxford University Press, 1975.

Burns, Walter Noble. *The Saga of Billy the Kid*. New York: Grosset and
Dunlap, 1926.

Callon, Milton W. *Las Vegas, New Mexico . . . The Town That Wouldn't
Gamble*. Las Vegas: Las Vegas Daily Optic, 1962.

Cawelti, John G. "The Gunfighter and Society." *American West* 5 (March
1968): 30–35, 76–78.

Cline, Donald. *Alias Billy the Kid: The Man Behind the Legend*. Santa Fe:
Sunstone Press, 1986.

Coe, Frank. "A Friend Comes to the Defense of Notorious Billy the Kid."
El Paso Times, September 26, 1923.

Coe, George W. *Frontier Fighter: The Autobiography of George W. Coe*, as related to Nan Hillary Harrison. Boston and New York: Houghton Mifflin Co., 1934. 2d ed., Albuquerque: University of New Mexico Press, 1951. Lakeside Classics ed., ed. Doyce B. Nunis, Jr., Chicago: R. R. Donnelley and Co., 1984.

Cunningham, Eugene. "Fought with Billy the Kid." *Frontier Times* 9 (March 1932): 242–47.

Curry, George. *An Autobiography*. Albuquerque: University of New Mexico Press, 1958.

DeMattos, Jack. "The Search for Billy the Kid's Roots—Is Over!" *Real West* 23 (January 1980): 20–25.

———. "John Kinney." *Real West* 27 (February 1984): 20–25.

Denton, J. Fred. "Billy the Kid's Friend Tells for First Time of Thrilling Incidents." *Tucson Daily Citizen*, March 28, 1931.

Dobie, J. Frank. "Billy the Kid." *Southwest Review* 14 (Spring 1929): 314–20.

Dykes, J. C. *Billy the Kid: The Bibliography of a Legend*. Albuquerque: University of New Mexico Press, 1952.

Earle, James H., ed. *The Capture of Billy the Kid*. College Station, Texas: Creative Publishing Co., 1988.

Fulton, Maurice G. *History of the Lincoln County War*, ed. Robert N. Mullin. Tucson: University of Arizona Press, 1968.

Garavaglia, Louis A., and Charles G. Worman. *Firearms of the American West, 1866–1894*. Albuquerque: University of New Mexico Press, 1985.

Garrett, Pat F. *The Authentic Life of Billy the Kid*. Santa Fe: New Mexican Printing and Publishing Co., 1882. Ed. and with an introduction by Maurice G. Fulton, New York: Macmillan Co., 1927. With introduction by Jeff C. Dykes, Norman: University of Oklahoma Press, 1954.

Gibson, A. M. *The Life and Death of Colonel Albert Jennings Fountain*. Norman: University of Oklahoma Press, 1965.

Haley, J. Evetts. "Jim East, Trail Hand and Cowboy." *Panhandle-Plains Historical Review* 4 (1931): 48–61.

———. *Charles Goodnight, Cowman and Plainsman*. Boston, 1936. Reprint, Norman: University of Oklahoma Press, 1949.

———. *George W. Littlefield, Texan*. Norman: University of Oklahoma Press, 1943.

Hertzog, Peter. *Little Known Facts about Billy the Kid*. Santa Fe: Press of the Territorian, 1963.

Hinton, Harwood P. "John Simpson Chisum, 1877–84." *New Mexico His-*

torical Review 31 (July 1956): 177–205; 31 (October 1956): 310–37; 32 (January 1957): 53–65.

Hobsbawm, Eric J. *Social Bandits and Primitive Rebels*. Glencoe, Ill.: The Free Press, 1959.

Hoyt, Henry. *A Frontier Doctor*. New York: Houghton Mifflin Co., 1929. Lakeside Classics ed., ed. Doyce B. Nunis, Jr., Chicago: R. R. Donnelley and Sons, 1979.

Hutchinson, W. H., and Robert N. Mullin. *Whiskey Jim and a Kid Named Billie*. Clarendon, Texas: Clarendon Press, 1967.

Hutton, Paul A. "Billy the Kid as Seen in the Movies." *Frontier Times* 57 (June 1985): 24–29.

Hyde, Albert E. *Billy the Kid and the Old Regime in the Southwest*. Ruidoso, N. Mex.: Frontier Book Co., n.d.

Irwin, Helen. "When Billy the Kid Was Brought to Trial." *Frontier Times* 6 (March 1929): 214–15.

Kadlec, Robert F., ed. *They "Knew" Billy the Kid: Interviews with Old-Time New Mexicans*. Santa Fe: Ancient City Press, 1987.

Kajencki, Francis C. "Alexander Grzelachowski: Pioneer Merchant of Puerto de Luna, New Mexico." *Arizona and the West* 26 (Autumn 1984): 243–60.

Keleher, William A. *The Maxwell Land Grant: A New Mexico Item*. Santa Fe: Rydal Press, 1942.

———. *Violence in Lincoln County, 1869–1881: A New Mexico Item*. Albuquerque: University of New Mexico Press, 1957.

———. *The Fabulous Frontier: Twelve New Mexico Items*. Albuquerque: University of New Mexico Press, 1962.

Klasner, Lily (Casey). *My Girlhood among Outlaws*, ed. Eve Ball. Tucson: University of Arizona Press, 1972.

Koop, Waldo. *Billy the Kid: Trail of a Kansas Legend*. Kansas City: Kansas City Westerners, 1965.

Lavash, Donald R. *William Brady: Tragic Hero of the Lincoln County War*. Santa Fe: Sunstone Press, 1987.

McCarty, John L. *Maverick Town: The Story of Old Tascosa*. Norman: University of Oklahoma Press, 1946.

McCright, Grady E., and James H. Powell. *Jessie Evans: Lincoln County Badman*. College Station, Texas: Creative Publishing Co., 1983.

McDonald, A. B. "Tascosa's Lone Settler [Mrs. Mickie McCormick] Recalls Wild Days." *Frontier Times* 8 (February 1931): 234–36.

Metz, Leon. *Pat Garrett: The Story of a Western Lawman*. Norman: University of Oklahoma Press, 1973.

Mullin, Robert N. *The Boyhood of Billy the Kid*. Southwestern Studies Monograph No. 17. El Paso: Texas Western Press, 1967.

———. "Here Lies John Kinney." *Journal of Arizona History* 14 (Autumn 1973): 223–42.

———, and Charles E. Welch, Jr. "Billy the Kid: The Making of a Hero." *Western Folklore* 32 (1973): 104–12.

Nolan, Frederick W., ed. *The Life and Death of John Henry Tunstall*. Albuquerque: University of New Mexico Press, 1965.

O'Neal, Bill. *Encyclopedia of Western Gun-Fighters*. Norman: University of Oklahoma Press, 1979.

———. *Henry Brown, the Outlaw Marshal*. College Station, Texas: Creative Publishing Co., 1980.

Otero, Miguel. *The Real Billy the Kid: With New Light on the Lincoln County War*. New York: Rufus Rockwell Wilson, 1936.

Pearce, T. M., ed. "Billy the Kid Symposium." *New Mexico Folklore Record, 1949–50* 4 (1950).

Perrigo, Lynn W. *Gateway to Glorieta: The History of Las Vegas, New Mexico*. Boulder, Colo.: Pruett Press, 1982.

Poe, John W. *The Death of Billy the Kid*. Introduction by Maurice G. Fulton. Boston and New York: Houghton Mifflin Co., 1933.

Poe, Sophie A. *Buckboard Days*. 2d ed., introduction by Sandra L. Myres. Albuquerque: University of New Mexico Press, 1981.

Rasch, Philip J. "A Note on Henry Newton Brown." Los Angeles Westerners *Brand Book* 5 (1953): 58–67.

———. "The Twenty-One Men He Put Bullets Through." *New Mexico Folklore Record* 9 (1954–55): 8–14.

———. "Five Days of Battle." Denver Westerners *Brand Book* 11 (1955): 295–323.

———. "A Man Named Antrim." Los Angeles Westerners *Brand Book* 6 (1956): 48–54.

———. "The Pecos War." *Panhandle-Plains Historical Review* 29 (1956): 101–11.

———. "Prelude to War: The Murder of J. H. Tunstall." Los Angeles Westerners *Brand Book* 7 (1957): 78–96.

———. "Amende Honorable—The Life and Death of Billy Wilson." West Texas Historical Association *Year Book* 34 (1958): 97–111.

———. "The Murder of Huston I. Chapman." Los Angeles Westerners *Brand Book* 8 (1959): 69–82.

———. "The Story of Jessie J. Evans." *Panhandle-Plains Historical Review* 33 (1960): 108–21.

———. "The Short Life of Tom O'Folliard." Potomac Westerners *Corral Dust* 6 (May 1961): 9–11, 14.

———. "Death at the Baile." Potomac Westerners *Corral Dust* 6 (August 1961): 30.

———. "John Kinney: King of the Rustlers." English Westerners *Brand Book* 4 (October 1961): 10–12.

———. "Alias 'Whiskey Jim.'" *Panhandle-Plains Historical Review* 36 (1963): 103–14.

———. "The Olingers, Known Yet Forgotten." Potomac Westerners *Corral Dust* 8 (February 1963): 1, 4–6.

———. "Garrett's Favorite Deputy [Barney Mason]." Potomac Westerners *Corral Dust* 9 (Fall 1964): 3–5.

———. "He Rode with the Kid: The Life of Tom Pickett." *English Westerners Tenth Anniversary Publication*, 11–15. London, 1964.

———. "War in Lincoln County." English Westerners *Brand Book* 6 (July 1964): 2–4.

———. "The Hunting of Billy, the Kid." English Westerners *Brand Book* 11 (January 1969): 1–10.

———. "The Quest for Joseph Antrim." *NOLA Quarterly* 6 (July 1981): 13–17.

———, Joseph E. Buckbee, and Karl K. Klein. "Man of Many Parts [Doc Scurlock]." English Westerners *Brand Book* 5 (January 1963): 9–12.

———, and Robert N. Mullin. "New Light on the Legend of Billy the Kid." *New Mexico Folklore Record* 7 (1952–53): 1–5.

———, and Robert N. Mullin. "Dim Trails: The Pursuit of the McCarty Family." *New Mexico Folklore Record* 8 (1954): 6–11.

———, and Lee Myers. "The Tragedy of the Beckwiths." English Westerners *Brand Book* 5 (July 1963): 1–6.

Rickards, Colin W. "Better for the World That He is Gone." English Westerners *Brand Book* 2 (April 1960): 2–8.

———. *The Gunfight at Blazer's Mill*. Southwestern Studies Monograph No. 40. El Paso: Texas Western Press, 1974.

Roberts, Gary L. "Violence and the Frontier Tradition." *Kansas and the West: Bicentennial Essays in Honor of Nyle H. Miller*. Topeka: Kansas State Historical Society, 1976.

Rosa, Joseph G. *The Gunfighter: Man or Myth?* Norman: University of Oklahoma Press, 1968.

Rudulph, Charles Frederick. *"Los Bilitos": The Story of "Billy the Kid" and His Gang*. New York: Carlton Press, 1980.

Shinkle, James D. *Fort Sumner and the Bosque Redondo Indian Reservation*. Roswell, N. Mex.: Hall-Poorbough Press, 1965.

———. *Robert Casey and the Ranch on the Rio Hondo*. Roswell, N. Mex.: Hall-Poorbough Press, 1970.

Shipman, Jack. "Brief Career of Tom O'Folliard, Billy the Kid's Partner." *Voice of the Mexican Border* 1 (January 1934): 216–19.

Siringo, Charles A. *A Texas Cowboy; or, Fifteen Years on the Hurricane Deck of a Spanish Pony*. Chicago: M. Umbdenstock & Co., 1885.

———. *A Lone Star Cowboy*. Santa Fe: n.p., 1919.

———. *History of "Billy the Kid."* Santa Fe: n.p., 1920.

———. *Riata and Spurs*. Boston and New York: Houghton Mifflin Co., 1927.

Sonnichsen, C. L. *"I'll Die Before I'll Run": The Story of the Great Feuds of Texas*. New York: Devin-Adair, 1962.

———. *Tularosa: Last of the Frontier West*. 2d ed. Albuquerque: University of New Mexico Press, 1980.

———, and William V. Morrison. *Alias Billy the Kid*. Albuquerque: University of New Mexico Press, 1955.

Stanley, F. *Dave Rudabaugh: Border Ruffian*. Denver: World Press, 1961.

———. *Notes on Joel Fowler*. Pep, Tex.: n.p., 1963.

Steckmesser, Kent Ladd. *The Western Hero in History and Legend*. Norman: University of Oklahoma Press, 1965.

Tatum, Stephen. *Inventing Billy the Kid: Visions of the Outlaw in America, 1881–1981*. Albuquerque: University of New Mexico Press, 1982.

Traylor, Leslie. "Facts Regarding the Escape of Billy the Kid." *Frontier Times* 13 (July 1936): 506–13.

Tuska, Jon. *Billy the Kid: A Handbook*. Lincoln: University of Nebraska Press, 1986.

Utley, Robert M. *Four Fighters of Lincoln County*. Albuquerque: University of New Mexico Press, 1986.

———. *High Noon in Lincoln: Violence on the Western Frontier*. Albuquerque: University of New Mexico Press, 1987.

Wallace, Lew. *Lew Wallace: An Autobiography*. 2 vols. New York and London: Harper and Bros., 1906.

Watson, Marilyn. "Was Sallie Billy's Girl?" *New Mexico Magazine* (January 1988): 57–60.

Weisner, Herman B. "The Prisoners Who Saw the Kid Kill Olinger." *Rio Grande History* 9. Las Cruces: New Mexico State University Library, 1978.

White, Richard. "Outlaw Gangs of the Middle Border: American Social Bandits." *Western Historical Quarterly* 12 (October 1981): 387–408.

Wilson, John P. *Merchants, Guns & Money: The Story of Lincoln County and Its Wars*. Santa Fe: Museum of New Mexico Press, 1987.

Wilson, Roscoe G. "Billy the Kid's Youth Is Topic for Argument." *Arizona Republic* (Phoenix), December 30, 1951.

Woody, Clara T., and Milton L. Schwartz. *Globe, Arizona*. Tucson: Arizona Historical Society, 1977.

INDEX

Diedrick, Moses, 142

Diedrick, Sam, 134, 142, 149, 190

Dills, Lucius, 264

District of New Mexico (U.S. Army), 83

Dixon, Joe, 93

Dodge City, Kans., 131

Dodge City gang, 130

Dolan, James J., 25, 26, 35–36, 41, 43, 48, 51, 52, 54, 55, 56, 58–59, 62, 69, 76, 80, 82–83, 90, 102, 103, 107, 111, 117, 120, 121, 135, 171, 176, 205, 206, 207, 219, 223, 232; described, 29, 36; and attachment of McSween's property, 39–40, 42, 43; and Tunstall killing, 44, 45, 47, 49, 225; and Chisum, 56; indicted, 77; bankruptcy of, 77, 102; breaks leg, 77; in Santa Fe, 83–84; and Peppin, 84; in San Patricio fighting, 86; in Five-Day Battle, 90, 93, 99, 240; and Chapman killing, 113–14; arrested, 116; indicted, 120

Dolan cow camp, 43, 56; Regulator raid on, 81–83, 236–37

Dolan store, 50–53, 64, 65, 79, 90, 230; closed, 77, 235; Kid's escape from, 178–83

Doña Ana County, N.Mex., 5, 121, 125, 176

Don Jenardo, 197

Dow's store, 81

Dowlin's Mill, N.Mex., 32

Dudley, Lt. Col. Nathan A. M., 82, 84, 103, 105, 107, 110, 111, 112, 114, 232, 245; described, 80; intimidates Copeland, 80–81; in Five-Day Battle, 92–101; removed, 115,

240; indicted, 121; and court of inquiry, 122–23

Dudley Court of Inquiry, 122–23

"Dummy," 95–96, 98, 240

Dwyer, Thomas, 212–13

Dykes, Jeff C., 211

Ealy, Mary, 53, 78, 90, 97, 231

Ealy, Rev. Taylor F., 74, 97; at Tunstall's funeral, 53; and Brady killing, 65–67, 230–31; in Five-Day Battle, 91, 92

East, James: and O'Folliard killing, 155–56, 255–56; in Stinking Springs fight, 159–60, 257–58; in Las Vegas, 161, 163, 165–67, 259

Easton, David M., 73, 234–35, 239

Edwards (posseman), 226

Edwards, Buck, 140, 141

Ellis, Ben, 91–92, 111, 262–63

Ellis, Isaac, 53, 67, 99, 172, 232, 263

Ellis store, 67, 79, 173, 230, 263; in Five-Day Battle, 90–91, 92, 94, 99, 100, 239

Emory, Tom, 155, 159, 163, 165, 167, 255, 257, 259

Erwin, Allen A., 220

Evans, Jesse, 21, 28, 37, 39, 49–51, 54, 56, 60, 62, 91, 117, 119, 120, 172, 204, 223; described, 22–23; Cooke's Canyon to Beckwith ranch, 24–26, 215–16, 223; theft of Tunstall's horses, 27; arrested and jailed, 27; jail break, 29–30, 32, 33, 35, 219–20, 223; in attachment of McSween's property, 41–44; wounded, 42; taunts Widenmann, 43; and Tunstall killing,

290

Wilson, John B. (*cont.*)
225; wounded, 65; and Kid
bargain with Wallace, 117–18,
259; in Stinking Springs fight,
157–60
Wilson, William, 130, 134, 137,
138, 149, 150, 151, 152, 153,
70, 260; described, 131; and
Greathouse ranch fight, 140–
45; and O'Folliard killing,
155–56; in Stinking Springs
fight, 157–60; in Las Vegas,
163–65; in Santa Fe jail, 168
Wolz, Charles, 224

Wood, Miles L., 10–12, 213–14
Woods, David, 178
Wortley, Samuel, 49, 181
Wortley Hotel, 49; in Five-Day
Battle, 90, 92, 93, 99; in Kid's
escape, 180–82

Yerby, Nasaria, 127, 194, 248
Yerby, Thomas G., 126, 127, 152
Yerby ranch, 126, 131, 148, 150,
151, 152
Young Guns (movie), 201

Zamora, Francisco, 91, 98